国际商务谈判实训

赵立民　编　著

首都经济贸易大学出版社

·北　京·

图书在版编目(CIP)数据

国际商务谈判实训/赵立民编著. —北京:首都经济贸易大
学出版社,2012.1

(21 世纪高职高专精品系列规划教材·国际商务专业)

ISBN 978 – 7 – 5638 – 1959 – 1

Ⅰ.①国… Ⅱ.①赵… Ⅲ.①国际商务—商务谈判—英、汉
Ⅳ.①F740.41

中国版本图书馆 CIP 数据核字(2011)第 230702 号

国际商务谈判实训

越立民 编著

出版发行	首都经济贸易大学出版社	
地 址	北京市朝阳区红庙 (邮编 100026)	
电 话	(010)65976483 65065761 65071505(传真)	
网 址	http://www.sjmcb.com	
E – mail	publish@cueb.edu.cn	
经 销	全国新华书店	
照 排	首都经济贸易大学出版社激光照排服务部	
印 刷	人民日报印刷厂	
开 本	787 毫米×980 毫米 1/16	
字 数	281 千字	
印 张	16	
版 次	2012 年 1 月第 1 版 2017 年 1 月第 1 版第 2 次印刷	
书 号	ISBN 978 – 7 – 5638 – 1959 – 1/F·1130	
定 价	27.00 元	

前　言

随着经济全球化的不断深入,我国的国际贸易得到了很大发展,越来越多的人从事外经外贸工作。很多高等院校开设了国际贸易相关课程,其中,国际贸易谈判成为重中之重。商务谈判师在国际贸易以及其他商务活动中扮演着极其重要的角色。为配合广大外贸工作者、高等院校学生们学习外贸谈判的需要,我们编写了《国际商务谈判实训》一书。

本书共分为十三章,每章分对话、常用词汇及词组、翻译练习、句型练习以及参考译文和答案五大部分。各课内容主要包括我国对外经济贸易谈判中的各个重要环节,涉及公司和产品介绍、询盘、报盘、还盘、订单、价格、合同、装运、付款、包装、保险、代理与佣金、商检与仲裁、索赔等内容。

本教材提供了不同情景下的范例会话共104篇,与实际贸易谈判紧密结合。常用词汇及词组为会话内容做了注释,方便读者学习理解会话。常用句式总结了贸易谈判中的一些基本用语,非常具有实用性,若能加以背诵,必能举一反三,触类旁通。参考用语提供了与会话内容相关的词汇,有利于读者扩大词汇量。翻译练习、听力练习、句型练习又有利于加深对对会话内容的理解。参考译文和答案可以帮助学员巩固所学知识,操练所学词汇用语,提高应用技能。

本书结构新颖,内容翔实,贴近实际,实用性强。在本书重视经贸谈判意识和口语谈判实践,适用于对外经贸类大学和职业学院经贸英语口语教学。

为了减少纸张的使用,以节约资源,以及便于读者参考使用,我们把参考译文及答案做成电子文件,请广大读者登录首都经济贸易大学出版社网站 www. sjmcb. com 注册后下载,或者发送电子邮件到 publish@ cueb. edu. cn 索取。由于编者的英语和业务水平有限,错误缺点在所难免,敬请各位前辈、专家及广大学员批评指正。

目　　录

Contents

第1章 公司与产品介绍

Company Introduction—Overview

The first Presentation Example takes you through a Company Introduction of a robotics company. Your presentation may look quite different than the one we are providing here, but you can view and listen to it as an example of how a presentation like this can be delivered.

This presentation is provided in 6 different slides:

1. Welcome and Introduction
2. Overview of the Presentation
3. Company History
4. Closer Look at the Product Line
5. Overview of Relevant Industries
6. Business Goals & Core Capabilities; Closing

Pay close attention to how the visual aids are used and how the text matches up with the slides. In creating your own presentation, look for ways to incorporate new Key Expressions and our Words & Phrases.

Company Introduction—Slide 1

Good evening ladies and gentlemen. I would like to welcome all of you to SYK Robotics Corporation. My name is Duke McCloud, and I am the marketing manager for SYK Robotics. It is my honor to be introducing our company to such a distinguished group.

女士们,先生们,晚上好。欢迎各位到蓝天机器人研发公司参观。我叫麦考特·杜克,是蓝天机器人公司的营销部经理。非常荣幸能够向尊贵的朋友们介绍我们公司。

Company Introduction—Slide 2

Today I am going to introduce you to our company and give you a brief introduction of the fast-paced and rapidly expanding industry that we compete in. Then I will give you a brief overview of our product line, and finish my presentation with our business goal and our core capabilities. We have a number of other presentations lined up for today, so I am planning to keep this presentation brief. If you have any questions, please

1

hold them until the end of the presentation, and I will be happy to answer them for you.

今天,我将向你们简要介绍我们公司是怎样在竞争中快速成长壮大的。然后简要介绍我们的生产线,最后,谈谈我们的经营目标和核心竞争力。考虑到今天还有其他情况要介绍,因此,我尽量简单扼要,如有问题,请在介绍后提出,我很愿意回答。

Company Introduction—Slide 3

So why don't we get started? Let me tell you a little bit about our history. SYK Robotics was established in October 1975 in Toronto. As you can see, SYK Robotics is the oldest Robotics manufacturing company in Canada, and one of the oldest in the world. SYK originally started as a manufacturing firm that developed and manufactured bionic limb replacements, which was a fledgling industry at that time in the mid 70's. Within less than two years SYK Robotics was able to establish itself as the leading producer of limb replacement devices in the world, with annual sales totaling 89. 2 million dollars in 1977. In fact, why don't we look at our sales figures at this point? I would like to direct your attention to this graph.

我们开始吧。先简单谈一下我们公司的历史,蓝天机器人研发公司于1975年10月在多伦多成立。正如你们所知,它是加拿大历史最悠久的机器人研发公司,也是世界上成立早的此类公司之一。公司起初是研发仿生人体假肢,在20世纪70年代中期只是崭露头角,然而在不到两年的时间里便发展成为世界上生产此类产品的领头羊。1977年年销售额达8 920万美元。让我们看一看销售数字。请看这个图表。

Company Introduction—Slide 4

As I've said before, we started out in 1975 producing limb replacements. During the next decade, SYK Robotics was able to accumulate a great amount of technical know-how as well as business expertise. Our investment in research and development finally paid off in 1982, when SYK Robotics, for the first time in the world, was able to perfect the Biosynchronous Neuron Algorithm technology, which gave our products a greatly enhanced capability.

我前面说过,我公司成立于1975年,生产仿生人体假肢。10年后,该公司积累了充足的技术秘诀和业务经验。我们在科研方面的投资终于在1982年有了回报。我公司在世界上头一次完善了神经同步运算技术,这使得我们的产品质量大大提高。

This algorithm allowed us to produce artificial arms and legs, which could respond to nerve commands from the patient. This was a great advance for our firm as well as for the industry. With this new technology, SYK began developing robotic home appliances in 1988, which are still our main product line. The first devices were crude compared to today's products, but were amazing devices back then. SYK Robotics was one of the first companies to develop and produce the automatic lawn mower, the ALM 1300, which was manufactured in 1999. This was a very early model and it was quite expensive as well, but the ALM 1300 proved to skeptics that such devices were technically feasible.

这一技术使得残疾人通过神经中枢指挥假肢运动。这一创举,不仅是我公司而且在同行中都是极大的进步。运用这一技术,我公司在 1988 年开发了家用机器人产品。这是我们的主要生产线。与现在的产品相比,刚开始时产品显得粗糙,以后愈发精密。蓝天机器人研发公司是世界上首次生产自动除草机的公司之一。ALM 1300 型是 1999 年生产的。这是一个老型号自动除草机,那时很昂贵,但技术过关。

Today, SYK Robotics has 12 500 employees. Our headquarters are in Toronto, with our research facilities in nearby York and Windsor. Our main production plant is also located in York, with subsidiary plants in nearby industrial areas. We also run a bioengineering program with the University of Toronto, at the McPherson Biomedical Center.

而今,蓝天机器人研发公司拥有 12 500 员工。总部设在多伦多,研发机构设在约克和温莎附近。我们的主要生产工厂也在约克,辅助生产工厂在不远的工业区。在 McPherson 生物技术中心,我们与多伦多大学共同开发了生物工程项目。

Company Introduction—Slide 5

So far, I've shared with you a little bit of our company's background. Before I move on and talk about some of our exciting products, I'd like to give you a brief overview of the biomedical and robotic home appliances industry.

在谈到我们的一些精良产品前,我已向你们介绍了我公司的背景情况。现在简略介绍一下生物工程和家用机器人产业的有关情况。

As I've mentioned, our two primary fields of operation are those two industries. Although it's true that we started out as a bioengineering firm and our sales in this field eclipse our sales of automated appliances, it is our projection that the automated home appliance market will continue to become more important to us. So, I would like to give you a brief overview of both industries.

正如我刚才所说,我们所经营的两大领域是两个不同的产业。我们是以生物工程产品起家,但自动化产品后来居上。自动化产品对我们而言,更为重要。现就这两个产业介绍如下。

Bioengineering is essentially the application of engineering knowledge to the fields of medicine and biology. The area of bioengineering that SYK Robotics focuses on is the development and manufacturing of artificial means to assist or replace defective body parts. Our major product, limb replacements, falls into this category. Total sales for the entire bioengineering industry amounted to around 2.8 billion dollars in 1999, and experts say that the industry will continue to expand almost indefinitely.

从本质说,生物工程是将工程技术运用于生物医学。我公司着力发展的生物工程就是生产能够帮助和替换残疾人肢体的人工假肢。这是我们的主要产品。1999 年其销售总额为 28 亿美元。专家预测,该产业在将来会有更大的发展。

Now I'd like to describe the robotics industry. The robotics industry is huge. It involves everything from industrial robots used in automobile production to tiny devices used in artificial hearts. SYK Robotics is mainly engaged in automated home appliances. This is a brand new field. The dream of having robots to clean our houses is not science fiction any more. From robot vacuum cleaners to robot lawn mowers, the future is getting closer and closer. If I were to have another opportunity, I would go over some of these stunning new inventions with you. For now, it suffices to say this is the ultimate growth industry.

现在谈一谈机器人工业的有关情况。机器人工业的前景是广阔的。大到自动化生产的工业机器人,小到人工心脏器件。我公司主要生产家用机器人设备。这是一个崭新的领域。科幻小说中让机器人打扫房间已不再是梦想。从机器人真空吸尘器到机器人除草机,未来美景日益接近。如果再有机会,我一定会与诸位共享新的发明创造的成果。现在,我所能说的是:这是目前的最新产业。

Company Introduction—Slide 6

Now let's move on and look at some of SYK Robotics' business goals and our unique capabilities. Our dream is to usher in an age where everyone can enjoy the fruits of modern science. I know what you are thinking. Sure, robot vacuum cleaners are nice, but who's going to buy them? At SYK Robotics, we're not talking about producing products just for the rich few who can afford neat little toys; we are not talking about things that might look impressive to neighbors; we are talking about things that will actually make lives better. We're talking about a life free from disabilities. We're talking about a world where physical problems and limitations won't keep us from doing what we want to do. This is our goal: to make products that help everyday people with everyday problems.

让我们继续看一看蓝天机器人研发公司的经营目标和独一无二的能力。我们的梦想是引导大家进入一个新的世纪,每一个人都能享受到现代科学的成果。我知道你们在想什么。是的,机器人除草机是不错,谁购买呢? 在蓝天机器人研发公司,我们不是谈论只为少数富人生产干净的小玩意儿,也不是让邻居看得眼馋的东西,而是生产那些使人们生活更好的产品,摆脱疾病困扰的产品,我们在谈论这样一个世界,在那里,人们的身体缺陷和限制不会成为我们想要干任何事情的障碍。这就是我们的目标:生产能够帮助人们克服困难的产品。

And we believe we have the capabilities to do so. As I've mentioned already, we've built up our expertise and built automated products to improve human welfare. We have a highly qualified R&D team and a management team armed with business know – how. And we have a history of successful products. We think we are in a position to become the leading developer of new and successful products in the bioengineering and robotics industries.

我们相信我们能够做到这一点。因为,如刚才提到的那样,我们已拥有了专门技术和自动化生产线,用以改善人类福祉。我们拥有高素质的研发队伍和具有丰富经营才干的管理层,我们拥有成功的产品历史。我们认为我们能够成为新兴的生物工程和家用机器人产业的领军企业。

I believe that will end my presentation for today. SYK Robotics is a goal – oriented company that has had a history of successful products. We believe we are ready to carry our company and our industry into the next millennium. Since we're short of time, I will finish my presentation at this point. If you have any questions, feel free to ask me about anything. I hope that I'll have more opportunities during this conference to introduce our company to you. Thank you for listening.

今天的介绍就到这里。蓝天机器人研发公司经营目标明确,产品成功。相信我们已做好准备,将公司和产品带入到新的世纪。因时间关系,就到此为止。如有问题,请尽管提问,希望我能有更多的机会向诸位介绍我公司情况。谢谢。

Key Expressions

Starting a Presentation 开始介绍

Greeting, Name, Position 问候、姓名、职务

Let me introduce myself

Let me just start by introducing myself. I'm…

be in charge of

be responsible for

I'm in charge of

I'm responsible for

Good morning, ladies and gentlemen, let me just start by introducing myself.

女士们,先生们,早晨好。让我先自我介绍一下。

I'm in charge of the Human Resources Department.

我负责人力资源部工作。

I'm responsible for the benefit policy of our company.

我负责我公司福利政策工作。

Title/Subject 题目

I'd like to talk today about

The topic of today's presentation is

I'm going to + [inform, introduce, discuss, go over]

Today, I'd like to talk about our product line for the year 2002.

今天,我要讲一下我公司 2002 年生产线的问题。

Today, we're going to take a look at our new business model.

今天,我们将看一看新的业务模式。

For this phase of my presentation, I would like to go over the major features of this new product.

在这一部分介绍中,我想讲一下这种新产品的主要特点。

Outline/Main Parts 概要、要点

I've divided [split] my talk into ~ parts [sections]

First/Second/Third

I'm going to split my talk into four parts.

我的讲话分为四个部分。

First, I want to start by distributing some handouts for reference.

首先,我将散发一些介绍提纲,供参考。

Finally, we'll go over our financial report for the year 2001.

最后,我们将看一看 2001 年的财务报告。

Length 时间的长短

take

last

This presentation will take [last]

I will speak [talk] about for - minutes

The presentation will take about 15 minutes.

介绍大约占 15 分钟。

I will speak for about 20 minutes.

我将讲约 20 分钟。

I plan to be brief.

我将简明扼要地讲。

Policy on Questions 提问方式

feel free to interrupt

at the end of my talk

after my talk

If you have any questions, please feel free to interrupt.

如有什么问题，可以打断我的谈话，提出来。

I'd be glad to answer any questions at the end of my talk.

介绍结束后，我将高兴地回答任何问题。

After my talk, there'll be time for any questions.

介绍结束后，给大家留出提问题的时间。

Practice 1

1. Ladies and gentlemen. My name is Michael Lee. I'm the new Managing Director.

2. Welcome to Office X. I am in charge of production.

3. As you know, I want to talk today about the marketing plans.

4. I'm going to inform you about our new product.

5. I've divided my talk into four parts.

6. First, I want to start by giving you some background information.

7. This presentation will take about 30 minutes.

8. I plan to be brief, about 5 minutes.

9. Please, feel free to interrupt anytime during my presentation.

10. I'd be glad to take any questions at the end of my presentation.

Practice 2

Good morning, let me just start by introducing myself. My name is Laura Marie, and I'm the new marketing director at Marathon Athletics. I'd like to talk today about our new line of crosstrainer athletic shoes which we will be introducing next spring. Firstly, what I want to do is show the progression of our target market from older to younger clients. I plan to be brief so we can get on with the rest of today's meetings. If you have any questions please feel free to interrupt.

早晨好。先自我介绍一下。我叫玛丽·劳拉。我是马拉松运动公司新来的营销主管。今天，我要讲的是我们的新款交叉松紧扣运动鞋，明年春季即将推出。首先，介绍目标市场发展过程，从老年顾客到青年顾客。我计划简单扼要地讲，以便继续今天的其他会议。如有问题，请不要客气可以随时提出来。

Practice 3

Ladies and gentlemen, my name is Michael Lee, I'm the new managing director at Horizons Human Resources. Today, I plan to talk about the new benefits policy of our company. I've divided my talk into four parts so you can see how each aspect affects you personally. I will speak for about 20 minutes so we can get out of here before lunch. I'd be glad to answer any questions at the end of my talk.

女士们，先生们，我叫迈克尔·李。我是地平线人力资源公司新来的常务董事。我来讲一讲我公司新政策的有益之处。我将我的讲话分为四部分，你们可以看得出，每一部分都与你们个人息息相关。我的讲话大约需要 20 分钟，午饭前结束。讲话结束时，我很高兴回答任何问题。

In the Middle of the Presentation I 介绍进行中（Ⅰ）

Beginning the Main Body 主题开始

Let's start with…

We can begin by talking about…

To begin with…

Now, OK, right…

What I'd like to talk about first is the new business strategy.

我首先要讲的是新的经营战略。

Right. Let's start off by looking at the annual report.

对啦，首先看一看年度报告。

To begin with, I would like to tell you the major features of this new product.

首先，我想讲一下这种新产品的主要特点。

Sequencing the Idea 讲话顺序

First, Second, Third…

There are four stages to the project…

At the beginning, Later, Then, Finally…

There are three things to consider.

有三件事需要考虑。

Our next focus area is Total Quality Management.

我们下一个重点是全面质量管理。

The third key point I'd like to address is market share.

我要强调的第三要点是市场占有率。

Finally, we will start focusing on diversification.

最后,我们的重点放在产品多样化上。

Ending a Section 结束一部分介绍

That's all for this topic…

That covers everything on this topic…

To summarize…

That's all for this topic.

这个话题就到此为止吧。

I think that covers everything on this topic.

关于这个话题,该说的都该谈到了。

To summarize, I think that invention leads to success.

总之,那个发明定会成功的。

Opening a New Section 开始另一段内容

Moving right along…

That brings me to…

Moving right along, I would like to demonstrate how this product works.

接下来,我要展示一下该产品的功能。

Now let's move on to the last page of the report.

下面,让我们接着看报告的最后一页。

That brings me to the next point, which is that our sales are lagging.

我下一个要讲的是销售状况仍萎靡不振。

Practice 1

1. Now let's move to the first part of my talk, which is about our new business model.

2. Right. We can begin by looking at some of the sales figures.

3. There are four stages to the project.

4. The first point I'd like to address is market share.

5. I think that covers everything on this topic.

6. That's all I wanted to say about this topic.

7. I'd like to summarize it before I move on to my next topic.

8. Now let's go on to the next section of this chart.

9. Moving right along, now I want to look at our budget for next year.

10. Let's go on to the each transaction cost.

Practice 2

Now let's move on to the first part of my talk, which is about the product release schedule for our new video game console. There are three things to consider. First, we have to target the specialty markets and online retailers. Second, we must target general retail stores. Third, we will allow wholesalers to take part in the action. I think that deals with the sales revenues. Now I'd like to turn to the promotions and marketing aspects of our release.

现在来谈第一部分,关于新的计算机游戏控制台产品销售计划,要考虑三件事:一是目标定在专业市场和在线零售商;二是目标定在普通零售店;三是我们要让批发商参与销售。我认为这决定了销售收入。下面谈一谈有关促销和营销的问题。

Practice 3

OK. Let's start with the first point, which is what our test audience should be. At the beginning, we will test with teenage males from 13 ~ 18 years. Later, we will test with teenage females from the same range. Finally, we will screen with both males and females in the audience. I think that covers everything on this topic. Moving right along, now I want to look at the box office sales for similar genre films within the last two years.

好啦,让我们先看第一点。我们的影片试销的对象应是哪些人呢? 初期,应是13 ~ 18 岁的男孩子;然后是同等年龄的女孩子;最后,在他们中间测试筛选。这是第一点的全部内容。下面,看一看近两年内,同类影片的票房收入。

In the Middle of the Presentation II 介绍进行中(II)

Emphasizing 强调

emphasize, stress

I'd like to emphasize [stress]

I'd like to emphasize that customer dissatisfaction has been increasing.

我要强调的是,顾客不满意度一直在增加。

We did achieve many things last year.

去年,我们的确取得了多项成绩。

This is a very, very important question.

这是一个非常、非常重要的问题。

Proposing 建议

recommend, suggest, propose

I suggest [recommend, propose]

My suggestion [recommendation, proposal] is

I suggest that we reshape the existing development plans.

我建议重新修改现有的发展计划。

In my opinion, our only option is to increase production.

依我看来,我们的唯一选择就是增加生产。

My recommendation is that we reevaluate our relationship with this company.

我建议重新评估我们与该公司的关系。

Engaging Your Audience 与听众互动

How can we explain this?

Does anyone want to comment about this?

哪位愿对此发表意见?

How many people here have ever predicted a stock's downfall?

这里有多少人预测股票将下跌。

Tom, you have a lot of knowledge in this area. Do you have anything to add?

汤姆,这方面你知识渊博。你要补充什么吗?

Practice 1

1. This is a very, very difficult problem.

2. We need a solution and we need it now.

3. We did think very carefully about this.

4. I'd like to emphasize the low performance of this particular month.

5. It does seem to be the best solution.

6. Peter, I know you have a lot of experience. Could you comment?

7. Is there anything we can do about this?

8. In my opinion, the only way forward is to cut back on staff.

9. I suggest that we reschedule phase four.

10. I propose that we consult our design team on this one.

Practice 2

We had an extremely good year. As you can see, the sales for this year are 10% higher than for the same period last year. Does anyone want to comment on this? Well, I'm sure you're all as excited as I am. My recommendation is that we try to improve on these figures and not just try and maintain these kinds of sales numbers.

我们今年业务状况格外的好。如你所知,今年的销售比去年同期高 10%,对此有谁要发表意见吗? 我相信你们和我一样振奋不已。我建议不能停留在目前水平上,要百尺竿头,再进一步。

Practice 3

This is a very, very important question. How can we attract new customers to our product? Tom, I know you have a lot of experience with this, could you comment? I feel we have to make subtle changes to the design that will attract new customers but will not alienate our old ones. I suggest that we consult our design team on this one.

这是一个非常、非常重要的问题。怎样才能让新的消费者对我们的产品感兴趣呢？汤姆，我知道，在这方面你有很多经验，你来讲一讲？我认为，应将设计做一些改动以便吸引新顾客，但不能因此而丢掉老顾客。我建议我们和设计组的人员商量一下。

Using Visuals 利用可视图形、表格

pie chart

bar graph

table

line graph

flow chart

organigram

Let's take a look at

I'd like to show you

OK. Let's take a look at the figures for this month.

好，让我们看一下本月的数字。

I'd like to show you the pie chart, which shows sales figures for the year 1999.

我想让你看一下统计图表，它显示出 1999 年的销售数字。

I have some flip charts to show you.

我向你展示一下几张配套挂图。

Check with the Audience 与听众沟通

Can you see

Is that clear

In focus

Can everyone see that?

每个人都看得清楚吗？

Is that clear for everyone?

都清楚吗？

Is that in focus?

都清楚吗？

Describing the Visual 对视图加以描述

illustrate, refer to

This graph shows [illustrates, refers to]

This graph shows our latest sales figures.

这个曲线图显示出最近以来的销售数字。

Here we can see a comparison between the two divisions.

这里,我们看得出这两部分之间的差别。

This is a graph, which represents the rise of our stock over the last five years.

这个曲线图显示出最近 5 年以来的股价增长情况。

Comparison 比较

compare

This compares A with B

Let's compare the

Here you see a comparison between

Let's compare the new product line to the old one.

让我们比较一下新老生产线的区别。

Here you see a comparison between our product and those of our nearest competitors.

这里,你们看得出我们的产品与离我们最近的竞争者产品的差别。

This graph compares the west coast and east coast branches performances.

这个曲线图显示出东西海岸两分公司的工作状况的差别。

Practice 1

1. I have some visuals that I'd like to show you.

2. Now let's take a look at the latest sales figures.

3. I'd like to show you the new design for our primary product.

4. Can everyone see that?

5. Can everyone see what these figures represent?

6. As you can see, this is a chart that shows our earnings.

7. Here we can see our latest sales figures.

8. Let's compare these two figures.

9. Here you can see a comparison between A and B.

10. This graph compares the new line with the old one.

Practice 2

I'd like to show you a chart detailing the profit margins for this quarter in comparison to those from the last four years. As you can see, we've steadily declined in this period every year despite rising sales in our other quarters. Can everyone see that? This shows that we're focusing too much on our seasonal sales and not enough on our year –

round potential. Let's compare the other quarters to find out where our problems might lie.

让我们看一下这个图表。它详细地标明了本季度与过去 4 年同期相比的利润率。你可以看得出来,每年这个季度利润额都在下降,而其他季度都在上升。这说明我们太过于强调季节性销售,而忽视全年的销售潜力。比较一下其他季度销售额,就会发现问题所在。

Practice 3

Let's look at this. This is the new logo for our sports team. The design adds an edge to our outdated logo that falls more in line with those of other teams. Is that clear for everyone? As you can see, this is quite a departure from our previous logo and will hopefully cause quite a stir with the media. Here you see a comparison with other teams. Their merchandise sales went up after a logo change.

让我们看一看。这是我们体育用品新的标识。新的标识的设计比起原来过时的标识做了较大的改动,与其他品类的标识更趋于一致。清楚吧? 这与以前的大不一样。希望经媒体炒作后会引起轰动。你们可以看得出比较情况。他们改动一下标识设计,销售额大增。

Ending the Presentation 结束介绍

Signaling the End 示意结束

bring to the end

end my talk

That brings me to the end of my presentation.

介绍到此为止。

OK, that ends my talk.

好,讲话到此为止。

That covers all I wanted to say today.

今天我要讲的就这么多。

Summarizing 总结

To sum up, in brief

summarize

go over

Let me just run over the key points again.

再次扼要复述一下要点。

To sum up, we need to reestablish our brand in a younger image.

总而言之,我们需要重新建立起较年轻一点的品牌形象。

In brief, we're losing money.

简言之,我们赔钱了。

Concluding 结束

summarizing

conclude

To conclude, In conclusion

I'd like to finish by saying

In conclusion, we need to refocus our online business.

总之,我们需要重新调整我们的在线业务。

To conclude, I'd like to say that this is our best year ever.

最后,我要说,这是有史以来最好的一年。

I'd like to finish by saying that we've exceeded expectations but we can't get lazy.

最后,我要说我们已超过了人们的期待,但应再接再厉。

Inviting Questions 邀请提问题

Are there any questions?

So, now I'd be interested to hear your comments.

I'd be glad to try and answer any questions.

Practice 1

1. That brings me to the end of my presentation.

2. That covers everything I wanted to say today.

3. So, that's all I have to say.

4. Before I finish, let me just go over these points.

5. To sum up, we must focus on cutting back on labor costs.

6. In conclusion, I think this is a very significant discovery.

7. I'd like to finish by saying we need to refocus our online business.

8. Are there any questions?

9. I'd be glad to answer any questions.

10. Now I'd like to invite your comments.

Practice 2

That covers all I wanted to talk about today. I hope it's not been too discouraging. To sum up, we must focus on cutting back on labor costs to offset our dropping profit margins. I'd like to conclude by saying that this doesn't mean we need to have massive layoffs. I'm just trying to show how our current workers must become more efficient. Now

I'd like to invite your comments as I'm sure you're all worried how this will affect your place here.

今天的介绍到此结束。希望你们不感到枯燥无味。总之,我们必须削减人工成本,以弥补利润下降所带来的损失。最后,我要说,这并不意味着大量解雇人员,而是我们目前的工作人员要更加努力,提高效率。我确信你们对自己的职位有所担心,请发表意见吧。

Practice 3

So, that's all I have to say about the accounting firms who've lobbied for our account. I'll briefly summarize the main points. This particular firm has offered us the most for our money, but these other firms have more established performance histories. Are there any questions about any of the other candidates?

有关那家会计师事务所的情况,我就说这么多。要点是:如我们花钱雇用这家事务所,它可以胜任。但其他事务所业绩更好。对于其他候选事务所,还有什么意见发表?

Handling Questions 回答问题

Positive Response 肯定回答

That's a good question.

Thank you for that question.

That's a good question.

Thank you for asking that question.

That's a really good one. It allows me to address the problems and offer some solutions.

Clarifying a Question 澄清问题

understand, catch, follow

If I understand you correctly, you want to know...

You're asking me about...right?

Sorry, I'm not sure I've understood. Could you repeat?

对不起,我不太明白。请再重复一遍。

If I understand you correctly, you want to know if there are other ways of dealing with the decrease in our profits.

如我理解正确的话,你是想知道,是否有其他办法来解决我们利润下降的问题。

Do you mean to ask how it might affect their ability to sell their stock?

你是说这怎么会影响他们卖股票的能力的？

Avoiding Giving an Answer 回避问题

I can't answer that.

That's not my field.

I'm afraid I can't really answer that.

恐怕我难以回答那个问题。

Perhaps we could deal with that later.

那个问题以后再说吧。

I'm sure Mr. Smith could answer that question.

相信史密斯先生能回答这个问题。

Checking the Questioner is Satisfied 核实提问者是否满意

Does that answer your question?

Is that clear now?

Does that answer your question?

这是否能回答你的问题？

Is that clear now?

清楚吗？

Can we move on?

我们还接着谈吗？

Practice 1

1. That's a good question.

2. Thank you for asking that question.

3. Sorry, I didn't catch your question.

4. Could you repeat that for me, please?

5. You are asking me about the possible problems that might arise with our new hiring policies, is that right?

6. I'm afraid I can't really answer that.

7. Perhaps we could deal with that later.

8. Does that answer your question?

9. Is that clear now?

10. Can we move on?

Practice 2

Thank you for asking that question. I guess I didn't make that clear enough in my presentation. You are asking me about the possible problems that might arise with our new hiring policies, is that right? I'm sure Mr. Smith could answer that question. He's much more familiar with the Equal Opportunity Employment act. May we go on to the next topic?

感谢你提出这个问题。我想可能我在介绍时没讲清楚。你问有关我们的雇工政策可能会带来的问题,是吗? 我想史密斯先生可以回答这个问题。他对公平机会就业法非常熟悉。好,下一个问题。

Practice 3

That's a really good one. It allows me to say that I don't think our shareholders need to worry about how this will affect their stocks. We've clearly shown that this kind of move has no effect on stock values. Do you mean to ask how it might affect their ability to sell their stock? I'm afraid I can't really answer that. Those kinds of decisions are up to the regulations board. Does that answer your question?

这个问题提得好。我只能说;我们的股东没有必要担心这一举措会对股票产生影响。我们已讲得很清楚,这不会影响股票价值的。你们是不是要问这会不会影响出售股票的能力? 恐怕我难以回答这个问题。这些决定取决于政策制定部门。这样回答满意吗?

Relative Expressions

Business Introductions

Informal:

This is my boss, Mr. Stratford.

Jared, this is my secretary, Barbara.

Good to meet you.

Nice to meet you too.

I'd like you to meet my co - worker, Collin Beck.

Collin, this is Susan Palmer.

Nice to meet you.

My pleasure.

Have you met, Jason?

Jason, this is Teresa.

Hi, I'm Jill Watson.

I don't believe we've met. I'm Greg.

Formal:

I'd like to introduce you to my dear friend, Mrs. Pleasant.

Allow me to introduce myself/my colleague, Ms. Winters

Let me introduce you to my colleague, Dean Richards.

Mr. Richards, this is David Porter from Aerospace Inc.

How do you do?

It's a pleasure meeting you.

Company Description

What company do you work for?

Which company are you with?

Who do you represent?

I work for ABC Company.

I'm with ABC.

I represent (the) XYZ (company).

What is the name of your company?

Where are you located?

The name of our company is...

Our company is located in...

Our headquarters is in...

What (type of business) do you do?

What business are you in?

We are in the computer business.

We're in computers

We sell...

We produce...

We manufacture...

Our major products are...

Describing Business Activities

What do you do at ABC Company?

I am in charge of marketing.

I'm responsible for sales.

I program computers.

I recruit and train employees.

What does your company do?

We design software.

We build storage units.

We produce small appliances.

We're in the insurance business.

Describing Products

Tell me about (this product)

What can you tell me about (this product)?

Can you give me some information/details about this?

What is special/unique about this?

What are the specifications?

Let me tell you about...

This is our (newest) product.

This is one of our latest designs.

It is made of...

It can be used for...

You can use it to...

You can...with it

This has/contains...

This one features...

This comes with...

This is equipped with...

This particular model...

This is priced at...

This costs...

Describing Projects

What are your current projects?

What are you working on (at present)?

What are your major initiatives in this area?

We are currently working on...

We are in the process of...

We are developing...

We are designing...

We are building...

We are marketing...

Information about Company

What does your company do?

What is your specialty?

What do you specialize in?

What is your main line of business?

We produce marketing materials.

We specialize in art and design.

What are your major products?

What services do you provide?

We produce office machines.

We design software.

We provide technical support.

Information about Products

Could you give me some (more) information on this?

What can you tell me about this (product)?

Tell me about this one/model.

This is one of our top brands.

It's our best selling refrigerator.

This one is the best in its class.

We're really pleased with its performance.

It's an excellent computer.

I highly recommend this one.

This model comes with several features.

This particular one has two components.

useful Phrases

Starting the presentation

Good morning/good afternoon ladies and gentlemen.

The topic of my presentation today is...

What I'm going to talk about today is...

Why you are giving this presentation

The purpose of this presentation is...

This is important because...

My objective is to...

Introducing the first point

Let's start/begin with...

Showing graphics, transparencies, slides etc.

I'd like to illustrate this by showing you...

Moving on to the next point

Now let's move on to...

Giving more details

I'd like to expand on this aspect/problem/point.

Let me elaborate on that...

Would you like me to expand on/elaborate on that?

Changing to a different topic

I'd like to turn to something completely different...

Referring to something which is off the topic

I'd like to digress here for a moment and just mention that...

Referring back to an earlier point

Let me go back to what I said earlier about...

Summarizing or repeating the main points

I'd like to recap the main points of my presentation.

—first I covered

—then we talked about

—finally we looked at

I'd now like to sum up the main points which were...

Conclusion

I'm going to conclude by...saying that/inviting you to/ quoting...

In conclusion, let me...leave you with this thought/invite you to...

Questions

Finally, I'll be happy to answer your questions.

Now I'd like to invite any questions you may have.

Do you have any questions?

Useful expressions for negotiation

Starting Negotiations 开始谈判

Next, let's turn to...

Let's move on to Item 2.

Let's move on to the next topic.

We need to move on.

The next item (of business) is...

We need to go on to the next item.

Shall/Should we move on?

Let's move on to number two.

The next item on the agenda is...

What's next on the agenda?

We would have to study this. Can we get back to you on this later?

We'll have to consult with our colleagues back in the office.

We'd like to get back to you on it.

Before we move on, I think we should...

Wait a minute. We haven't discussed...

Don't you think we need to...

I will now hand you over to Mr. Brown, who is...

I will now hand the floor over to Mr. Adams, who is...

Now let me hand the meeting over to my colleague, Ms.

Jones, who...

Not so fast. We haven't (yet)...

商务谈判之产品描述和公司介绍术语

制作精巧 skillful manufacture

工艺精良 sophisticated technology

最新工艺 latest technology

加工精细 finely processed

设计精巧 deft design

造型新颖 modern design

造型优美 beautiful design

设计合理 professional design

造型富丽华贵 luxuriant in design

结构合理 rational construction

款式新颖 attractive design

款式齐全 various styles

式样优雅 elegant shape

花色入时 fashionable patterns

任君选择 for your selection

五彩缤纷 colorful

色彩艳丽 beautiful in colors

色泽光润 color brilliancy

色泽素雅 delicate colors

瑰丽多彩 pretty and colorful

洁白透明 pure white and translucence

洁白纯正 pure whiteness

品质优良 excellent quality (high quality)

质量上乘 superior quality

质量稳定 stable quality

质量可靠 reliable quality

品种繁多 wide varieties

规格齐全 complete in specifications

保质保量 quality and quantity assured

性能可靠 dependable performance

操作简便 easy and simple to handle

使用方便 easy to use
经久耐用 durable in use
以质优而闻名 well – known for its fine quality
数量之首 The king of quantity
质量最佳 The queen of quality
信誉可靠 reliable reputation
闻名世界 world – wide renown

久负盛名 to have a long standing reputation
誉满中外 to enjoy high reputation at home and abroad
历史悠久 to have a long history
畅销全球 selling well all over the world
深受欢迎 to win warm praise from customers

实训综合习题

I . put the following sentences into Chinese.

1. Let me introduce our company to you.

2. Please ask questions at any time.

3. This is our sample room.

4. Our factory specializes in office furniture.

5. Our factory manufactures toys.

6. Our product ,has a solid reputation.

7. I'll get a couple of product catalogues for you.

8. Let me show you the workshops.

9. Let's have a look at the layout of the exhibition.

10. Our products are of the best quality and the lowest price.

II . put the following sentences into English.

1. 我们的绝大多数产品是为成年人生产的。

2. 我们的产品在国内国际都很畅销。

3. 我们在中国各地都有销售网点。

4. 这是我们新开发的计算机。

5. 欢迎您试试。

6. 我们只卖家用电器。

7. 我们的办公室计算机化程度很高。

8. 做出决定之前请您再考虑一下。

9. 几天内如果货物备好,我会通知您。

10. 我们进出口业务都做。

11. 我们刚刚开发出一个新型号。

24

12. 车间自动化水平很高。

13. 我们保证产品达到国际标准。

III. Role play.

Task 1

Role simulation：One plays the role of a Chinese businessperson；the other, as a foreign business person.

Your role：

You are the sales managers of the Tianjin Home Textiles Corporation. Your products include towels, bedclothes and curtains. You are now having a talk with an American business person about your company, the line of business and the products, trying to persuade him to buy your products.

Your partner's role：

You are a novice（新手）at the import and export business. This is your first visit to China. You are not sure whether you can close a deal or not. The goods you want to purchase are bedclothes. After going over the catalogues, you find some items very attractive. So you ask a lot of questions.

Task 2

Mr. Anderson, an American businessman, is visiting an exhibition. He is rather interested in a new product, a pair of socalled "air cushioned" shoes, which are manufactured by a small business. Mr. Zhang, an exhibitor from the company, is trying his best to provide Mr. Anderson with detailed information on both his company and the new product.

IV. Topics for Group Discussion.

1. If you find some items attractive and want to purchase, what questions should you ask?

2. Try to discuss the ways to provide your new customer with detailed information on both your company and your new product.

第 2 章　询盘

Inquiries（Ⅰ）

G. Good morning.

S：Good morning.

G：Through the introduction of Mr. Smith, our mutual friend, I got to know your name and address. As my customers in India want to buy machine tools, I've come to make some inquiries. Do you happen to export machine tools?

S：Yes. As a matter of fact, we specialize in this range of goods and have an experience of over thirty years.

G：Can I have a copy of your catalogue?

S：By all means. Here's a catalogue for some popular ones. They enjoy fast sales in your neighboring countries. Demand always exceeds supply. I'm sure your customers in Singapore will be greatly interested in them.

G：We've been thinking of placing an order if they are of the types we want.

S：Never mind the types. We also take special orders. That is to say, we can make machine tools according to our customer's samples and exact specifications. You know, service is the motto of our company.

G：That sounds very encouraging. Now, Please tell me, do you offer FOB, or CIF?

S：Either. Which do you prefer?

G：I'd rather you quoted us your CIF prices.

S：We'll see to it when we make you offers.

G：All right. Here's a list of our requirements. I hope you will make us your most favorable offer on the basis of CIF Singapore.

S：Thank you for your inquiry. We'll make a careful study of your list and do everything possible to meet your requirements.

Words and Expressions

Singapore 新加坡

inquiry 问问,询价

specialize 专门化,专营

exceed 超越

place 放置

order 订单,订货

type 型号

sample 样品

specification 规格

motto 座右铭

FOB(free on the board) 离岸价

CIF (cost, insurance and freight) 到岸价

Karachi 卡拉奇

quote 报价

enjoy fast sales 畅销

happen to do something 恰巧做某事

by all means 想办法一定要

place an order 订货

see to it 注意,料理

do everything possible 尽一切可能

Notes

see to 注意,料理

We'll see to your requirements when we have fresh supplies.

我们有新货可供时,将考虑你们的需要。

I hope you will see to the matter immediately.

希望你们能立即处理此事。

see to it that 或者 see that 从句

We shall be glad if you will see to it that the contract is duly signed.

如果你方对合同完满签字能给予关照,我们将十分高兴。

Inquiries(Ⅱ)

Y:Now you're seen our samples, what do you think of them?

J:I should say the quality and finish are all right. Nevertheless they are not exactly what I want.

Y:Is there anything wrong with them? Let me know your opinions frankly. I'll be only too anxious to have them.

J:Well, for one thing, I don't think I like the color. Besides, the design is a little out of date.

Y:That can be adjusted very easily. Just tell me the color and design you have in mind. I'll change them accordingly. Believe me, we can make them to everything of your desired specifications.

J:But before coming to concrete business, there is yet one point I wish you to make quite clear.

Y:What is it?

J:When can I expect delivery? Is it possible for you to ship the goods in May?

Y:If you place your order with us in a week or so, I can delivery the goods in May. But then, you will certainly have to advise us of your opinions on the improvement of the products as soon as possible.

J：There will be no problem. Another thing. Could I have discount if my order is a large one?

Y：I can hardly give you an answer right now. It all depends on how large your order is.

J：Right. We'll leave this problem for some other time. At the moment I'll get in touch with my customers right away and let you know their responses immediately.

Words and Expressions

finish 最后工序   shipment 装船
concrete 具体的   be only too anxious 十分着急的
nevertheless 尽管如此   out of date 过时的
hesitate 犹豫不决   make clear 澄清
frankly 坦率地   get in touch with 与……联系
desire 渴望   leave for some other time 留待其他
delivery 交货   时间

Notes

I should say the quality and finish are all right.

I should say 我得说。常含有"我确实认为"的意思。

At the moment I'll get in touch with my customers right away and let you know their responses immediately.

与某人联系可以用：

be(get) in touch with someone

be(get) in contact with someone

have contact with someone

contact someone

approach someone

keep in contact with someone

establish contact with someone

Sample Dialogue 1. An Enquiry for Refrigerators

Mr. Zhang is Sales Manager of a Company, a firm which manufactures refrigerators. He is talking with a prospective American customer, Mr. mason, who is visiting the factory.

M：It was very kind of you to show me round your factory. Everything I saw was impressive, especially the quality control methods.

Z：Good. I'm pleased you like our whole operation here. I'm also glad you've found our quality control methods interesting. As you saw at the end of the assembly line, we conduct an overall test on every set of refrigerators instead of doing sampling test. No fridge will be allowed to go out of the factory unless everything is OK.

M: I heard a lot about your quality back home, and a business friend of mine think highly of your products. I thought it was publicity. Seeing is believing, so I'm now completely convinced.

Z: I can safely say that very few can match us on quality, and on price as well.

M: Sure. I'll say! Can you give me details of these fridges? As soon as possible.

Z: I'll give you our brochures for the fridges, which give the specifications of the models and also list the prices for different models.

M: Tell me, are the prices quoted firm to the end of the year?

Z: No, I am afraid I cannot guarantee that.

M: Do you grant any quantity or other discounts?

Z: Yes, we do. It certainly depends on the size of the order.

M: And the terms of payment?

Z: By letter of credit.

M: What about after - sales services?

Z: We offer two - years free of charge guarantee and life maintenance service. We have special maintenance services in most big cities across the United States.

M: OK, would you please let me have all the sales literature, and any other publicity material. I'd like to keep that sort of thing on file in my office and show them to my clients whenever it is necessary. You never know when it'll come in useful.

Sample Dialogue 2. Enquiry and Trial Order

Ali Husan, an Egyptian importer finds Chinese - made glazed tiles interesting and is talking on a trial order so as to develop the tiles business in the domestic market in Egypt.

D: Good morning. Welcome to the stand of the Ideal Tiles. What can I do for you. ?

H: Good morning. I'm Ali Husan, an importer from Egypt. I've shopped round the exhibition and found your ceramic tiles of better quality.

D: Ah, that is true, Mr. Husan. I'm Ding Chun, the sales manager. Here's my business card. We the Ideal Tiles are a leading manufacturer of glazed tiles in China. To tell you the truth, our products are of really good quality at moderate price .

H: That's good. It has recently become a fashion in our country to decorate homes, especially the floor with large sizes of glazed tiles. There is a large demand for tiles in the market. So I would like to know your supply position.

D: We can supply in a wide selection of tiles in every conceivable size and color.

Here's a copy of brochure. It gives in full details the designs, sizes and colors in which the tiles are available.

H: What about the tiles in big sizes?

D: We have sizes as large as 40mm, 50mm, 60mm and even 80mm. They're mainly used as tile flooring. Now come with me to our tile – decorated model room. This way, please.

H: Hmm. It's marvelous. Was the floor decorated with nature marble stone?

D: Oh, no, by no means. It was done with our tiles.

H: You don't say! Graceful and comfortable. They look like so real the marble that they can pass fake imitation for genuine.

D: You know, the imitation is even better than the genuine. For one thing, the natural marbles are apt to contain substance of radiation, which is harmful to the residents' health. The second advantage is that the surface of marble like tiles is not smooth so that the residents won't slip over as they sometimes do on the real marbles.

H: Oh, that's impressive. But are the tiles likely to be affected by rising damp when they laid on the ground floor? What special preparation would be necessary for the under-flooring?

D: We have a sales rep and a technician working in your part of the world. They will, once summoned, call on you to inspect your customers' floors and will advise you on what preparation is necessary and how to prevent dampness to create a problem. If necessary in the future, you can set up a service team and we can provide them with training.

H: You're really considerate. Now what about the price?

D: Here's the price list. If you order in large quantities, we can offer 10% discount.

H: To start with, I'm afraid what I can do is to place a trial order to test the market. If the tiles prove to be satisfactory to our customers, I'm sure considerable orders will flood in. I'll have a close look at your catalogue and price – list, and then select some items for the trial order.

D: OK. To help you push sales of our products in your district, we would like to allow you 5 % discount for this trial order as an exception.

H: Thank you. I'll be back this afternoon or early tomorrow morning. Goodbye.

D: Goodbye.

Sample Dialogue 3. An Enquiry for Mountain Bikes

Wang Mei, the sales manager of a bicycle – manufacturing company, is receiving Mr. Green, an English. businessman who enquires for mountain bikes.

W: Good morning. Can I help you?

G: Yes. While I'm touring in China I've receive from my office an enquiry for mountain bikes. As this is new business to us, a friend in British Embassy told me you're the leading manufacturer of bikes.

W: Right. We've produced a wide range of mountains bikes, for men, women and children. Here's a brochure and a catalogue about our bikes. If you come with me to the showroom, this way, please.

G: Oh, such a large variety of colorful bikes. It's a real eye – opener for me.

W: What is it in particular you're interested in?

G: But first could you tell me something about them?

W: Well, of course. We have 3 – gear, 5 – gear, 10 – gear and 15 – gear mountain bikes.

G: Excuse me, I didn't quite catch what you said by things like 3 – gear.

W: Oh, they have 3, 5, 10 and 15 speeds respectively. Got that?

C: Yes. I see.

W: And in addition to all black and all blue, they are available in 5 different color combinations—his one is purple with yellow, but it also comes in green with blue, red with gold and so on.

G: Oh, what is the price?

W: US $ 75 each for men's model, US $ 80 for women's model, and US $ 50 for children's model.

G: Any chance for making it lower?

W: I'm afraid not. To be frank with you, our bikes are of the best quality in the trade, but some township factories are making similar mountain bikes of interior quality at a lower price. To maintain the market share, we have to undercut our competitors' price thanks to our mass production and, in fact, our prices hit the rock bottom.

G: What about discount? Would it be possible for you to give me a good discount?

W: Well, for an order of above US $ 100 000 in value, we could allow a discount of 8 %.

G: I see. What about delivery time?

W: We can deliver from stock.

31

C:Do you deliver the bikes with any free accessories?

W:Yes. Each with a small pump, a helmet and a set of simple tools like spanners.

G:Good. I'll get in touch with my head – office as soon as I'm back in the hotel and may bring you an order tomorrow. Thank you for all your information.

W:You're welcome.

Sample Dialogue 4

G:Mr. Cheng, Thank you for inviting me to visit your company. I hope we can conclude some business with you as soon as possible.

C:It's our pleasure, Mr. George, to have the opportunity of meeting you here in our company. After you have seen the displays in our show room, may I have what particular items you are really interested in?

G:I had studied your catalogs before I saw your displays in the show room. We are interested in your silk blouses. I think some of them will find a ready market in Europe. Here is a list of our requirements, for which I hope to have your lowest quotations CIF Singapore.

C:Thank you for your inquiry. Could you please tell us the quantity you require so that we can work out the offers?

G:I'll do that. Meanwhile, would you give me an indication of price?

C:Sure. Here are our FOB price lists. All prices in the lists are subject to our final confirmation. You can see the prices are reasonable.

G:What about the commission?

C:As a rule ,we do not allow any commission. This is our usual practice.

G:From European suppliers, in the general practice, we usually get a 3 to 5 percent commission for imports. You see, we do business on commission basis. And furthermore, a commission will make it easier for us to promote sales.

C:Well, if the order is really large enough, we may consider the commission. I think it's better to discuss this when you place your order with us.

G:OK. Then I will put down the quantity for each item on the enquiry list. When do you think I can get your offer?

C:Tomorrow morning. Could we meet again tomorrow afternoon for a further discussion?

G:Fine.

Sample Dialogue 5

J:Is that Mr. . Zhang? I am John from ABC Corporation. We met at the fair two weeks ago.

Z:Hello,John. What can I do for you?

J:I want to know,if we can place an order recently,when the delivery can be arranged at the soonest.

Z:It should be in August if your order is not excessively large.

J:As to the offer you gave to me at the fair,is it firm?

Z:Our offer is valid for two weeks. If you can tell the exact quantity of the order,I will renew the offer for you.

J:Thanks. I am preparing the order sheet. It will be sent to you as soon as possible.

Z:We are looking forward to it and will give you a prompt reply when we receive it. Thanks for your inquiry.

Sample Dialogue 6.

Ms. Jones,a textile importer,has been invited to the East China Trade Fair. A member of the Fair Office staff greets her in the hall. After introducing herself,Ms. Jones is ushered into a colorfully decorated showroom of the Shanghai Silk Import & Export Corporation.

Staff member:This is Ms. Liu,Sales Manager of the Shanghai Silk Import & Export Corporation. This is Ms. Jones from ABC Trading Co. , Ltd. (Liu and Jones shake hands).

L:How do you do?

J:How do you do? It's a pleasure to meet you,Ms. Liu.

L:My pleasure. Have a seat,please.

J:Thank you. Ms. Liu,you must have heard of our company——we are one of the largest textile importers in the world. We used to buy silks from Japan and India. But now we are thinking of expanding into the Chinese market.

L:I'm glad to hear that. We would be only too pleased to start business with you.

J:Yesterday I walked around the hall and found the exhibits so attractive. Your corporation seems to handle a great variety of silks. May I know the main items you export?

L:Our line covers pure silk fabrics,synthetic fabrics and mixed fabrics. We deal mainly in crepe de Chine,velvet,spun silk,satin plain,brocade,etc. Silks are one of China's traditional exports. They are well received wherever they go. Here are the catalogues and the pattern books that'll give you a rough idea of our products.

J:Thank you. (Glancing over the pattern books) What a dazzling display,fantastic!

L:As you know,Chinese silks are highly reputed for their quality and designs. I'm sure they can compete with the products from any other country. Look here, these are the latest fashions.

J: May I have a price list with specifications, Ms. Liu?

L: Sure. But if you have something particular in mind or if you inquire specifically, we could give you an offer.

J: There's such a wide variety to choose from, I'm really at a loss as to which to take. May I take the catalogues and pattern books so that I can examine them further?

I'm sure I'll come back here for another meeting.

L: Fine. Come again anytime you like. Just give us a call before you come.

J: Thanks, I will. Good－bye.

L: Good－bye.

Useful expressions for negotiation

Asking for an Opinion 征求意见

I'd like to know your opinion about this.

I'd like to hear your views on this.

What do you think/feel?

What's your opinion?

What's your view on this?

What's your position?

How do you see this?

What do you think about/of...

What do you feel about...

Have you got any comments on...

Do you have any opinions on...

Do we all agree (on that)?

Does everyone agree?

What should we do about it?

What needs to be done?

What do you think we should do?

What are we going to do about it?

Do you have any suggestions?

Any questions about that?

What do you think about that, Charley?

Does that fit in with your objectives?

Is that compatible with what you would ike to see?

Does that seem acceptable to you?

Is there anything you'd like to change?

Is this okay with you?

May l ask,please,what your proposal is in connection with our company?

What in general terms are you looking for here?

May we leave that till later and first look at...

Can we deal with...first?

实训综合习题

I . put the following dialogue into Chinese.

A：May I see the manager?

B：I'm afraid he isn't in. Is there anything I can do for you?

A：Yes, I have brought some catalogues of machine tools. I wonder if any of your endusers would like to have a look at them.

B：They certainly would. Would you leave them with me?

A：We are suppliers of machine tools of various types. I think your endusers will be interested in some of our new products.

B：We're thinking of ordering some special kinds of machine tools. We would be interested in your products if they are of the types we want.

A：As you probably know, we also take orders for machine tools made according to specifications.

B：How long would it take you to deliver the orders?

A：Three months at most after receipt of the covering L/C. It would take longer to deliver the special orders, though never longer than six months.

B ：Very well. I'll send your catalogues to those who are interested in. Meanwhile, may I have an indication of the price? Can I have your price sheet?

A：Yes, of course, here you are. Our prices compare most favourably with quotations you can get from other manufacturers. You'll see that from our price sheet. The prices are subject to our confirmation, naturally.

B：All your quotations are on an FOB. Vancouver basis. May I ask if you allow any discount?

A:Please tell me what you have in mind.

B:From European suppliers we usually get a 5% discount, and sometimes 10%.

A:If your order is large enough, we'll consider giving you some discount.

B:Fine! We'll negotiate after we decide how many machine tools we are going to order from you.

A:When shall I hear from you?

B :Next Friday.

Ⅱ. Substitution Exercises.

Drill 1   What/Which…are you interested in?

Complete the above sentence by using the following:

—model

—kind of car

—type of material

—category of the commodities

Drill 2   In addition to bamboo and rattan products, I'd like to take a look at your…

Complete the above sentence by using the following:

—china ware

—embroideries

—porcelain ware

—arts and crafts items

Drill 3   Bamboo and rattan products are considered to be arts and crafts items.

Substitute the subject part "Bamboo and rattan products"

in the above sentence with the following:

—silk rugs

—ivory items

—embroideries

—Chinese snuff bottles

Drill 4   Do you mind if I…

Complete the above sentence by using the following:

—ask a question

—take a copy of this catalogue

—move this stuff out of your way

—take a closer look at this sample

Drill 5   I can't resist commenting on the fact that…

Complete the above sentence by using the following:

—your Trade Fair is satisfactory.

—you have so many more varieties this year.

—the quality of many of your products is improved.

—the co - operation between our two companies in the past year is successful.

Drill 6   I can't tell you for sure now, because...

Complete the above sentence by using the following:

—we have too many orders on hand.

—there is a short supply of this item.

—we haven't heard anything from the manufacturer yet.

—we have sent out an inquiry already, but there's no answer yet.

Drill 7   I'll have to confirm this with...

Complete the above sentence by using the following:

—the wholesaler

—the supply department

—the Korean Airline Ticket Office.

—the university president's office.

Drill 8   Please make your quotation on the...basis.

Complete the above sentence by using the following:

—ex works(EXW)

—free carrier(FCA)

—free on board(FOB)

—free alongside ship(FAS)

Ⅲ. put the following sentences into English.

1. 这些商品能马上供应吗？我们希望先看一看样品。

2. 接到你们的询价后，我们可以马上报价。

3. 这种商品型号很多，你们要哪一种？

4. 如果需要的话，我们可以按照你们的要求，接受特殊订货。

5. 这种商品的质量跟你们要的完全一样，只是厂家不同。

6. 这个问题等你们订货的时候再说吧。

7. 能不能给我们寄30公斤货样来？

8. 我忍不住要对今年的交易会评论几句。

9. 由于我们在沿海和特区搞起了好多新厂，所以今年的花色品种大为增加。

10.尽管这没什么问题,但我们最近收到的订单太多,我还是要和总公司核对一下。

IV. Role play.

Work in pairs. Make up a dialogue on one of the following situations:

Task 1

You represent a cosmetics company. You are selling fat – reducing soap that is very popular in China. A businessman from the United States heard about your soap and wants to place a trial order. You start from inquiry and proceed to offer. Your offer is USD12 per dozen.

Task 2

At a fair, you are selling green tea, which enjoys great popularity. A businesswoman from Japan is very keen on it. Your offer is USD22 per kilogram. You start from inquiry and proceed to offer, and finally you settle on price and date of delivery.

V. Oral Practice.

Work with your partner. You are a importer for chemicals. One of your prospective customers seems to be able to supply the items you wanted at reasonable price. So you make inquiries and expect to try some quantities. Have a talk with him/her.

第3章 报盘与还盘

Offer(Ⅰ)

S:Look,all these articles are our best selling lines.

B:Oh,how wonderful! I had no idea that I could see such beautiful things here. They are so charming and attractive in design,color,and taste. Please give me two samples each of the toy bear and the doll. What prices do you quote for these two items?

S:They are on the catalogue. You'll see all the prices are highly competitive. It's always our practice to supply superior quality goods at competition prices.

B:Are they on the basis of CIF terms?

S:All prices are FOB with a commission of two percent for you.

B:But I'd rather have your lowest quotation CIFC2% San Francisco.

S:That can be done easily. We'll work out our CIF offer this evening and give it to you tomorrow morning. But could you give us a rough idea of the quantity you require?

B:I think it would be better for you to quote your price first. The size of my order depends very much on your price.

S:All right. We'll see what we can do.

B:How long do you generally keep your offers open?

S:The prices on the catalogue are without engagement. In case of firm offers we usually keep our offers valid for one day.

B:Could you leave your offers open for three days? You see,I'll? have to send a fax to my customers and ask about their opinions. It takes time,doesn't it?

S:You have a good point. OK,we'll consider it when we come to the concrete transactions.

Words and Expressions

quotation 询价

rough 粗糙的

engagement 诺言,约定

valid 有效的

commission 佣金

consider 考虑

at competitive prices 按照竞争性价格

work out 制定

a rough idea 初步意见

without engagement 不受约束

in case of 万一

ask about 询问

you have a good point 你说得有理

Notes

Look, all these articles are our best selling lines.

瞧,这些商品都是我们的畅销品。

line 在商贸中用法特别多,在不同场合有不同的意义。

What's your line of business?

你经营什么行业?

We've been for many years in the textile line.

我们经营纺织品已有多年。

This article is under our line of export.

这项商品属于我们的出口范围。

This is a low – priced line of table cloths.

这是一种低价的台布。

Your price is entirely out of line with the market level.

你们的价格与市价完全不符。

Your price is in line , but the date of shipment is too far away.

你们的价格尚可,但交货期太远。

We don't think we can fall in line with your views.

我们认为不能同意你们的意见。

We can't continue doing business along the old lines.

我们不能再按老办法来做买卖了。

We shall write to you again along these lines.

关于此事,我们将再给你写信。

quotation quote 与 offer:

quotation 和 offer 都可以解释为"报价",可以替换。一般用 make/send/give/ cable/fax...for/of/on 结构。

quote 动词的"报价",一般用 quote someone a price for something。

offer 动词的"报价",比 quotation 更常用。

We'd rather you make us your best quotation/offer for Men's Shirts CIF London.

我们希望你们报男衬衫最低到伦敦的报价。

It is quoted at 25 dollars. 该商品报价为 25 美元。

We offer the goods on the basis of FOB. 我们报船上交货价。

Offer（Ⅱ）

L：Suppose we get down to do business now?

S：Yes, that would be fine. To begin with, are you ready to make us an offer?

L：Absolutely. We have here an offer for you. It's something like this: 500 cases of black tea at the price of US $ 6 per kilogram, CIF New York. Shipment will be effected in July. This offer holds good for two days.

S：But your 500 cases is not enough, I'm afraid.

L：To the best of my memory, you booked only 500 cases last year, didn't you?

S：That's true. But the whole thing was rapidly sold out in less than two months. As I'm sure I can do better this year, I hope you will increase your supply at least by 300 cases.

L：I'm afraid I can't meet your needs to the full. Owing to the drought this year's tea crop has sharply decreased while demand both at home and abroad has tremendously increased. As a result 500 cases is the most I can grant you at present.

S：But if I don't see to my market, my customers will turn to other suppliers for their requirement.

L：I think I have made my position quite clear to you. The fact is that we've employed all possible means to get even these 500 cases for you.

S：I feel very much disappointed, Mr. Liang…all right, since nothing can be done, I'll take only 500 cases this time. But I hope you should supply more next year.

L：If supply position improves, we'll doubtlessly satisfy your requirement of all things. We can't afford to lose such an old customer like you.

Words and Expressions

absolutely 绝对地	to the best of my memory 据我记忆
black tea 红茶	to the full 全部,全数地
sharply 剧烈地	turn to somebody for 转向某人寻
tremendously 巨大地	求……
doubtlessly 毫无疑问	of all things 首先,在所有事物中
afford 提供	employ all possible means 竭尽全力,
get down to something 着手做某事	采用一切手段
to begin with 开始,作为开始	afford to do something 经得起做某事

Notes

This offer holds good for two days.

本报盘有效期两天。

表示报盘有效期的常见说法有：

This offer is open(firm/good/valid) for three days.

本报价 3 天有效。

We shall keep our offer open until next Friday.

我们的报盘有效直到下周五。

This offer will remain firm(effective) for a week from today.

本报盘自今日起一周内保持有效。

This offer holds good until 10th October.

本报盘有效期 10 月 10 日截止。

Offer(Ⅲ)

Hall: I've come to hear about your offer for exercise bicycles.

Jing: We've been reserving it for you, Mr. Hall. And here it is 800 pieces Forever Brand Exercise Bicycles at US $ 25 per piece, CIF European Main Ports, for shipment in May, 2002. This offer is subject to our final confirmation.

Hall: Does your price include any commission for us? You understand, we are commission agent.

Jing: Yes, it includes a commission of 2% for you.

Hall: This price sounds workable. It has the edge on competition. Now how about your offer for Butterfly Brand Folded Chairs?

Jing: Sorry. Butterfly Folded Chair is not available at present. If you need the goods urgently, we suggest you try Golden Lion Brand Folded Chairs. It's similar to Butterfly in price.

Hall: But it's new to our market and we can't be sure of its quality. You can't count on sales of a new product and make profit by it, can you?

Jing: Well, we just happen to have a sample here in the room. You may see for yourself if the quality meets your requirement. Our records have it that Golden Lion enjoys a ready sale on the Mediterranean markets.

Hall: (Examining the chair) Umm, the quality looks excellent. Will you quote us the price CIFC 5% Hamburg?

Jing: It's US $ 50 per piece CIF Hamburg including a commission of 2 %. What do you think of it?

Hall: Your quotation is worth considering. I will think it over and inform you of my decision about the trial order in a few days.

Jing: I'll be waiting for your favorable news. But if you don't mind, I'd like to tell you that demand for these two items have been growing rapidly. I don't want to sound pushy, nor can I force you to make a deal right now. But for your own good, you'll have to make haste if you really want to get them.

Words and Expressions

port 港口	hear about 听取有关……
subject to 以……为条件	count on 依赖
Mediterranean 地中海	see for yourself 亲自看看
Hamburg 汉堡	our records have it that 我们的记录表明
pushy 催促的	make haste 赶快
deal 交易	

Notes

European Main Ports(EMP)欧洲主要口岸。按照航运会统一规定,包括 Genoa(热那亚),Marseilles(马赛),Antwerp(安特卫普),London(伦敦),Rotterdam(鹿特丹),Hamburg(汉堡),Copenhagen(哥本哈根)。

to sound pushy 听上去好像是催促

Sample Dialogue 1. Counter Offer

Mr. Fox is the manager of a furniture company. Miss Mei, Fox's secretary, is showing into his office Mr. Mark, a sales rep who has been here to push sales of their microwave ovens.

F: Good morning, Mr. Mark, it's nice to see you again.

M: Good morning, Mr. Fox, glad to see you too.

F: Come on in and sit down.

M: Mr. Fox, how are you?

F: I'm fine, I'm fine.

M: Great.

F: Mr. Mark, I've looked through all the brochures, catalogues and the price – list you left me last time and tried the sample microwave oven you sent us later. Our chef finds it very useful.

M: I'm glad you like it.

F: Hmm. We were thinking to buy 6 sets, but after doing some market research, we've found your price is on the high side, out of line with the market price in the shops and supermarkets.

M: In all fairness, there's no comparison at all between our products with those on sale in the stores. They are only for domestic use for two or three people, while our ovens are much bigger with a lot more functions, which cater for the canteens.

F: Then, we can buy a few more ordinary microwave ovens. Guess the cost is less than your price.

M: In that case, your cooks will have more work to do and it'll take them a good deal more time. Your employees in turn will have to wait to buy their food in a longer queue.

F: Anyhow, we're reluctant to make the deal with you unless you make a price reduction, say at least 2 %.

M: Since any further reduction in price is beyond my power, I'll have to ask my superior for instruction. I'll give you a reply in a day or two.

I hope that is a favorable one.

F: I hope so, too.

Sample Dialogue 2. Make a Bargain

Joe and Mr. Liang meet again for a heated discussion on price…

J: Mr. Liang, I've just received the feedback from our home office. They think the new quotation is still too high to accept.

L: May I ask what they have in their mind?

J: They suggested a 5 percent cut on the CIF price you quoted at first time.

L: Look, Joe. I believe this report on Business Express will convince them. According to their marketing investigation, the price of this item is soaring right now.

J: Mr. Liang, you see, we can't always let news guide us in business. Moreover, have you noticed that newspaper also predict a downward tendency owing to the new sanitary regulations in Europe? More than a piece of news, the fact is that the new regulations have scared most buyers and make them hold their orders in the last weeks.

L: Well, anyway, a 5% reduction is not workable for us. I have to say that again, a 2% discount is the best I can do.

J: To start business, and to develop a new market, let's meet half way to bridge the gap on a fifty – fifty basis? That would be a 4.5% reduction on your previous offer.

L: Personally, I would like to give you any support you may need. But it is really beyond my authorization. I need to consult my general manager and will let you know.

J: Understand. I can't say yes either without our home office's consent. When do you think I can get a reply?

L: Tomorrow morning.

J: Then, let's meet again tomorrow morning to finalize the price before we have to discuss another price fluctuation, and go on a further discussion on terms and conditions in details.

L:OK. I'll call you as soon as I hear from our home office.

Sample Dialogue 3. Making an Offer

Before a buyer places an order for the goods he wishes to buy, he has to find out what the price is, what the terms are, how soon the goods can be delivered, etc. In order not to be misled, he must have a clear grasp of all the relevant information.

(In the reception room of ABC Import & Export Corporation)

M:Mr. Chen, do you have offers for all the articles listed here?

C:Oh yes, this is the price list, but it serves as a guide line only. I wonder, Mr. Mohammed, if there is anything you are particularly interested in?

M:I'm interested in your Lead Crystal Glassware, the Pressed Tumbler. But as we are just taking up the line, I'm afraid we can't do much right now. Could we have 2 000 gross for a start? if the sales go well, big business is sure to follow. I hope you could offer us your most favorable terms, though the quantity we are ordering is by no means an attractive one.

C:I'm sure you will find our price most competitive. The trial price is US $ 15.00 per gross CIF Colombo.

M:I have business with other corporations, so I'm thinking of arranging container shipment for all my goods. Could you make an offer on FOB basis?

C:It's US $ 12.70 FOB Shanghai. If the order was for a larger quantity, say, 5 000 gross, we could give you a 5 per cent discount.

M:That does seem to be a nice offer, but 5 000 gross is certainly too large a figure to be used for a trial. Still Mr. Chen, you have given me something to think about. Now what would be the earliest possible date of shipment?

C:Three months after the signing of the contract, that is, for an order of less than 5 000 gross. For larger orders, we can arrange partial shipments.

M:How long will you keep your offer open?

C:24 hours.

M:Thank you very much, Mr. Chen. I shall telephone you from my hotel tomorrow morning with my decision.

C:Thank you, Mr. Mohammed. It's nice talking with you.

Sample Dialogue 4. An Offer for an Old Customer

Ms Zhou Chun, Manager of Chinese Export Corporation, is discussing business with an Egyptian businessman Mr. Housain at the Guangzhou Fair.

Z: How are you, Mr. Housain?

H: Fine, thanks. You look the picture of health, Ms Zhou. Glad to see you again.

Z: Me, too. When . did you arrive and where are you putting up at?

H: I arrived only late last night, and I'm staying at the Baiyun Hotel. Mr. Muhammad should have been here at the opening of the Fair, but unfortunately he was ill. I've been touring to this part of the world, doing a project. So the boss asked me to make a detour to come here. You see, I'm two days late.

Z: Now shall we get down to business?

H: Yes. What about the traditional item we have been buying from you?

Z: What's the quantity you have in mind?

H: 100 metric tons, ready shipment.

Z: It's no go, I'm afraid. If you had come two days earlier, perhaps we might have satisfied your demand. But now our stocks are temporarily all but drying up.

H: Oh, goodness. Am I to understand you can't offer us anything at all?

Z: Oh, no. Since we're old friends and your boss informed us that someone from your company would come to the fair, we felt we had to do something for you.

H: What can that something be?

Z: You see, we have luckily earmarked 40 tons for you. The quantity, such as it is, is the best we can do for an old friend. They can be shipped from immediate stock. If you should come another two days later, this lot would be sold out.

H: I was just going to say the quantity is too small and not half of what we need. On second thoughts, however, I felt we ought to be content with what you've kept for us. What about some additional quantity for forward shipment?

Z: To tell you the truth, we've sold far into the last quarter.

H: I tell you what. Would you please try and check up your position and see if you can gather together enough 100 tons for our production. Say 20 tons each for June, August and October.

Z: All right. I'll look into your request and let you know what we can do, say, in a day or two.

H: A thousand and one thanks. An old friend is an old friend. Now please name for 40 tons spot goods your price CIF Alexandria.

Z:USD 450 per metric ton.

H:Why,that high。 You quote twice the price of that when I came here a year ago.

Z:That was the water under the bridge.

H:How come?

Z:You've been away from the business for quite some time and let me put you in the picture. Supplies are slender because of the rough weather throughout the world and price has been soaring. Taking the international market as the criterion,our price can even be said to be preferential. I'm sure your boss will praise you to the sky instead of blaming you.

H:Praise or not. I'll thank god if my trip's been worthwhile.

Z:Shall I prepare the contract?

H:Not for now. I think it's better you make us a firm offer first and I'll send it back home by e – mail. If the boss gives me the go – ahead,I will confirm it in the afternoon or at latest in the evening. If you can put the forward shipments in the contract,so much the better.

Z:OK. I'll be expecting your good news.

Sample Dialogue 5. Let's Talk About the Offer

Joe. the representative of the buyer,is at Mr. Liang's office,discussing the offer with Mr. Liang…

J:Mr. Liang,thank you for your prompt offer. I have studied your offer carefully and consulted our home office. Our investigation and comparison show that your price is about 7 percent higher than those offered by your competitors

L:I hope you also put the quality into consideration. I'm sure you know fully well that our product is made of pure wool. This,of course,adds to the cost but promises the much superior quality.

J:I will agree with you about the importance of quality. But anyway,7 percent is a big difference which is unacceptable for us. The intense competition on the world market doesn't allow us to sacrifice too much for the high quality;otherwise we need to do sales promotion for this new type.

L: We can give you a 1. 5 percent discount if you can adjust your order up to 7 000 pieces. And we have the confidence in our new design.

J:I am afraid 1. 5 percent is not enough to help us develop a new market for your products. We believe 5 percent lower will make your product more competitive.

L:I'm afraid we can't give a 5 percent cut by all means. Considering you are a new

47

customer, a 2 percent cut is really the best we can do.

J: Well, Mr. Liang, does this price include seaworthy packing?

L: The outer packing is for container transportation. That is the general practice.

J: How long will this offer be available?

L: Within one week.

J: I'll try to persuade our head office to accept the price with a 2 percent discount and let you know the answer as soon as possible. By the way, could you also make us an offer on FOB basis for the same quality and quantity?

L: If it is more convenient for you to arrange the transportation on your own end. I can let you have FOB right away. That will be US $ 23. 5 per dozen FOB Dalian.

Key Sentences 经典必备句

● 报价:

We are waiting for your offer.

我们正等您的报价。

Please make us a cable offer.

请来电报盘。

We have the offer ready for you.

我们已经为你准备好报盘了。

Our offer was reasonable instead of wild speculations.

我们的报价合理,而不是漫天要价。

We've kept the price close to the costs of production.

我们已经把价格压到生产费用的边缘了。

I think our first offer in last week is the best one.

相信我们上周的第一报是最好的。

We will make you a special offer.

我们会给你一个特别优惠价。

We'll give you the preference of our offer.

我们将优先向你们报盘。

After a comparison. you'll see that our offer is more favorable than the quotations you can get elsewhere.

比较之后你会发现,我们的报价比别处要便宜。

This offer is competitive.

此报盘很有竞争性。

All prices in the price lists are subject to our confirmation.

报价单中所有价格以我方确认为准。

We'll try our best to get a bid from the buyers.

我们将尽全力获得买主的递价。

We'll make the official offer next Monday.

下周一我们正式报盘。

We can offer a quotation based upon the imitational market.

我们可以按国际市场价格给您报价。

We'll let you have the firm offer tomorrow morning.

明天早上我们就向你们发实盘。

We want to make you a firm offer at this price.

我们愿意以此价格为你报实盘。

Our offers are for one week.

我们的报盘一周有效。

We have extended the offer as per your request.

我们已按你方要求将报盘延期。

The offer holds good until 6 o'clock p. m. 6 th of January,2004.

此报价有效期到 2004 年 1 月 6 日下午 6 点。

This offer is subject to your reply reaching here before the end of this week.

该报盘以你方答复本周末到达我地为有效。

The offer is not workable.

报盘不可行。

It is difficult to make an offer without full details.

未说明详尽细节难以报价。

Buyers do not welcome offers made at wide intervals.

买主不欢迎报盘间隔太久。

No headway is made with your offer.

你们的报盘未得到任何进展。

Would you like to renew your offer on the sale terms and conditions?

请按同样条件恢复报盘。

We are regretful that we have to decline your offer.

很抱歉,我们不得不拒绝你方报盘。

The offer is withdrawn.

该报盘已经撤回。

We prefer to withhold offers for a time.

我们宁愿暂停报盘。

Buyers are worried at the lack of offer.

买主因无报盘而苦恼。

● 还盘：

We are sure no other buyers have bid higher than this price.

我们肯定没有别的买主的出价高于此价。

This price is much higher than we offered to other suppliers.

此价格比我们给其他供货人的出价要高。

May we have your counter – offer?

您可以还个价吗？

Would you like to make a counter—offer?

您是否还个价？

We highly appreciate your prompt counter—offer. Unfortunately , we find it too low.

十分感谢您的及时还价，遗憾的是我们觉得还价太低了。

We are looking forward to your reply to our offer in the form of counteroffer.

我们正等待着你们能以还盘的形式对我方报盘予以答复。

The price is too high to interest any buyers in counter—offer.

过高的价格会让买方没有兴趣还盘。

Your counter—offer is relatively modest.

你们的还盘相对来说比较保守。

Your offer is unacceptable unless the price is reduced by 5%.

除非你们减价5% ,否则我们无法接受报盘。

We don't find your price competitive at all.

我们认为你们的报价毫无竞争力。

We have accepted your firm offer. I'm afraid the offer is unacceptable.

我们已收到了你们报的实盘。恐怕你方的报价不能接受。

Frequently Used Words and Phrases 常用词汇和短语

bid n. 递价,出价,递盘（由买方发出）;v 递盘

combined offer 联盘,搭配报盘

competitive 有竞争性的

concentration of offers 集中报盘

cost of production 生产费用

counter offer 还盘,还价

firm offer 实盘

lump offer 综合报盘（针对两种以上商品）

non—firm offer 虚盘

offer and acceptance by post 通过邮政报价及接受

offer letter 报价书

offer list/book 报价单

offer price 售价

offer sheet 出售货物单

offer subject to export/import license 以获得出口（进口）许可证为准的报价

offer subject to first available steamer 以装第一艘轮船为准的报盘

offer subject to goods being unsold 以商品未售出为准的报盘

offer subject to our final confirmation 以我方最后确认为准的报盘

offer subject to our written acceptance 以我方书面接受为准的报盘

offer subject to prior sale 以提前售出为准的报盘

offer subject to sample approval 以样品确定后生效为准的报盘

offer subject to your reply reaching here 以你方答复到达我地为准的报盘

offer 报盘，报价

offeree 被发价人

offerer 发价人，报盘人

offering date 报价有效期限

offering period 报价日

offering 出售物

offeror 发价（盘）人

official offer 正式报价（报盘）

preferential offer 优先报盘

quotation 价格

quote 报价

subject to 以……为条件，以……为准

the preference of one's offer 优先报盘

to accept an offer 接受报盘

to cable an offer(or to telegraph an offer) 电报（进行）报价

to decline an offer 或 to turn down an offer 谢绝报盘

to entertain an offer 考虑报盘

to extend an offer 延长报盘

to forward an offer(or to send an offer) 寄送报盘

to get a bid 得到递价

to get an offer(or to obtain an offer) 获得……报盘

to give an offer. 给……报盘

to make a bid 递价

to make an offer for 对……报盘（报价）

to offer for 对……报价

to renew an offer 或 to reinstate an offer 恢复报盘

to submit an offer 提交报盘

to withdraw an offer 撤回报盘

unacceptable 不可接受的

wild speculation 漫天要价

workable 可行的

Useful expressions for negotiation

Stating an Opinion 陈述意见

I think that…

I believe that…

In my opinion,…

In my view

From my point of view,...

If you ask me

As I see it,...

It seems to me,...

As far as I'm concerned

I definitely think that...

I firmly believe that...

I certainly believe that...

I really think that...

I tim convinced that...

Now, I'd like to talk about...

I tend to think that...

I'm inclined to think that...

t would think that...

I suppose that...

It seems to me that...

Don't hold me to this, but...

I'm not sure, but...

I could be wrong, but...

Interrupting and Blocking 插话和阻止插话

Sorry to interrupt, but...

Am I interrupting?

May I interrupt for a moment?

May I ask a question?

I might odd that...

Excuse me, but...

Excuse me, but may I soy something?

Excuse me, but may I ask something?

Excuse me, but may I remind you of something?

Excuse me for interrupting, but...

May I add one thing?

May I interrupt?

I'd like to add something here.

I'd like to ask you a question. How much...

I've got a question for you. Who is...

I have a question. When will you...

Here's a question for you. What does...

I need to know something. How mare...

Do you mind if I ask a question?

May make a point here? I think...

May say something here? I believe...

Can say something? In my opinion...

Can add something? It seems to me that...

Can point out something? The fact is...

Can make a comment? It is true that...

Just a moment, please.

Let me finish, please.

Let me make my point first.

I'd like to say this first.

Pardon me, I'm not through. Just give me a few seconds to finish my point.

实训综合习题

I. put the following dialogue into Chinese.

A: We've studied your offer on wheat and find it out of line with the world market.

It doesn't seem very hopeful to close the deal on that basis. Would you please reconsider it?

B: Well, this is our rock – bottom price, Mr Li. No further concession can be made.

A: Mr Smith, if that is the case, there is no need for further discussion.

B: I'm thinking that we might as well call the whole deal off. What I mean is that the gap between your price and ours is too great. There is no way out.

A: To be frank with you, Mr Smith, the price you quoted is impossible. I can show you that we can buy wheat from Australia at a price 20% lower than yours.

B: The price varies according to the quality. I can quote you on wheat of low quality and the price will be comparatively low.

A: You needn't tell me this. The reason that we sent you inquiries is that we usually found your quotations rather reasonable. I think it unwise for either of us to insist on his price.

B: How about meeting each other halfway? In this way we may be able to conclude the business.

A: What is your concrete proposal?

B: When I suggest that we meet eachother halfway, I mean it literally.

A: You mean you reduce the price by 10%. I still think it is rather high.

B: I'm disappointed at what you have just said. That's really our rock – bottom price. I have to take the cost into consideration. There is nothing more I can do now.

A: Let me see. Can we once more meet each other halfway on that basis? Then if you agree, We'll close the deal. I hope you will not miss the chance to get this business. We can very well buy wheat from Australia. However, you are our old supplier. In order to keep up our good business relations, we choose to negotiate business with you and to buy from you. May I repeat that if you are not interested in this business. We'll soon purchase from Australia. We cannot afford to wait for you very long.

B: You have a way of talking me into it. All right, let's meet each other halfway again.

A: I'm very glad that we have finally come to an agreement. We'll go on to other terms and conditions tomorrow. Is it all right to you?

B: Very good. See you tomorrow.

II. Substitution Exercises.

Drill 1　I'd like to have your lowest quotations.

Complete the above sentence by using the following:

—FOB Dalian

—FAS Xingang

—CFR San Francisco

—DES Long Beach, California

Drill 2　Could you also tell me the...you desire?

Complete the above sentence by using the following:

—patterns

—date of delivery

—number of the items

—quantity of the commodities

Drill 3　...an indication of price.

Complete the above sentence by using the following:

— I hope you can give me...

— You don't mind giving do you?

— I was wondering if you could give me...

— Would it be possible for you to give me...

Drill 4　...is/are subject to our final confirmation.

Complete the above sentence by using the following:

— the prices of these commodities

— the delivery date of this aircraft

— the availability of the airline ticket

— the final delivery date of this consignment

Drill 5　We have received many inquiries for our...

Complete the above sentence by using the following:

—woolen knitwear

—surgical dressings

—sorbic acid（山梨酸）

—aluminum sulphate（硫酸铝）

Drill 6　Here's our latest product catalogue, but the...are/is subject to change without notice.

Complete the above sentence by using the following:

—prices

—specifications

—quality of supply

—appearance and color of the design

Drill 7　What's your CIF quotation of these products to…

Complete the above sentence by using the following：

—Montreal, Canada

—Barcelona, Spain

—Marseilles, France

—Liverpool, England

Drill 8　Our primary concern is…

Complete the above sentence by using the following：

—whether your price is competitive

—whether you can make the delivery on time

—the percentages of discount and commission

—the quality and durability of these products

Ⅲ. put the following sentences into English.

1. 你们的价格太高了,令人难以接受。

2. 我们的产品都是上等货,当然价格会有所不同。

3. 参照国际市场的做法,我们的报价有效期是三天。

4. 等您确定了订货数量之后,我们可以详细讨论价格问题。

5. 我对你们的化工产品很感兴趣,请你是否能就下列产品报给我纽约港的到岸价。

6. 询价中需要明记的一条原则是,询价只询两三家,而且不能明确具体数量。

7. 发盘是实际贸易磋商中的第一步,习惯上是由卖方向买方发出的。这种发盘称为卖方发盘。有时买方也会向卖方发盘,这种发盘称为买方发盘,也称为递盘。

8. 发盘包括实盘和虚盘两种。实盘是有约束力的发盘,是指发盘人有肯定的签订合同的意图。此项发盘一经受盘人的有效接受,发盘将受约束。发盘人对其发盘的内容不得变更和反悔,否则将承担违约的法律后果。

9. 要价必须是肯定的。对商品名称、规格、数量、价格、装运期和支付条件必须是明确的、完成的、无保留条件的。

10. 实盘一定要明确具体的有效期。如遇在发盘期间行情上涨,就要严守有效期的限制,凡过期者一律不予承认。哪怕只过期一个小时,也不予承认。如遇发盘期间行情无大变动,也可灵活掌握,即便有稍许迟复,也可确认。有些商品市场比较稳定,实盘有效期可略长;对那些市价波动快的商品,实盘有效期要短。

IV. Role play.

You, the representative from Hebei Textile Imp. & Exp. Corp., are talking with Mr. Simpson, a Canadian businessman, who is interested in Chinese cotton piece goods. Mr. Simpson is not quite satisfied with your designs and asks you to produce patterns provided by him. You agree to make him an offer provided he increases the quantity for each design to 1 000 yards. As to payment terms, you succeed in persuading him to accept your usual practice.

V. Oral Practice.

Work with your partner. You are a salesman for a famous brand. One of your prospective customers seems to be attracted by low prices offered by other producers Have a talk with him/her.

VI. Topic for Group Discussion.

When making an enquiry, what questions should you ask to begin with?

第4章 订单

Orders(I)

Mr. Norwich, an American auto distributor, places an order for Toyota Vois cars with Tianjin Auto Co. at a car exhibition.

H:Good morning. I'm Huang Wei, a sales rep from Tianjin Auto Co. Can I help you?

N:Yes. I'm Norwich, an auto distributor from the States. We are in the market for a batch of cars. I've looked around the car exhibition for two days and found your range of Toyota Vios cars particularly interesting.

H:Well, we've got a new model here. If you come over here, this way. It's this one.

N:The car's shape and appearance are very impressive. Can you tell me something about it?

H:OK. This is a fuel - saving model with an engine of 4 cylinders. The exhaust is 1. 3 L/min. It is equipped with driver and front passenger air bags. Special heat - treated glass is used in side and rear windows. It's only been on the market for a few months, but it's very popular.

N:What's the oil consumption?

H:It's 5. 3 gallons per hundred kilometers.

N:How many colors do you have for the cars?

H:They're all in five colors respectively: black, white, red, blue and gold.

N:What does it cost?

H:CIF American Western ports unit price is US $ 14 500 for Model DLX range and US $ 9 800 for the range of Model GL.

N:I would like to place an order for some models chosen from your catalogue.

H:Certainly. I'll just note down the details. What models in particular do you have in mind?

N:I'd like to order 200 Model DLX Vios cars equally in 5 colors and 300 Model GL Vios cars also equally, in 5 colors. It comes to 500 cars. What's the total value?

H:Let me see…Oh, a total of 2. 8 million US dollars for Model DLX and…a total of 2. 94 million US dollars for Model GL. The grand total is US $ 5 740 000.

N: I think I'll deserve a good quantity discount for so large an order.

H: Yes, you do. For an order like this we could offer a discount of 15%.

N: How much shall I pay?

H: The total amount of US $ 5 740 000 off 15% of discount, i. e. US $ 861 000, is 4 879 million dollars. So the amount should be 4 879 million US dollars, all told.

N: How should I pay?

H: Since it's your initial order, we'd like you to make payment by letter of credit.

N: OK. What about delivery?

H: Within 2 months from the date upon receipt of your letter of credit.

N: It's a deal! I'll fax back to my head – office to this effect and they perhaps will place a firm order by fax in a day or two.

H: Thank you very much. I'm looking forward to your head office's favorable reply.

N: Goodbye.

H: Goodbye.

Orders(Ⅱ)

Mr. Gary Lom, a foreign agent, is discussing with Mr. Qin Jin, the sales manager of a Chinese furniture company , a large order for office furniture to furnish a foreign company's new office building.

Lom: Mr. Qin, I'm delighted to meet you.

Qin: I'm very grateful that you could see me at such a short notice.

Lom: Well, since this is a large order, I'd like to make sure you're able to make a suitable offer.

Qin: And we've just learnt that our competitors are still undercutting their prices.

Lom: Yes, yes, they are. But frankly, we're still more interested in your products if your quality is as good as your catalogue prints.

Qin: Ah, we have a large number of highly satisfied customers all over the world. So, we're confident about our products.

Lom: However, I must say that my clients are especially cautious and I'm told to let them have the offer first for their approval by fax or e – mail before I can make any decision. Are you ready to revise your offer? We must remind you that if this order turns out to be satisfactory and there follows a repeat order to furnish all their branches everywhere.

Qin: Well, now let me see. First of all, we'd like to suggest an overall reduction of two and a half percent on the unit price of all the articles.

Lom：Two and a half percent?

Qin：Two and a half percent, which means that a filing cabinet would be five pounds cheaper, a desk four pounds, a chair one and a half pounds and so on.

Lom：Yes, I see. We'd like you to ship the goods in separated articles to be assembled in our client's offices.

Qin：That's all right. We'll send someone to supervise the assembly of separated parts and in doing so the expenses will of course be less.

Lom：That's good. And this will also reduce freight charge by about 15％.

Qin：You're right.

Lom：What about payment?

Qin：I suggest the most suitable arrangement should be by an L/C, valid for 30 days, that is until 30 October.

Lom：Well, if you don't mind my saying so, I think my client will prefer some other arrangement. I would suggest a bill of exchange payable at the sight after 60 days. I think my client's reputation will be sufficient to guarantee payment on time.

Qin：I'm not doubtful that your client's a reputable organization. I must admit, however, that at the moment I'm unable to agree with this before I get my head – office's say – so.

Lom：All right, Mr. Qin, See what you can do. I understand your position.

Qin：What about the delivery time?

Lom：We believe you can have the goods in store by the middle of August. Delivery in Alexander will be by the 20th of October. What do you say?

Qin：It's a deal!

Words and Expressions

in the market for 打算购买	to this effect 带有那个[这个]意思
batch 一批	undercut 廉价出售
Toyota Vios 丰田威驰	revise 修改
exhaust 排气	furnish 供应, 提供
heat – treated 对……热处理	filing cabinet 档案橱柜
oil consumption 耗油量	assemble 装配
deserve 应受, 值得	supervise 监督, 管理, 指导

Sample Dialogue 1. Winning an Order

Mr. Fan Hong, Marketing Manager of a Chinese company, is haggling with Mr. Neu, a foreign agent, over the rate of discount for a large order.

Fan：Good morning, Mr. Neu. Have you heard anything from your client about our offer?

Neu：Yes, I've just got an e – mail from them, saying they're comparing your price with those offered by the other suppliers.

Fan：Does that mean they haven't made up their mind to place an order with us?

Neu：As things stand at present, they seem to take a wait and see attitude towards your offer, because they also have other supply channels.

Fan：Is there any chance of their placing an order with us, do you think?

Neu：Yes and no. They're a very big buyer, but traditionally, they are inclined to purchase from Europe and Japan. I've done all I can to talk them into buying from you, at least for a trial order.

Fan：If it's just a small order, I still have some other customers waiting for the supply.

Neu：Well, all I can say, Mr. Fan, is that I can let you have orders for at least… um…five hundred tons a year depending on the price and quality, like I said at the last meeting. I told you so, if your quality is no good and your prices are not competitive, that's the end of our deal.

Fan：Say no more, Mr. Neu. Now, all I want to know is how much you are putting in an order for, I mean what sort of quantity we're talking about?

Neu：I can safely say my client is…er…a very large company, and needs by next month, at first, eighty to a hundred tons. Well, you know, they have a distributing network across the United States, and even some parts of Canada.

Fan：That's all right. We are flexible and we can do that.

Neu：In that case, Mr. Fan…if the quality is satisfactory, I am sure that we can do business.

Fan：But, Mr. Neu, it must be stressed that we do require considerable figures, or quantities, I mean, especially if you want a discount.

Neu：I'm not talking less than a hundred tons.

Fan：That's good. We'll give you a good price on that.

Neu：If we order immediately two hundred in total, then can I expect a good discount?

Fan：If the order is placed, yes, that is not going to be a problem.

Neu：One more thing, the condition of the product must be perfect, A1 quality. Otherwise we can't do business.

Fan: Of course, it goes without saying. As you know, we only deliver goods in perfect A1 condition. We do have a good reputation. .

Neu: But, if we find the price you're quoting too high and the quality is not good, then, Mr. Fan, we...

Fan: I'm sure you'll find our product is guaranteed A1.

Neu: If there's a guarantee, then we...oh, they are prepared to take two hundred tons.

Fan: OK. That's good, Mr. Neu. We can allow you...oh, allow you an 8 % discount on the total.

Neu: But as far as I know, they received 10% from other supply sources. You even allowed me a 6% discount on a much smaller order I placed last time.

Fan: Ah, well, I'm sorry, but we quoted a higher price last time, you see, and this is just two hundred tones.

Neu: Look, I'll sign for two hundred and fifty tons and you give them 10% discount, what do you say, Mr. Fan?

Fan: OK. Done!

Sample Dialogue 2. Getting an Order Confirmation Right

Ted Koch, Purchasing Manager of the British TK Telecom Trading Ltd, is talking on the long distance telephone with Xu Qing, the sales manager of Motorola Company, asking him to correct the wrong confirmation of their order.

Xu: Good morning. Motorola Company.

Koch: Good morning. I'd like to speak to Mr. Xu, Manager of Sales Department.

Xu: Xu here. Who's that speaking, please.

Koch: This is Koch speaking from a British company TK Telecom Trading Ltd. You might still remember my name as I placed an order with you by express – mail three days ago.

Xu: Yes, thank you. Can I help you?

Koch: Yes. We've just received an e – mail from you confirming our order for the mobile telephone, but there seems to be a mistake. What we've ordered is Motorola Model T720, not T170.

Xu: Oh, goodness, I'm awfully sorry, but I'll just have a quick check and get on to it fight away. Would you please hold on a minute, Mr. Koch?

Koch: That's all right.

Xu: Ah, right, Mr. Koch. I've got it right already. We'll make all the adjustments and you'll receive the confirmation by e – mail in an hour or so.

Koch:Thank you very much.

Xu:It is we who must thank you for pointing out our mistake and also for the trouble. We'll be in touch before delivery.

Koch:Fine. Goodbye,Mr Xu.

Xu:Goodbye,Mr Koch,

Sample Dialogue 3. Increasing the Quantity of the Order

An European businessman Mr. Lorch has come personally to China to visit his supplier Mr. Chen Ying,requesting him to increase the quantity of his order.

Chen:Do come in,Mr. Lorch. How are you?

Lorch:As well as can be expected,under pressure as usual. We haven't heard about you very often recently.

Chen:I was on a training course for half a year,just back last week. What Can I do for you?

Lorch:I have been here for an order.

Chen:Oh let me check my file…Hmm,here,we're producing 500 units for you,as usual for the last two years.

Lorch:As usual? No,as a matter of fact,this time we're going to place an order for 800 units. That's why I came here personally.

Chen:I'm afraid we cannot change our production schedule to increase your quota at the moment.

Lorch:You see,we've recently obtained a big customer,who would like to order 300 units for trial sale,not only in our country but also in other parts of Europe. If your products turn out satisfactory,they might get all their supplies from you in the future.

Chen:Since there will be a good market for this product,we'll move heaven and earth to supply you with 800.

Lorch:All in one lot?

Chen:It's no go. Let me see what we can do…We've been fully booked this month. To do this,we will have sent you your order in two installments. You will receive 400 units at the end of this month and the remainder at the middle of next month. I hope this won't be putting me out.

Lorch:It's a deal! That's very kind of you. Thank you.

Chen:You're always welcome.

Useful Expressions for Negotiation

Don't worry. Everything will be Okay.

1 wouldn't get upset if I were you.

I'm sure it'll be all right.

It could happen to anybody.

It's just one of those things.

I assure you that…

Let me assure you that…

There is really no reason for you to be worried.

Be assure (that)…

I am sure about…

I am certain about…

I am positive about…

I've no doubt…

I'm quite convinced (that)…

It's my conviction (that)…

I have every confidence in…

Please rest assured there's no danger at all…

You will certainly find this perspective more rewarding.

We do understand your concern, it's not always easy to…

Let me reassure you that…

I can promise you that…

Have no doubts that we will…

实训综合习题

I. put the following dialogue into Chinese.

A: Good morning, Mr Smith.

B: Good morning, Mr Chen.

A: We're meeting again. I suppose you've decided to accept our offer of the day before yesterday.

B: You know, Mr Chen, although I myself feel your quotation is acceptable, I still can't accept it now as the authority given to me is limited. I called my home office up immediately after our talk the day before yesterday, and told them of our talk and your quotation, and I also suggested that they accept it.

A: Did they agree to your proposal?

B: I just received their reply this morning and they accepted the proposal in principle.

A: Good. I'd say, Mr Smith, you've done your share in pushing the conclusion of this transaction between us, because you took the initiative when you reported to your home office.

B: Mr Chen, I'm extremely anxious to do my part in pushing the development of trade between our two firms.

A: We appreciate your efforts very much. Shall we prepare the contract at once, along the lines of our last talk?

B: Yes, but as to the arbitration terms, my home office thinks that it's better to summit our arbitration case to an organization in a third country if any disputes arise. I do not mean that the Foreign Trade Arbitration Commission of the China Council of the Promotion of International Trade is not reliable, nor do I mean that any disputes should be referred to arbitration. It is not necessary to submit a case to arbitration as long as our two parties can discuss the matter in a friendly manner. But, Mr Chen, business is business, and isn't it better to make the stipulations complete before we sign the contract?

A: Has your home office cabled acceptance of all the other terms?

B: Yes, all the other terms are accepted provided that you agree arbitration be held in a third country in Sweden, for instance.

A: Oh, I see. Alright, we will take this transaction as an exception and accept your request, to hold arbitration in Sweden.

B: Very good, Mr Chen. The transaction is now concluded and our talk has been a success.

A: Yes. Congratulations to you.

B: The same to you. When shall I come to sign the contract?

A: What about tomorrow morning, at 10:00.

B: Fine. It's perfectly alright for me.

II. Substitution Exercises.

Drill 1   I think some of your products may find a market in our country, particularly...

Complete the above sentence by using the following:

—garden tools

—candle making machines

—cookers and kitchen knives

—your machinery and hand tools

Drill 2   For a trial sale, we'd like to order...

Complete the above sentence by using the following:

—100 sets of your hand tractors

—2 000 sets of your Model T bearings

—150 sets of your F35 Pearl River cameras

—200 sets of your Flying Swallow(飞燕牌)measuring and cutting tools

Drill 3 According to our...the minimum order for this kind of goods is...

Complete the blanks in the above sentence by using the following:

— rules,100 sets

— practice,20 tons

— regulations,500 cases

— way of doing business,1 000 pieces

Drill 4 Yes,we do take special orders from our customers. For example,we could...

Complete the above sentence by using the following:

— alter the design

—change the color

— modify the specifications

— add on or take away some parts

Drill 5 I'm thinking of placing an order,but I'd like to know...of your product first.

Complete the above sentence by using the following:

—the quality

—the availability

—the delivery date

—the after sale service

Drill 6 We're unable to increase our supply because...

Complete the following by using the following:

—we have too many orders on hand

—we ran out of the raw materials we needed

—the manufacturer has gone out of business

—we want to wait until the price is increased again

Drill 7 Since there's a shortage of this commodity right now,it's most likely that...

Complete the above sentence by using the following:

—the price will go up

—the number of buyers will increase

—many middlemen will stock up on it

—other manufacturers will start producing it,too

Drill 8 The price we offer compares favorably with quotations you would get...

Complete the above sentence by using the following:

—elsewhere

—from our competitors

—from other companies

—from other manufacturers

Drill 9   We've already begun...

Complete the above sentence by using the following:

— training our employees

— giving out memos to the staff

— decreasing the company's work force

— the process of hiring someone to be in charge of this job

Drill 10   We've got to add...to...

Complete the two blanks in the above sentence by using the following:

—sales tax, the total amount

—insurance, the total expenditure

—a service charge, the listed price

—transportation fees, the cost of labor

Drill 11   of course. we'll bear the cost of...

Complete the above sentence by using the following:

—processing fees

—the marketing campaign

—making those extra parts

—labor and transportation

Drill 12   If...is all right. I'll...

Complete the blanks in the above sentence by using the following:

—the schedule, fly Lufthansa(德国汉莎)

—the lottery drawing result, buy a Cadillac

—the interest rate of the loan, buy a villa at the beach

—the transportation, stay at the Holiday Inn Downtown Beijing(北京金
都假日饭店)

Drill 13   That's something I know of. But it's also true that...

Complete the above sentence by using the following:

—marketing your product is difficult

—foreign workers are discriminated against

　　—this kind of commodity has become less popular

　　—market price will be different 6 months later

Drill 14　Really, there's no point for you to…

　　Complete the above sentence by using the following:

　　—open a letter of credit in US dollar

　　—inquire about the shipping space now

　　—deliver the goods within one month

　　—confirm your order at so early a stage

Drill 15　…is out of the question.

　　Complete the above sentence by using the following:

　　—to get a 10% discount

　　—to get a 5% commission

　　—to increase the price at this stage

　　—to advance the shipment of the goods

Ⅲ. put the following sentences into English.

1. 我向您推荐一种我们今年最新的光电产品(1aser and electronics),我们这种产品代表今后十年的发展趋势。

2. 你们这种产品的起订数量是多少?

3. 我们是不是先少订购几台,如果确实好销,我们再来。

4. 这不要紧,但目前生产这种产品的厂家,就是在美国和日本,也只有一两家。

5. 既然如此,那我们就多订购几台吧。

6. 虽然过去也有商品脱销的情况,但没有今年这样紧张。

7. 的确,与去年相比,我们的价格是高了一点;然而,其他公司的同等商品的价格更高。

8. 我承认你们商品的质量好,但这不等于我们的用户也能接受你们的价格。

9. 你若能保证我三个月内收到货,我现在就可向你订货。

10. 你知道我们做每一笔生意的时候,各种风险都要考虑到,时间差也是其中之一。

11. 去年我们订购了 5 000 件这样的女上衣,销路不错;今年我们再订 5 000 件吧。

12. 按照我们去年的做法,我们还是照付标签的加工费。

13. 今年的原材料等都涨了价,所以完全跟去年一样恐怕不行。

14. 但如果价钱太高的话,我们就只好转向其他的供货商了。

15. 我们也知道这个情况,但今年的价格上调是普遍的,别的公司也和我们差

67

不多。

16. 我们经营的加湿器曾获国际展览会金奖。它是一种集加湿雾化和医疗两种功能于一身的家庭医疗仪器。

17. 我们对这种加湿器的起订数量没有什么特别的规定;但一般地说,最少500台以上才能接受订货。

18. 我们经营的乌龙茶,有几个不同的品种。请看一下我们的样品及您想要哪个品种。

19. 301 号乌龙茶是高档茶。由于对健康有益,愈来愈受到欢迎。尤其是这几个月,国外订单不断地来,已经有些供不应求了。

20. 如果你们同意分批交货的话,我们可以保证如数供应。

Ⅳ. Role Play.

Work in pairs. Make up a dialogue on one of the following situations.

Mr. Botha, an Italian importer, discusses with you about an offer on 5 000 sets of cooking utensils. Having bargained for sometime, he accepts your revised price. After going over the payment and other general terms, the business is concluded. Both you and Mr. Botha take one more look before signing.

Ⅴ. Oral Practice.

Work with your partner. You are an importer and you place an additional orders for the articles you regularly buy from your old supplier.

第5章 价格

Price(I)

Bragg: What is your price per set for laser printer?

Zhang: Our price is two hundred dollars per set FOB Guangzhou. It can be supplied from stock for prompt shipment.

Bragg: I'm afraid your price is rather on the high side. To be honest with you, we have another offer for a similar one at a much lower price.

Zhang: I can assure you that our price is most realistic. A trial sale will convince you of what I say.

Bragg: But it will be impossible for us to make any sales at this price. If you can go a little lower, I'd be able to give you an order on the spot. You see, I have here a buyer who intends to book 50 sets. But the price he offers me is only one hundred and ninety dollars per set.

Zhang: This price of yours is out of the question. You must be aware that the cost of production has risen a great deal in recent years. What's more, we have worked hard on improving the efficiency and reliability of this product. Advanced features have also been added. As a consequence, this product runs a lot more efficiently. It's much easier to operate and user – friendly. Any other model in its class is not comparable with ours. Better quality deserves higher price, anyone in trade knows the rule.

Bragg: That all sounds very hi – tech. Still I can't accept your price as it is well out of line with the market level. One hundred and ninety is my customer's final bid and I can't help it. That's my actual position. I hope you'll give a second thought to the bid. 50 sets is no small quantity.

Zhang: (Writing something in calculation in his notebook) OK. Since it is a big order, I think I'll accept your price of one hundred and ninety as an exception. It's quite a bargain. I hope you will appreciate it.

Bragg: Thank you for your cooperation.

Zhang: It will leave us very little profit indeed. But I trust our first supply will induce your customers to place regular orders with us in the future.

Words and Expressions

laser 激光

stock 库存

model 型号

induce 引导

supply from stock 供现货

on the high side 偏高

to be honest with you 老实说

convince somebody of 使某人信服

go a little lower 价格稍降

on the spot 当场

out of the question 不可能

be aware 知道,认识到

what's more 还有,此外

work on something 就……展开工作

as a consequence 结果

out of line with 不相一致

I can't help it. 我无能为力

give a second thought to 再考虑一下

as an exception 作为例外

It's quite a bargain. 这笔买卖真是赚(赔)了

Notes

order 作为"订货"常有以下用法:

accept (book/enter) an order 接受订单

place an order 订货

repeat an order 续订

carry out the order 执行订单

cancel the order 撤销订单

refuse an order 拒绝接受订单

Price(Ⅱ)

Smith:I'm afraid your prices are not acceptable at all,Mr. Zhang.

Zhang:Nothing would have surprised me more than to hear you say so,Mr. Smith.

Smith:But we've obtained quotations from other sources,which are about 8% lower than yours.

Zhang:How can that be? As an old client of ours,Mr. Smith,you know perfectly well that our quotations come in line with the ruling prices in the world market.

Smith:But you can't be ignorant of the fact that goods of Japanese make are sold at only ＄180.4 per piece.

Zhang:Well,speaking of goods of Japanese make,you must be aware our quality is far superior to theirs. Ours is a little more expensive than our competitors,but do you remember the extra features of our model,I think you'll agree that it gives much value for money. When we compare prices,we must first of all take into consideration the quality of the goods,mustn't we?

Smith:Sure we must. But the difference in price should,in no case,be so much as 8%.

Zhang:To be frank with you,there are many other customers who have approached us with some higher prices. If it weren't for our good relationship, we'd hardly be willing to make you a firm offer at this price.

Smith: Still it would be difficult for us to put your products onto the market at this price. Will you consider cutting down your price by 6%?

Zhang: That's more than we can promise you. But to comply with you, we are prepared to reduce our price to $ 190 per piece. This is bottom price and we can't go any farther.

Smith: All right, Mr. Zhang. In order to get the business, we accept this price.

Zhang: I'm glad we've settled the question of price at last.

Words and Expressions

acceptable 可接受的
willing 愿意
client 客户
comply 顺从
perfectly 完全地
settle 解决
compare 比较
frank 坦率的
in line with 与……一致
ignorant of 对……无知

goods of Japanese make 日本制造的产品
superior to 比……优越
take into consideration 考虑到
be frank with 坦率地
be willing to 愿意
cut down 减少
comply with 顺从,配合
at last 最后

Notes

讲到价格低廉和行得通时可以说:

reasonable 合理的
workable 可行的
practicable 可行的
attractive 有吸引力的
realistic 现实的
competitive 有竞争力的
popular 通行的

keen 低廉的
low 低廉的
cost price 成本价
market price 市价
bottom price 最低价
in line with the market 与市价相符

"达成交易"的表达方法有:

to come to terms with you
to come to business with you on the following terms
to close business at the price of

to close a deal with your offer
to conclude business
to enter into business with you
to see/pull the business through

Price(Ⅲ)

Lakins: Well, to come straight to the point, could you give us an indication of your new price?

Liang: Most willingly. It's $ 516 per ton, FOB Dalian.

Lakins: That's a high price I must say I'm shocked.

Liang: But you know, Mr. Lakins, the price of this article has soared up since last year.

Lakins: I know that very well. And I also know that you'll stand no chance if you don't bring your price into line with the world market.

Liang: You seem to be very well informed. As our old customer and friend, you might very well speak out your mind in a more direct way.

Lakins: By all means. Just for your information, goods of same quality are being offered at a much lower price by some other suppliers. If you cannot see your way to reduce your price by, say, 5%, it will be hopeless for you to get the business.

Liang: 5%? I'm afraid you are asking too much. To tell the truth, ours is the rock – bottom price. For friendship's sake we may exceptionally consider reducing our price a little, but never to that extent. The gap is too wide.

Lakins: Then how big a step are you prepared to take?

Liang: 2%, which would be a sacrifice on our part.

Lakins: My counter bid is well founded. Still, I think it unwise for both of us to insist on his own views, Mr. Liang. How is this, then? My request is 5% reduction in price. As you think you can allow 2% reduction, there remains only a difference of 3%. To pull this transaction through, let's both move together. Suppose we meet halfway? You see, joint efforts would help carry us each one more step forward.

Liang: You certainly have a way of talking me into it, Mr. Lakins. All right, I give up. Let us meet each other half way.

Words and Expressions

straight 直的

indication 指明

soar 飞翔,飞涨

well – informed

rock – bottom 最低的

sake 缘故

exceptionally 例外地

counter bid 还盘

to come to the point 直接谈到话题,
开门见山

indication of price 价格意向

stand no chance 没有机会

speak out 说出来

for your information 供你知道

see one's way to do/doing something
设法做某事

to tell the truth 真实地说

for friendship's sake 为了友谊的缘故

to the extent 达到……程度

insist on 坚持

meet halfway 各让一半

talk somebody into doing something 劝
说某人做某事

give up 放弃

Notes

on one's part/on the part of 就……而言,在……方面

We have carried out the contract to the letter on our part.

就我们而言,是忠实履行合同的。

Sample Dialogues 1. Driving a Bargain

Mr. Ali from Egypt has taken a keen interest in the pen "Hero330", a quality product of Dongling Stationery & Sporting Goods Corporation. He is forthright, but very shrewd as well. Profit after all, is the whole point of doing business. That's his idea. See how hard he is negotiating with Mr. Zhu, his counterpart.

A: Now, what is the price? That's the big thing.

Z: Well, for "Hero 330", we are quoting US $ 6.50 per dozen CIF Alexandria.

A: My goodness! You can't be serious, Mr. Zhu. At that price we are not playing in the same ball park.

Z: I'm not joking, of course. Our price has always been reasonable.

A: What do you mean by reasonable?

Z: The price which comes in line with the prevailing market level.

A: Business is rather slow nowadays. Few buyers have been in the market recently.

Z: Oh, yeah? Just last week we received several orders. One was from your place.

A: I wonder who it was? It must have just been a small order. Our business operates on a much larger scale.

Z: Oh yes, you have mentioned nothing about quantity yet.

A: Well, if the order is a substantial one, how much will you come down?

Z: But what's your idea of a substantial order?

A: It seems I'll have to break the ice. OK, if I ordered, say, 5 000 dozen, what would you charge then?

Z: That would be a nice order, but one can hardly call it substantial.

A: Mr. Zhu, surely there's a difference between an order of 5 000 dozen and one of only 1 000 dozen.

Z: You know we don't do much bargaining. We go in for business on the basis of mutual benefit.

A: Sellers are naturally reluctant to reduce their price. If I were the seller, I would do the same, but Mr. Zhu, you certainly realize that lower prices are an effective marketing tool, in the short or the long term.

Z: I'm afraid I don't quite agree with you there. It's only part of the matter.

A: A very significant part, I believe.

Z: More and more people are looking for quality. A market secured by a reputation for quality is far more difficult to dislodge. Quality is the thing that counts most.

A: Quality, yes. I admit your pens are of good quality. If you are prepared to give me a 5 per cent reduction, I'll consider placing an order for 10 000 dozen.

Z: You are asking a great deal, Mr. Ali.

A: But I'm offering a great deal as well.

Z: Five per cent reduction is absolutely out of the question. Now Mr. Ali, to help you sell our product, we'll make an exception—give you a special discount of 2 percent. That's the best we can do.

A: That's the first step. With one more, we could strike a deal. To make things simpler, let's split the difference and meet each other half way. You must leave us some margin to cover the advertising expenses. We'll work very hard to make your pen a competitive brand, to establish a "brand image" in our market through promotion.

Z: I appreciate your straightforwardness, Mr. Ali. Well, for a good start to our business relationship, we'll make it 3 per cent.

A: Done, Mr. Zhu. Thanks a lot. You've come a long way to meet me.

Z: There is yet a long way to go, Mr. Ali.

Sample Dialogues 2. Price Negotiation

Mr. Hu, a sales rep of Tianjin Metals, is negotiating with a new customer Mr. Herd about the price of welding electrodes at a foreign exhibition.

Hu: Good morning. Welcome to Tianjin Metals stand.

Herd: Good morning. Great exhibition you've got here!

Hu: Thank you. I'm Hu, in charge of the welding electrodes.

Herd: How do you do, Mr. Hu? Here's my card.

Hu: How do you do, Mr. Herd? We are here at the Exhibition every year and our products are very popular. You see, so many people are around inquiring about them. It seems you're quite interested in our welding electrodes.

Herd: Quite right. You see, a British friend of ours did some business with you last year. They bought from you a parcel of welding electrodes. They turned out to be very satisfactory to their customers. For this reason, some of our customers asked me to order a parcel for them.

HU: What quantity do you have in mind, Mr. Herd?

Herd: Well, maybe er…It really depends on the price. What's the current price?

Hu: In US dollars?

Herd: You were quoting in pounds sterling or euros, weren't you?

Hu: Yes, we're also giving prices in pounds sterling or euros. How would you like it?

Herd: Better in euros.

Hu: Let me see…3 150 euros per metric ton, CIF European Main Ports. Ah,. we've got to tell you straight that the price's a little bit higher than that of last year. As you know, this is just because inflation, the rising cost of material, and greater demand for this product.

Herd: Much too high. Well, I wonder why my friend hasn't mentioned these things to me. Price is a crucial factor in our business.

Hu: I understand that. I – mm. I can keep the same level if you can increase the quantity of the order you're going to place with us.

Herd: OK. Well, what quantity are you talking about?

Hu: You'll have to increase your quantity up to 20 tons and then we could keep the unit price at 3 065 euros. How's that?

Herd: Hold on for a moment, Mr. Hu. 3 065 euros per metric ton. You'll have to do better than that. If I was told correctly, the unit price last year was 3 025 euros. The company next to your stand but one offered me 2 895 euros per ton.

Hu: You see, Mr. Herd. As the saying goes: Penny plain, two pence colored. The better the quality the higher the price. Ours is a famous international brand and is of top quality. This is the truth everybody in the trade knows.

Herd: I'll say! But for your information, our client has obtained a few more big projects, and they're considering to get in a larger quantity. Quantity is also an important factor that determines the price.

Hu: Look, Mr. Herd. I'll tell you what I'll do. If you can get in an order for 50 tons by the end of the month, I can cut the price to 3 015 euros. Order a hundred tons and you can have them for 3 000 euros per ton. How about that?

Herd: I'll think about that, Mr. Hu. And what about delivery?

Hu: As usual. Within two months on receipt of your letter of credit.

Herd: OK. I'll get in touch with my client immediately and get back to you as soon as possible.

Hu: How soon, I would like to know?

Herd: Not later than tomorrow afternoon.

Hu: Well I'm expecting your reply.

Herd: Goodbye for now.

Sample dialogues 3. Demanding a Lower Price

Mr. Wang, Chief Negotiator of R&D Co. is negotiating with Mr. Scott; a sales rep of Exxon about the price for asphalt R&D is going to buy for their construction of roads.

Wang: Good morning, Mr. Scott. Fancy your coming here!

Scott: I'm touring in this part of the world and call on you in passing to see what's happened to our offer. We sent it to you a week. ago, but so far haven't heard anything from you.

Wang: It did reach us in time, but we haven't decided yet. I've been up to my ears in doing some desk research and haven't had time to get in touch with you.

Scott: You, desk research? That's interesting. Anything you've found?

Wang: Yes. Your price is much too high.

Scott: But that's the prevailing price.

Wang: Maybe prevailing in the past.

Scott: I didn't catch you by prevailing in the past?

Wang: You're well aware of that. Six month ago, we bought from you 5 000 tons at US $ 320 per ton. At that time, the world oil price was US $ 28 a barrel. Three months later, the oil price dropped to 21, and has remained to this level up to now, without any prospects for rising. On the contrary, your offer this time makes it 332 per ton, 12 dollars higher than your previous price. How can it be prevailing now?

Scott: The reason may be that our refineries are using their past crude oil reserves.

Wang: You are a born salesman and should know better than not to find supplies, which are made of the current cheap stock.

Scott: We'll try our best. Could you accept our last price?

Wang: No, I'm afraid it's still unacceptable because it was not reasonable then and is even less reasonable now.

Scott: Sorry, but I don't follow.

Wang: The Italian company who's just completed their road in this country, sold us

300 tons bitumen which had been left unused at US $ 290, at which they told us they bought. That shows we bought our last shipment at a much higher price than they did. Their bitumen was of better quality than what we bought from you. Certainly this was because we built a road with a lower grade. You're their suppliers?

Scott: Oh, no, they have their own supply channels. But you see, Mr. Wang, their roads more than 200 kilometers long while yours only about 80. They needed a lot more bitumen than you did. They must have obtained a quantity discount.

Wang: I agree with you there, but even a quantity discount would not be allowed to such an extent. So one thing is for sure...the price you've just offered us is higher than it should be.

Scott: Oh, Mr. Wang, er...the best I can do is 315.

Wang: For your information, we've received quite a few offers recently from other sources, which have actually been keeping in touch with us. One offer is 285 US dollars.

Scott: One penny plain and tow penny colored. Their goods must be inferior in quality.

Wang: Judging from the long list of quality analysis and test data they've telexed us, it is quite adequate for us, considering the grade of road we're building. Since we're old friends, we've decided if your price can come down to that level, we'll still cooperate with you.

Scott: No way!

Wang: Then there's nothing I'll have to say.

Scott: Oh, look, Mr. Wang. We'd better continue to negotiate. Negotiation works wonders, you know. If you buy quality bitumen...

Wang: What's in this for us in building not high – grade road?

Scott: Fame and fortune.

Wang: Can we make a fortune if at a higher cost?

Scott: You see, Mr. Wang, R&D has just broken into the international market for a couple of years and are now building only mad of ordinary grade. Quality asphalt, among other things, will help you build better road; better roads will in turn bring you fame and more and larger contracts. For that matter, you will need a great deal greater quantity of asphalt, for which you'll be allowed a good quantity discount. Fame and fortune, isn't it? A higher cost . you may pay, but it pays.

Wang: I go along with your view on that. What are you driving at?

Scott: I'm prepared to make an exception in this case. Our last offer is 297 US dollars, and it is certain that our quality is much better than your other suppliers'.

Wang: Hmm. All things considered, your last price is acceptable on the understanding that the technical data of your product would prove a lot better than those of our other suppliers'.

Scott: No problem. I'll get on to it as soon as I get back. Thank you, Mr. Wang.

Wang: Thank you for coming. This ,. trip of yours is really worth – while.

Sample dialogues 4. Insisting on the Price Offered

Mr. Corey, art American businessman wants to place an order with a Chinese company but is reluctant because of the high price. Now he is haggling over the price with Mr. Zhang, the sales manager of the Chinese company.

Corey: Mr. Zhang, I've studies your offer against our order. To tell you the truth, we are greatly surprised at the price you quoted us. It's much higher than we had expected.

Zhang: Oh, let's be honest, Mr. Corey, you'll not be surprised if you have a better idea of the world supply position. Now the world oil price goes up every day, quoting for forward shipment at 54 US dollars per barrel, the highest ever in history. As the saying goes, when the water rises, the boat goes up with it. The same is true of the prices for raw materials and product. I can safely say our price can never be fairer at present.

Corey: I'm afraid I can't agree with you there. In fact, I've received other quotations that are lower than yours.

Zhang: That's no news to me. It's sure that your quotation comes from the Indian suppliers. Price is mainly determined by the quality of products. I'm sure it's just to buy goods of inferior quality at a lower price that you can never make your business prosperous.

Corey: It's true. I grant you that yours are of better quality. But a friend of mine told me that some European suppliers are offering a price lower than yours.

Zhang: Well, nothing of the kind. It's a mere hearsay. As a matter of fact, a Canadian businessman, who used to buy their requirements from Europe, found our price favorable and placed a large order the day before yesterday. Their costs for labor, storage, and things like that cannot make their price lower than ours. In doing business, we can't put two and two together and make five. Am I right?

Corey: There's something in what you say, but still I don't think we can succeed in persuading our clients to buy at such a high price. Would it be wiser for you to adopt a policy of small profit and quick turnover? If so, you can sell at a lower price.

Zhang: It's actually our traditional policy and usual practice. If I were in your shoes, I wouldn't worry about persuading your clients. A comparison will tell its own story. I can assure you the prices we offer are very favorable. I don't think you'll have any difficulty in pushing sales.

Corey: But the market prices are changing frequently. How can I be sure that the market will not fall before the arrival of the goods at our port?

Zhang: Judging from the current world situation, it's impossible for oil price to go down in a foreseeable future. I don't see why there's such a possibility. It's, however, up to you to decide.

Corey: If you can promise delivery before April, I'll be able to decide. It looks as if the market won't go down till then.

Zhang: Well, delivery in May is the best we can do for you. The demand for our products has kept rising. If you placed your order today, even May delivery wouldn't be possible. But since you ordered three days ago, we'll try to make delivery in May. Frankly speaking, even the July production is under offer now.

Corey: How long will your offer hold good?

Zhang: For three days, as a rule. I hope you'll make up your mind soon.

Corey: I'll try my best to talk our clients into placing a firm order.

Sample dialogues 5. Your Price is Really High

Green: Now, Mr. Chen, I've compared your quotation with the prevailing market prices and with that of other origins, and I find your price is really high.

Chen: But this is the best quotation we can make. We consider it a rock bottom price indeed.

Green: I'm sorry to hear that. But we still find no way to accept your quotation.

Chen: Mr. Green, I think you will agree that our products are of the best quality compared with similar products in the world. What's more, they are brightly colored and beautifully designed.

Green: I agree. But you know, no material, however attractive, will sell well if it's too expensive. We must always bear in mind the fact that all of us are operating in a highly competitive world market.

Chen: Well then, what's the price you would pay?

Green: The best we can accept is US $ 280 per bale, CIF Sydney.

Chen: Did you say 280?

Green: Precisely.

Chen: But, the best we can do is to reduce our price by $ 10 and I should think we could strike a deal at $ 310.

Green: I do appreciate the effort you're making towards reaching an agreement, but frankly speaking, the gap between your price and mine is still enormous. I really don't see how we can go above $ 290.

Chen: Sorry, we may not be able to sell anything near that price.

Green: That would be a pity, indeed.

Chen: One thing I want to make clear is whether the quantity you ordered can be bigger.

Green: If that is the question, then the answer is yes. I would order 300 bales more.

Chen: Then, the price will be US $ 295 per bale, CIF Sydney.

Green: Is it possible 290?

Chen: I couldn't have said it any more.

Green: I'm in a difficult position. It's beyond my capability to decide it.

Chen: In that case, let me think it over. Now I have to say that my rock – bottom price is US $ 292 per bale, CIF Sydney. Anything lower than this is impossible.

Green: All right. Considering our newly established business relationship and the good quality of your product, I accept your lowered price of $ 292 per bale, CIF Sydney to be delivered in July this year.

Chen: Then, with this settled, I hope we will have no difficulty in reaching an agreement concerning terms of payment.

Green: I hope so.

Sample dialogues 6. Can We Meet Each Other Half Way?

Smith: What do you have there, Mr. Yang?

Yang: Some of our new products. Would you like to have a look at the patterns?

Smith: Yes, please.

Yang: Here they are, Mrs. Smith.

Smith: I like this printed poplin. How much is it a yard?

Yang: 45 pence per yard, CIF London.

Smith: Your price is higher than I can accept. Could you come down a little?

Yang: What would you suggest?

Smith: Could you make it 40 pence per yard, CIF London?

Yang: I'm afraid we can't. This is the best price we can quote.

Smith: Let's leave that for the time being.

Yang：Are you interested in our pongee?

Smith：Yes. Please show me the latest product.

Yang：Here it is.

Smith：The quality is very good. But nowadays nylon is pushing this material out.

Yang：I don't think so. We've sold a lot this month.

Smith：Well, anyway, I'll book a trial order. The price?

Yang：Same as we offered last time.

Smith：What about the quantity?

Yang：200 pieces for September shipment.

Smith：All right. I'll take the lot.

Yang：How about printed poplin, then?

Smith：There's still a gap of 5 pence. Will you give me a trade discount?

Yang：Sorry. Can we meet each other half way?

Smith：What do you mean?

Yang：Let's close the deal at 43 pence per yard, CIF London.

Smith：You drive a hard bargain, but I'll accept this time.

Yang：We will provide good service and quality.

Smith：That will be deeply appreciated.

Yang：Shall I make out the contract for you to sign tomorrow?

Smith：Fine.

Sample dialogues 7. Marketing Trend

After a counter – offer, an agreement is reached between two sides…

Minnie：What do you think about our counter – offer, Mr. Li?

Li：US $ 28 per bottle is too low for us. The gap between our offer and your expectation is apparently too big.

Minnie：Let me tell you why we think our price is reasonable. We made an investigation on the market situation in our country recently. The result shows that the competition for goods like this is really tough. We investigate the sale of 10 of these goods. Those 10 commodities together occupy about 82% of our domestic market. Frankly speaking, your offer is relatively high but the quality is after some of them.

Li：But your last order which was made with us 3 months ago seems to sell all right, don't they?

Minnie：That is right. But you know the marketing fluctuation is not expectable. In current market, at your price of US $ 35, we won't make any sales.

Li: Well, I think both of us need to make a compromise in order to come to agreement. Provided you can increase your order to 1500 bottles, I think we can meet each other half way.

Minnie: Mm…let me think…All right. That is a deal.

Sample dialogues 8. Price Comparison

After a bargain, James comes back to the supplier in order to finalize the price of tablecloth. Mr. Qin is waiting for him…

Qin: Nice to see you again, James…

James: Hi. Qin. Nice to see you, too. Are you ready to start another round?

Qin: You are a tough rival. What is the feedback from your head office? What do they think about our offer?

James: They still think your price is not competitive at all, compared with what is quoted from other suppliers. You know, business mainly depends on the price.

Qin: As you know, a slight but sustaining inflation leads to a rise in the cost of raw material. Considering the increasing cost of our production, our offer is very close to our bottom. And everybody in this field knows that our tablecloth is of top quality.

James: They are of the best quality, but we simply can't place an order at this Price. Frankly speaking, two of your competitors have offered us a price 10% lower than yours. After checking samples, we believe the quality is similar. Buyers won't pay more for similar quality. Otherwise, the increasing cost of production caused by inflation also happens to your competitors. But the fact is that they can offer a much lower price than yours.

Qin: Our price is a bit higher, but the quality of our products is far superior to those of other competitors, it is not similar. Then what's the moderate price in your mind?

James: Will you consider cutting your price by 10%?

Qin: That's much more than we can promise you. But to comply with you, we are prepared to reduce our price by 4% if you can take the quantity we offer, that is, 5 000 pieces. You know, business mainly depends on the size of your order.

James: We accept the quantity. But for this quantity, our final bid requires a reduction of 7%. I hope you'll give a second thought to the bid.

Qin: Since it is a big order, I think we'll accept your price. It's quite a bargain.

Key Sentences 经典必备句

● 高价格：

Price is advancing.

价格正在上涨。

Price has been hiking.

价格持续急剧抬高。

There is a spiral rise in price.

价格螺旋上升。

Experts predict the price will rise perpendicularly in the near future.

专家预测在不久的将来价格会直线上升。

Price has shot up unexpectedly.

价格意想不到地飞涨。

Price has skyrocketed.

价格猛涨。

We are happy that price is looking up.

我们很高兴看到价格看涨。

Price is up.

价格上涨。

Since the production cost has been raised, we have to adjust the prices of our products accordingly.

由于生产成本上涨，我们不得不对产品的价格做相应的调整。

The goods are priced too high.

货物定价太高。

The price is not attractive.

该价格无吸引力。

Your price is twice of the other countries.

你们的价格是其他国家的两倍。

Your price is not convincing.

你方价格无吸引力。

Your price is much higher than the price from other suppliers.

你方价格比其他供货商的都高很多。

The price is on the high side.

价格偏高。

Your price is impracticable.

你方价格行不通。

The offer is prohibitive.

报价高得让人望而却步。

Your price is rather stiff.

你方价格相当高。

● 低价格：

Commodities for daily use are economically priced.

日用品价格低廉。

We simply can't stand such a big cut.

我们再也不能承受大幅度削价了。

Our rock – bottom price is $ 300/mt, and there cannot be a further reduction.

我们的最低价是 300 美元 1 公吨，不能再低了。

Price has declined.

价格已经跌落。

Price has sagged.

价格已下降。

Price is down sliding.

价格正在急剧下降。

Price has plummeted since last week.

上周以来价格暴跌。

The importer suffered a big loss since the price has tobogganed.

由于价格突然下降让进口商蒙受了巨大的损失。

We notice that price is easy off.

我们注意到价格趋于疲软。

Price is leveling off.

价格趋平。

The utmost we can do is to reduce the price by 5%.

我们最多能减价 5%。

I am afraid there is no space for any reduction in price.

恐怕价格再无降低的余地了。

To have this business concluded. you need to lower your price at least by 3%.

为达成这笔交易，你方应至少减价 3%。

We won't take anything off the price.

我们不会再减价了。

We agree to reduce the price by 3%.

我们同意减价 3%。

Our price has already been cut down to cost level.

我们已经将价格降到成本费的水平了。

We've already cut the price very fine.

我们已将价格减至最低限度了。

Your offer is competitive.

你方报价有竞争力。

Your price is feasible.

你方价格是可行的。

Your quotation is unacceptable.

你方报价无法接受。

Your price is inducing.

你方价格有吸引力。

Our price is realistic.

我们的价格合乎实际。

Our price is reasonable.

我们的价格合理。

Your price is workable.

你们的价格可行。

Our products are moderately priced.

我们的产品都定价适度。

● 讨价还价:

Having thought of our long – term business relationship, we gave you a special price.

考虑到我们长期的合作关系,我给你们报了特价。

If you take quality into consideration, you won't say Our price is unreasonable.

如果您考虑到质量,就不会说我们的价格不合理了。

Since this is our rock – bottom price. we can't move any more.

因为这是我们的底价了,不能再让步了。

Shall we meet each other half way so that an agreement will be reached?

为了能达成协议,我们能否各让一步?

We must take every means to keep this price so that we can gain a profit.

我们必须尽所有力量保证这个价格,才能让我们获利。

Frequently Used Words and Phrases 常用词汇和短语

acceptable 可以接受的,可以使用的

Australian Dollar(AS)澳大利亚元

average price 平均价格

bargain 讨价还价

base price 底价

bedrock price 最低价

buying price 买价

ceiling price 最高价,顶价

closing price 收盘价

cost level 成本费用的水平 cost price 成本价

current price 时价,现价

economically 经济地,便宜地

exceptional price 特价

extra price 附加价

going price 现价

gross price 毛价

Hong Kong Dollar(HK $)港元

hover 徘徊于……盘旋于

Japanese Yen(Y)日圆

market price 市价

maximum price 最高价

minimum price 最低价

moderate price 公平价格

moderately 适当地,合适地;适度

net price 净价

new price 新价

nominal price 有价无市的价格(虚价)

old price 旧价

opening price 开价,开盘价

original price 原价

Pound Sterling(Stg.)英镑

present price 现价

prevailing price 现价

price calculation 价格计算

price card 价格目录

price contract 价格合约

price control 价格控制

price effect 价格效应

price format 价格目录,价格表

price index 或 price indices 物价指数

price limit 价格限制

price list 定价政策,价格目录,价格单

price of commodities 物价

price of factory 厂价

price per unit 单价 price ratio 比价

price regulation 价格调整

price structure 价格构成

price support 价格支持

price tag 价格标签,标价条

price terms 价格条款

price theory 价格理论

price 价格,定价,开价

priced catalogue 定价目录

priced 已标价的,有定价的

pricing cost 定价成本

pricing method 定价方法

pricing policy 定价政策

pricing 定价,标价

retail price 零售价

rock bottom price 最低价

rock - bottom 最低的

ruling price 目前的价格

selling price 卖价

Singapore Dollar(S $)新加坡元

special price 特价

stainless steel 不锈钢

to adopt, to employ, to use(某种价格术语)采用某种价格

United States Dollar(US $)美元

wholesale price 批发价

Useful expressions for negotiation

Making a Proposal 提出建议

I propose that…

I'd like to propose that…

I hope you all agree that…

Well, don't you think we should…

How about if we do this by changing…

I strongly recommend that…

Do you suppose we could…

You might consider

Don't you think it might be a good idea to…

I was wondering if you'd ever thought of…

The way I see it, you should…

I have a proposal to make.

I would like to make a suggestion.

Here's an idea.

I suggest that we…

I say we should…

Maybe we should…

Why don't we…

How about…

Shall we…

I recommend that…

I would like to propose that…

Why don't we…

实训综合习题

I. put the following sentences into Chinese.

1. Your price has soared. It's almost 25% higher than last year's.

2. To support you in pushing sales, we grant you a special discount of 8%.

3. To get the business done, we can consider making some concessions in our price.

4. Unless you can reduce the price, chances for the business are remote.

5. In order to cope with the heavy competition, please reduce your price by 10%.

6. If you hang on the original quotation, business is impossible.

7. If you could make a 10% discount, we would be pleased to give you an order for 150 sets.

8. You could benefit from higher sale with a little concession, say a 2% reduction.

9. We feel that your quotation is not proper because the price for such material is on the decline at present.

10. This is our rock – bottom price, we can't make any further concessions.

11. As for the suggested 2% discount we regret we cannot accept your counter – offer.

12. It would leave US only a small profit to accept your proposal.

13. Due to the present price of raw materials, we are not in a position to change the conditions of our offer.

14. We are not in a position to entertain business at your price, since it is far below our cost price.

15. We find it difficult to reduce our price by 5% , because the freight and cost of raw material are going up.

16. The market is bound to advance with the coming season.

17. In the present circumstance, we are prepared to make a generous allowance off the price.

18. As this is our first transaction with you, we are prepared to reduce our price to $ 30 per set instead of $ 25 as you suggest.

19. To get business under way, we take your price.

20. The price is in line with the ruling price in the world market.

II. Substitution Exercises.

Drill 1   Your prices have...

Complete the above sentence by using the following:

—increased 25 96 over last year

—soared an additional 20 % over the last year

—soared 30 % over the past couple of months

—increased 15 % compared with the past 10 months

Drill 2   We have marked up (or "marked down") the prices by...

Complete the above sentence by supplying the following:

—25%

—30%

—35 % compared with last Christmas

—10 % compared with the same period last year

Drill 3   The reason is that...

Complete the above sentence by using the following:

—the in – service training is very effective

—our company's financial situation has improved

—working hours in our factory have become more flexible

—we've incorporated a new management system in our work

Drill 4　Our prices were consistently...

Complete the above sentence by using the following:

—on the low side

—on the high side

—lower compared with the prices on the international market

—lower compared with the prices of the same kind of product

Drill 5　We can first agree on the principle of...and then the specific...later.

Supply the missing words in the above sentence with the following:

—supply, delivery time

—volunteer work, requirement

—the coming meeting, procedure

—the contract, technical problems

Drill 6　We are not used to...

Complete the above sentence by using the following:

—working night shift

—giving customers samples

—dealing with this kind of situation

—providing a large percentage of commission

Drill 7　We'll give you a preferential treatment by...

Complete the above sentence by using the following:

—giving you a 10 % discount

—taking 5 % off the listed price

—providing you with a 5 % commission

—reducing our price to $ 900 per metric ton

Drill 8　I don't think you can avoid considering do you agree?

Complete the above sentence by using the following:

—the situation on the world market

— the better quality of our product

— the after sales service we offer

— the service network we have around the world

Drill 9　To clinch the deal, I really think we should both make some concessions.

How about...

Complete the above sentence by using the following:

　　　　— finding some alternatives

　　　　— meeting each other half way

　　　　— splitting the difference fifty – fifty

　　　　— using a different term to address the issue

Drill 10　That has been confirmed by…

　　　　Complete the above sentence by using the following:

　　　　— our market survey

　　　　— an agent's report

　　　　— a reliable source

　　　　— an independent study

Drill 11　I'll take 50% off your…

　　　　Complete the above sentence by using the following:

　　　　— listed price

　　　　— counter offer

　　　　— original offer

　　　　—suggested price

Drill 12　I'm surprised that your price…

　　　　Complete the above sentence by using the following:

　　　　— is so much higher compared to last year

　　　　— is almost 2 times higher than other companies

　　　　— has gone up almost 50 % compared to last year

Drill 13　I'd appreciate it if you could…

　　　　Complete the above sentence by using the following:

　　　　— give us some extra time

　　　　— consider the deal carefully

　　　　— reduce your price by another 10 %

　　　　— call your manufacturer as soon as possible

Drill 14　But surely you know…

　　　　Complete the above sentence by using the following:

　　　　— we'll help those retired workers

　　　　— the manager wants to set up a training course

　　　　— our company has always been wanting to attract more customers

　　　　— the government wants to introduce charges for health care

Drill 15　Competition for this kind of goods is tough.

Substitute the entire subject part before the verb "is" by using the following:

— to quit smoking

— to reduce tension

— to give up benefits

— to refuse a request from a friend of yours

Drill 16 I can assure you that...

Complete the above sentence by using the following:

— we hire managers from elsewhere

— our product has a ready market

— there're still a couple of positions open

— we don't provide bonus for workers who are absent a lot

Drill 17 Since I don't see how I can put this through.

Supply the missing part in the above sentence by using the following:

— our opinions are so different

— the interest rate is so high

— there's such a big gap in expenditure

— our production capability is limited

Drill 18 Why don't we meet each other half way, provided you...

Complete the above sentence by using the following:

— make the payment by letter of credit

— purchase 100 cases more of our product

— purchase 50 tons more of our fertilizer

— you use our trade mark on this consignment of goods

III. put the following sentences into English.

1. 我们的价格和国际市场上同类产品的价格相比一直是偏低的。

2. 你也知道,这里的主要原因是我们的劳动力便宜。

3. 由于我们双方对海湾战争有不同的看法,这个问题我们以后再说吧。

4. 国际市场上的原油供应一直比较丰富。

5. 我看还是先就原则性的问题达成协议,然后再谈具体问题。

6. 这个价格很难说服用户。

7. 由于原材料涨价,我们也不得不调整产品价格。

8. 如果你们大量订货的话,我们可以考虑减价。

9. 我们的价格还是合理的,你们再考虑考虑。

10. 这个价格已经是很低的了,你们的还盘我们实在没办法。

11. 我们双方报价的差别太大,这没办法成交。

12. 恐怕我只好取消这笔买卖了。

13. 这的确是我们的最低价了,我没办法再让你了。

14. 你看这样行不行,你在发盘的基础上减 5% ,我在还盘的基础上加 5% ,怎么样?

15. 产品的质量不一样,价格当然不一样。你要的是我们今年顶尖的产品,价钱当然不一样。

16. 你们的报价与国际市场的差别太大,请再考虑一下能否给我们更优惠的价格?

17. 我们双方若在价格问题上都坚持己见,那就很难谈下去了。

18. 我是说我们双方是否都可以让一点? 比如说我们双方在差价上各让一半?

19. 我很赞赏您的合作,但希望您能多买一点我们的产品。

20. 只要您同意多买 200 箱我们的产品,我们就可以按每箱 $ 138 新港离岸价成交。

IV. Role Play.

Work in pairs. Make up a dialogue on one of the following situations:

Task 1

You are going to import a quantity of chemical fertilizers for your endusers. But you find the price quoted by Mr. Smith of a Canadian firm on the high side compared with the ruling prices on the world market. Taking advantage of a weak market that is unfavourable to sellers, you try your best to persuade Mr. Smith to reduce his price.

Task 2

You sell exercise bicycles on behalf of Tianjin Recreation Equipment Imp. & Exp. Co.. A businessman from the Canada wants to buy 500 sets of your bicycles. Your price is USD200 per set FOB Tianjin, but his counter – offer is USD180 per set. You start bargaining.

V. Topics for Group Discussion.

1. What is the best strategy for a seller if the market is unfavourable to him, and how should he put it into practice when negotiating?

2. In order to conclude a business, what kind of concession can you make?

VI. Oral Practice.

Work with your partner. You are a Chinese exporter. An Italian importer wants to buy 20 000 tons of coal. Now, negotiate for an agreement.

第6章 合同

Contract(I)

A: Now, thanks for great efforts made by both of our parties, we have finally reached a basic agreement.

B: That's true. It is time to sign the contract now.

A: But, though everything seems clear after several revisions, to avoid possible arguments over some minor problems, I suggest that we'd better have another check.

B: That's a good idea. From your conscientious attitude, I understand why your company enjoys high prestige in this field. I think We made a right choice to cooperate with you.

A: Thank you. I believe a successful cooperation between us comes from good will and confidence in each other.

B: That's true. OK. Let's get down to our contract. We need to check all the items to make sure nothing has been overlooked.

A: OK. Let's start. Let me read it out. That is it. Is everything all right?

B: Yes. I believe we can sign.

A: Sure. We have written the content both in Chinese and English. They're equally authentic in terms of law after the signature.

B: OK. Let's sign now.

Contract(II)

Before signing the contract, the seller read through the contract together with the buyer for a final check.

Seller: I think there is one more provision which should be added to the contract.

Buyer: Yes?

Seller: We forget the "Force Majeure". In the international practice, if the production and delivery are affected by a "force majeure", we are not responsible.

Buyer: That is fair. But it must be stipulated at the same time that you are responsible to notice us the accident within 15 days with the enclosure of the accident certificate issued by relative organization.

Seller: Sure.

Buyer: And if the "force majeure" lasts over two months, we are entitled to cancel the contract.

Seller: I hope everything will go smoothly.

Buyer: That's also our wish. If there is no other question about the contract, I will get the contract revised right now so that we can sign it today.

Words and Expressions

reached agreement. 达成协议,成交   provision 规定

revision 修订,修改   Force Majeure 不可抗力

argument 争论   international practice 国际惯例

conscientious attitude 尽责的态度   be entitled to 有……的资格

equally authentic 同等有效

Sample Dialogue 1. All the Terms Should Meet with Unanimous Agreement

Allen: Good morning, Mr. Liu. Here is our contract. Please go through it and see if everything in order.

Liu. . Let me read it over and consider it. Don't you think we should insert this sentence here? That is, if one side fails to observe the contract, the other side is entitled to cancel it, and the loss for this reason should be charged by the side breaking the contract.

Allen: That's good. I think all the terms should meet with unanimous agreement. Do you have any comment to make on this clause?

Liu: I think this clause suits us well, but the time of payment should be prolonged, to say, two or three months.

Allen: We are accustomed to payment within one month, but for the sake of friendship, let's fix it at two months.

Liu: No wonder everyone speaks highly of your commercial integrity.

Allen: One of our principles is that contracts are honored and commercial integrity is maintained. Anything else you want to bring up for discussion?

Liu: There is still a minor point to be cleared up. Whom will this commodity inspection be conducted by?

Allen: The first inspection should be carried out by New York Administration for Quality Supervision and Inspection and Quarantine, whose decision is the final basis and binding on both sides. The reinspection should be carried out by Changsha Administration for Quality Supervision and Inspection and Quarantine, whose decision is the basis for the buyers to a lodge claim.

Liu: It contains basically all we have agreed upon during our negotiations. I have no questions about the terms.

Allen: Other terms and conditions shall be subject to those specified in the formal S/C signed by both parties.

Liu: Mr. Allen, your terms and conditions can be accepted. Then, when shall we sign the contract?

Allen: Would 9:00 tomorrow morning be all right for you?

Liu: That's Ok. See you tomorrow.

Allen: See you tomorrow morning.

Sample Dialogue 2. On the Whole the Contract Seems Perfectly in Order

Xiong: Good morning, Mr. Svenson.

Svenson: Good morning, Madam Xiong. I had a good look at the contract you left with me yesterday, and on the whole it seems perfectly in order.

Xiono: Oh, good. That'll make things simple. What about the terms of payment, do they suit you?

Svenson: I just have one point I'd like to clarify. Does Sinochem always buy FOBST (FOB stowed and trimmed) ?

Xiong: Not always. For small quantities we usually buy FOB or FAS. But for complete shiploads we prefer FOB stowed and trimmed.

Svenson: Oh, really. Why is that?

Xiong: Well, that way we ensure that the stowage and trimming charges are included in the price, and there can be no confusion as to whether the buyer or the seller is responsible. We've had our fingers burnt over this problem before.

Svenson: Oh, really? How's that?

Xiong: Once when the contract was completed, the seller sent us a bill for US $ 800 000 for the expenses incurred, as we had forgotten to write the term " stowed and trimmed" into . the contract.

Svenson: US $ 800 000! That's a bit steep. I'll make a mental note of it for future reference.

Xiong: Yes. It's actually quite difficult for us to keep abreast of the fluctuations in loading charges at the various ports around the world, so it's better for the sellers to include such charges in their price quotations.

Svenson: I was wondering about the wording of the quantity clause. Why do you stipulate 10% more or less than the contract quantity at the buyer's option?

Xiong: The only reason for that is for the convenience of chartering a vessel. Obviously ships' capacities vary, and we can't wait until we find a 100 % suitable vessel. That could cause everyone unnecessary delay.

Svenson: True. My final question is on the subject of demurrage. I notice you haven't fixed the demurrage and dispatch rates.

Xiong: That's right. The thing is that we can't fix them until we have chartered the ship because these rates vary from ship to ship, and fluctuate in line with the international freight rates.

Svenson: I see.

Xiong: Besides, they are also decided by the loading capacity of the port.

Svenson: Oh, I see. That makes sense.

Xiong: Anything more not clear?

Svenson: No more. Thank you.

Xiong: When should we sign the contract?

Svenson: We'll revise the contract this evening, and have it ready to be signed tomorrow morning at ten. How's that?

Xiong: Perfect.

Sample Dialogue 3. The Quality Be Guaranteed for Two Years

Harrison: We've negotiated about the agreement for seven days. I hope we can sign it today.

Lu: Mr. Harrison, I am sorry to say we are still not satisfied with Item 4 in your proposed agreement and I hope we can spend some time on it and see what we can do for our mutual benefits.

Harrison: Let me see. Yes, here, ah, "The quality of the equipment supplied under this agreement shall be guaranteed for a period of two years from the date after the completion of the installation of the equipment including the trial run of the equipment thus installed. " Yes, what is your opinion on it?

Lu: According to Item 4 the quality of the equipment you will lease us will only be guaranteed for two years, which we think is too short.

Harrison: Mr. Lu, I hope you understand that this proposed agreement is based on our letter of intent signed last year when I came to China for this project.

Lu: Yes, that's why I think you did not fully accept our proposal of last year. We talked about the guarantee period and we agreed that we would further discuss the period, but now you still insist on two years.

Harrison: I am sorry. Mr. Lu. I don't mean that I want to insist on that. The manufacturer is unwilling to give us a guarantee period of more than two years. If that is the case, how can we provide a guarantee longer than the manufacturer?

Lu: But is there anything you can do? For example, can you further negotiate with your manufacturer?

Harrison: Well I can try, but I can't guarantee anything, as in the United States, it is our usual practice to provide our customers with a guarantee of quality for two years.

Lu: Mr. Harrison, we've been quite happy about our cooperation for the past years, But this time, I feel...

Harrison: Excuse me, Mr. Lu. It could be hard for us to provide a longer guarantee, but I can give you a favored maintenance service after the guarantee period.

Lu: Well, that sounds a good compromise.

Harrison: We will charge you only 80% of the regular service charge for the maintenance service after the guarantee period. What do you think?

Lu: A good idea.

Harrison: So, I'll put the suggestion into the agreement as a supplementary item for your signature.

Lu: Yes, we have made it.

Harrison: All right. Can we sign the agreement tomorrow?

Lu: OK. Let's sign it tomorrow.

Sample Dialogue 4. Signing a Contract

Mr. Qian signs a contract with Mr. Wiseman for a joint venture in foods, in a reception room of the Shanghai International Equatorial Hotel. Also present at the signing ceremony are Mr. Wang from the Shanghai Municipal Foreign Economic Relations and Trade Commission, Ms. Li from the Shanghai Foodstuff Import & Export Corporation, and Ms. Hunter, assistant to Mr. Wiseman.

Qian: Shall we sign the contract now, Mr. Wiseman?

Wiseman: Certainly. This agreement is the result of our friendly negotiations.

(Signing the contract)

Qian: I think, the contract will bear fruit in no time, and I'm looking forward to our continued cooperation and further extension of our trade relations.

Wiseman: Thanks to your open policy, without which our cooperation would have been impossible.

(All sit again on couches and chairs.)

97

Qian: You've got a busy schedule these days, haven't you, Mr. Wiseman?

Wiseman: Yes. We did a lot of things, and we thank you for all that you've done for us. You've opened your hearts as well as your door to us.

Li: Well, would you mind telling us what impressed you most during your stay here?

Wiseman: Apparently, you've done a lot to attract foreign funds. China, I would think, is the first country in the world that has written into its Constitution articles for safeguarding the interests of foreign partners.

Qian: Yes. And at the same time we've been improving our legal system and establishing local laws to protect the interests of foreign investors.

Wiseman: Another thing we've been gladly informed of is that Shanghai has stipulated that foreign investors are allowed to invest in specialized hospital and school projects, infrastructure construction and tertiary industry, such as banking, insurance and consulting. This is really very good.

Qian: I'm very glad you've found Shanghai is becoming more and more attractive to foreign investors. Well, as people say "The outsider sees the best of the game". I wonder if both of you could let us know all the comments and suggestions you have in mind.

Wiseman: Oh, sure. China's modernization and policy of opening to the outside world has attracted the attention of the whole world. China is bound to become more prosperous through participation in the international market. But there is still a lot to be done.

Qian: Mr. Wiseman, could you give us some details?

Wiseman: Well, you see, some of our US investors have the impression that complex procedures and administrative problems might detract their interest to invest more in China.

Qian: Mm – hmm. That's why our State Council and Shanghai Municipal Government have worked out some regulations and measures to improve working efficiency. In order to make it more convenient for overseas businessmen to invest in China, the municipal government has set up the Foreign Investment Commission, which deals with all matters concerning examination and approval of foreign – invested projects. That makes the procedures more simplified and saves time as well.

Wiseman: That sounds great.

(An attendant comes in and tells the host that dinner is ready.)

Qian: It's dinner time. Today we'd like to treat you to a dinner here at the Shanghai International Equatorial Hotel.

Li:Its restaurant enjoys an abundant source of foods and beverages of all kinds. It is well reputed for its fine cuisine. I hope you'll like it.

Hunter:I'm sure we will.

Qian:Shall we go over to the dinner table?

Key Sentences 经典必备句

● 关于合同:

Any deviation from the contract will be taken as breach of contract.

任何违反合同之事都是违约行为。

We are already somewhere near a contract.

我们已经可以签合同了。

We make out a contract for every deal.

我们为每笔交易都订一份合同。

As one party fails to carry out the contract,the other party is entitled to cancel the contract.

当一方不执行合同时,另一方就有权撤销该合同。

I will sign the contract on behalf of our corporation.

我将代表我们公司在合同上签字。

Once a contract is signed,it must be strictly implemented.

合同一旦签订就应严格执行。

Once the contract is signed by two parties,it is legally binding upon both parties.

合同一经双方签字,对双方就有了法律约束力。

The buyer has the option to cancel the purchasing contract.

买主有权撤销购买合同。

If only contract comes into effect,we can't go back on our word.

合同一旦生效,我们就不能反悔了。

These are two originals of the contract we prepared for signature.

这是我们准备好要签字的两份合同正本。

We always carry out the terms of our contract to the letter and stand by our words.

我们一向重合同,守信用。

Both sides have to make some concessions if we really want to sign a contract.

如果我们都想签下这份合同的话,双方都要做些让步。

Sales contract NO. 105 is enclosed in duplicate.

附上第 105 号销售合同一式两份。

We signed a contract for steel plates.

我们签订了一份购买钢板的合同。

The contract is already ready for signature.

合同已经准备好待签字。

The contract only can be cancelled with the agreement from both parties.

合同只有在获得两方的同意后才能取消合同。

They have no grounds for backing out of the contract.

他们没有正当理由背弃合同。

● 合同内容：

A few problems with packing items under the old contract must be resolved.

老合同中的一些包装问题必须解决。

As per the contract the installation and trial run should finish at the end of this month.

根据合同规定,安装和调试应该在本月底完成。

May we make a small change on Article 5 of the Payment Terms and Conditions of the contract?

我们可以对合同付款条款的第五条有个小改动吗?

According to the contract, a delay in delivery will be charged a penalty.

合同规定延误交货期将被罚款。

Please see the arbitration clause in the contract.

请参看合同中的仲裁条款。

Before we repeat the contract on the same terms we need clear up problems arising from the old contract.

按照原来条款再签合同之前,我们需要清理一下老合同中出现的问题。

The seller didn't ship goods in accordance with the terms of the contract.

卖方没有按合同条款交货。

Both quality and quantity must be in conformity with the contract stipulations.

质量、数量都必须与合同规定相吻合。

When the goods aren't up to specification stated in the contract. the contract enables the buyer to get compensation from the seller for poor quality.

如果所交货物与合同所规定规格不符,合同让买方有权力由卖方处获得劣质产品的补偿。

There must be specific descriptions of the goods the quantity and the unit price in each contract.

每笔合同中都必须详细描述商品的性能、数量和单价。

Frequently Used Words and Phrases 常用词汇和短语

a long term contract 长期合同

a nice fat contract 一个很有利的合同

a short term contract 短期合同

a written contract 书面合同

breach of contract 违反合同

cancellation of contract 撤销合同

completion of contract 完成合同

contract for future delivery 期货合同

contract for goods 订货合同

contract for purchase 采购合同

contract for service 劳务合同

contract law 合同法

contract life 合同有效期

contract note 买卖合同(证书)

contract of arbitration 仲裁合同

contract of carriage 运输合同

contract of employment 雇用合同

contract of engagement 雇用合同

contract of insurance 保险合同

contract of sale 销售合同

contract parties 合同当事人

contract period(or contract term)合同期限

contract price 合约价格

contract provisions/stipulations 合同规定

contract sales 订约销售

contract terms(or contract clause)合同条款

contract wages 合同工资

contract 合同,订立合同

contractor 订约人,承包人

contractual claim 根据合同的债权

contractual damage 合同引起的损害

contractual dispute 合同上的争议

contractual guarantee 合同规定的担保

contractual income 合同收入

contractual liability/obligation 合同规定的义务

contractual practice/usage 合同惯例

contractual specifications 合同规定

contractual terms & conditions 合同条款和条件

contractual 合同的,契约的

contractual – joint—venture 合作经营,契约式联合经营

copies of the contract 合同副本

execution of contract 履行合同

expiration of contract 合同期满

interpretation of contract 解释合同

originals of the contract 合同正本

performance of contract 履行合同

renewal of contract 合同的续订

to abide by the contract 遵守合同

to alter the contract 修改合同

to annual the contract 废除合同

to approve the contract 审批合同

to be laid down in the contract 在合同中列明

to be legally bindin9 受法律约束

to be stipulated in the contract 在合同中予以规定

to break the contract 毁约

to bring a contract into effect 使合同生效

to cancel the contract 撤销合同

to carry out a contract 执行合同

to cease to be in effect/force 失效

to come into effect 生效

to countersign a contract 会签合同

to draft a contract 起草合同

to draw up a contract 拟订合同

to enter into a contract 订合同

to execute/implement/fulfill/perform a contract 执行合同

to get a contract 得到合同

to go(enter)into force 生效

to go back on one's words 反悔

to honor the contract 重合同

to land a contract 得到(拥有)合同

to make a contract 签订合同

to make some concession 做某些让步

to place a contract 订合同

to repeat a contract 重复合同

to secure one's agreement 征得……的同意

to ship a contract 装运合同的货物

to sign a contract 签合同

to stand by 遵守

to tear up the contract 撕毁合同

to terminate the contract 解除合同

Useful expressions for negotiation

Stating a Fact 陈述事实

It is a fact that…

The fact is that…

I know for a fact that…

There is no disputing the fact that…

Surely,everyone knows that…

It has been proven that…

Let me give you an example.

Allow me to cite an example.

An example of this would be…

Let me cite a few instances…

To show you what I mean,let's examine…

For example,let's take a look at…

To illustrate my point,consider…

A case in point is…

Let's take a look at the next…

As you can see from this chart.

We can see from this chart that…

You will notice from this graph that…

The table clearly shows that…

I acknowledge that…

The truth is…

I hate to admit,but you are right.

Here's what happened.

实训综合习题

I. put the following sentences into Chinese.

1. Enclosed iS our counter,signed Sales Contract NO. 147.

2. After I have signed the contract, please counter—sign it.

3. Please see to it that the stipulations in the relevant credit are strictly in accordance with the terms stated in the contract.

4. Let's go over the contract and see if everything is all right.

5. The contract stipulates that the goods should be shipped entire.

6. We have duly counter—signed the contract and are returning one copy for your file.

7. The main sticking point seems to be termination.

8. May I call your attention to Clause 4 of the Draft Agreement?

9. I have strong reservations about Paragraph 2.

10. I hope you will understand that Subsection 8 will have to be amended.

11. I think the wording of Clause 9 is misleading and should be changed.

12. I think we should include a Force Majeure Clause.

13. What struck me about Clause 10 is that no mention is made of demurrage.

14. I think that Clause 1 does not reflect what we agreed last Friday.

15. In my opinion we should add a standard arbitration clause.

16. I think clause 5 is substantially the same as clause 8. I think we could delete it.

17. If one side fails to honor the contract, the other side is entitled to cancel it.

18. It contains basically all we have agreed upon during our negotiation.

19. Have you any questions about this stipulation?

20. This copy is for you. Let's congratulate ourselves that this transaction has been brought to a successful conclusion.

II. Substitution Exercises.

Drill 1　Now, we've finally come to...

　　　　Complete the above sentence by using the following:

　　　　— a constructive idea

　　　　— a concrete suggestion

　　　　— something more tangible

　　　　— the point of making a breakthrough

Drill 2　As long as you I have no objections.

　　　　Complete the above sentence by using the following:

　　　　— can mail us the sample

　　　　— can complete the project on time

　　　　— have another copy of the journal

— can effect shipment according to the schedule

Drill 3   Therefore, in terms of law, they're equally...

Complete the above sentence by using the following:

— binding

— important

— significant

— restrictive

Drill 4   I want to point out here that...

Complete the above sentence by using the following:

— the validity of the L/C has expired

—we've made out a WPA coverage already

—the breakage results from maritime accident

—the insurance company has refused to admit liability

Drill 5   Should there be a problem, you can contact us anytime...

Complete the above sentence by using the following:

— today before 8 p. m.

— in the next several days

— tomorrow before midnight

— tomorrow before 12 o' clock at noon in my office

Drill 6   Here's the...we drafted according to the...

Complete the above sentence by using the following:

— clause, motion by our legislators

— stipulation, employees' suggestion

— motion, the votes from the Congress

— document, decision made by the executive meeting

Drill 7   Please take a look to see if there's anything that should be

Complete the above sentence by using the following:

— revised

— modified

— appended

— re – written

Drill 8   How do we resolve the case when both sides hold different opinions on...

Complete the above sentence by using the following:

— some fundamental issues

— the cause of the accident

— the quality of the commodities

— the interpretations of the provision

Drill 9   Oh, gee! I forgot to mention…

Complete the above sentence by using the following:

— the outer packing

— the processing fees

— the general shipping marks

— the materials we should use

Drill 10   If the…is not on hand now, you can mail it to us after you return to the United States.

Complete the above sentence by using the following:

— relevant information

— sample of that material

— design you want us to look at

— reference of the technical journal

Drill 11   Another thing on my mind is…

Complete the above sentence by using the following:

— we should revise this term

— we should change the tone here

— we should delete this provision

— we should add one more clause to the contract

Drill 12   I think that's fair. We really should…

Complete the above sentence by using the following:

— make it clear for both parties

— honor the contract without any excuse

— follow the stipulations in the contract

— be more direct when writing this contract

Drill 13   Looks good enough to me. You've really done a good job.

Complete the above sentence by using the following:

— Both the style and length are okay

— Everything is clear and to the point

— The use of tone and the wording are proper

— The contract itself is concise and accurate

Drill 14　Well then , why don't we proceed to our next item on the agenda…

Complete the above sentence by using the following :

— closing our negotiations and going home

— packing everything up and having a good break

— signing the contract and proposing a toast to our deal

— celebrating our contract and opening a bottle of champagne

Drill 15　We've done everything possible to…

Complete the above sentence by using the following :

— push the negotiations

— protect our interests

— prevent it from happening

— narrow the differences between us

Drill 16　I'm so pleased that…

Complete the above sentence by using the following :

— you could come personally

— the outcome of our negotiations is encouraging

— our talk has opened up an even broader scale of co – operation

— the first co – operation between our two companies is such a success

Ⅲ. put the following sentences into English.

1. 在我们签订这份服装合同之前,我们再来核对一下有关条款。

2. 这笔合同的成交价是 23 万美元成本加运费,旧金山交货。

3. 货物分两批装运,第一批在 7 月份,第二批在 10 月份。

4. 付款方式为 50% 承兑交单,50% 不可撤销信用证。

5. 我们已向中国人民保险公司投保了水渍险。

6. 我们非常高兴我们圆满地完成了采购任务。

7. 其中有些机械设备是我们急需的。

8. 像我们合同中的这批重型运输车辆,在我们上海浦东经济特区的开发中马上就要用。

9. 还有一批规格高、强度大的钢架也将在我们经济区的建设中发挥作用。

10. 我们也很高兴能为你们国家的建设提供一些帮助,也希望我们今后继续合作。

11. 在我们达成最后协议之前,还有两个问题要澄清一下。

12. 恐怕有几个地方给忽略过去了。

13. 你看是否对付款条件这一部分的说明做些改动?

14. 我对合同本身没有任何异议,只是想知道在发生争议的情况下,中国哪一个机构受理仲裁。

15. 这是我们根据会议的记录所草拟的合同文稿,请过目。

16. 哎哟,有一个重要的说明我们应该加在合同条款里的。

17. 我们应该明确无论在哪一方没能履行合同时,另外一方有权提出索赔。

18. 我同意,这体现了"公平竞争"精神,应该这样。

19. 艰苦的谈判终于结束了,现在是喝上一杯的时候了。

20. 是啊,为了我们的成交,为了我们今后的进一步合作,干杯!

IV. Role Play.

You are the Sales Manager representing Huabei Heavy – duty Machinery Imp. & Exp. Corp...Now a businessperson from Thailand has ordered a total of USD800 000 worth of your Heavy – duty Machinery equipment. The contract was drafted by the Thai company. You find one more provision should be added: the insurance premium should be born by the Thai party since the price is determined on a CFR basis.

V. Oral Practice.

Read through a contract together to make sure all items are made on an agreement between both parties.

VI. Topics for Group Discussion.

1. What should you examine carefully first when the contract is ready?

2. What would you say if you want the buyer to open the L/C in accordance with the contract?

3. If you find something wrong with the contract, what do you do?

第 7 章　付款

Payment(I)

The buyer is talking with the seller about payment terms…

A:Very well,we have settled everything in connection with this transaction,except the payment terms.

B:As you know. we prefer the L/C 20 days in advance which expires 1 5 days after the loading is completed.

A:After our long term cooperation,I suppose you have known our financial standing and credit well now. We know an irrevocable L/C can ensure that the seller gets paid in time. But,on the other hand,it would increase the buying cost. Therefore,could you consider giving us D/P?

B:I am sorry. But our rules don't allow us accept other payment terms except L/C,although the buyer has had two or three deals before.

A:But why not if you have known the buyer's credit after several deals?

B:We hope you can understand. We have got some serious lessons from the credulity. One of them was through D/P documentary collection. When the shipment worth US $50 000 was effected,the buyer refused to make the payment. But we could do nothing about it. And that buyer had had one or two deals before this one.

A:I see. But the flexibility of payment terms will definitely bring you more orders as well as suit the buyers' convenience.

B:Sure. We never mean we won't accept other payment terms at any time. As a matter of fact,we will do so when we have known well about the buyer's credit after a real long – term cooperation.

Payment(II)

The buyer placed an order for assembly lines from a German company. They are negotiating the terms of payment…

Buyer:Apparently,it is practical to make our payment for the complete set by installment,because the order includes not only your equipment,but also your service of installation,trial run and staff training.

Seller:Sure. What is your opinion on the installment payment?

Buyer: We think it is fair that we make a down payment on the delivery of the e-quipment. And then we will pay off the rest in three payments according to the progress of the project.

Seller: We may agree with your proposal. So, the down payment actually is worth the equipment that you purchase.

Buyer: We would like to pay it by L/C.

Seller: Sure. But you must open the L/C at sight one month before the shipment is made.

Buyer: No problem.

Words and Expressions

Letter of Credit = L/C 信用证

in connection with 与……有关, 连同

in advance 预先

expire 期满, 终止

financial standing 财务状况

irrevocable 不可撤销的

D/P = document against payment 凭单付款

credulity 轻信

documentary collection 跟单托收

installment payment 分期付款的支付

make a down payment 预付定金

pay off the rest 付清余款

Sample Dialogue 1 . Payment by Cash in Advance

Mr. Tao, the marketing manager of a Chinese company, is discussing with a foreign businessman Honeyman Lee on the terms of a sales contract.

Tao: What are going to talk about next?

Lee: Let me see, what about the terms of payment?

Tao: I'd like to, yes, but first we are doing business for the first time, we insist on payment by letter of credit. Now that the establishment of L/C involves certain expenses and trouble and this is a relatively small order, we can ask for payment with order.

Lee: You mean, we pay before we buy. Well, small as the order is, it is a trial order. You see, we're the sole supplier for bed sheets and towels to most of the hotels in our country. If your products prove to be satisfactory, large orders will flow in regularly. Can you see your way clear to reconsider it?

Tao ；Well, I think, in the circumstances, we might be able to accept payment on invoice, that is to say when we effect shipment of the goods, we'll work out an invoice and send it to you. You'll have to pay us cash as soon as you receive it.

Lee；That means I'll have to transfer the money from my bank in Bangkok to your bank here. I could arrange that easily. How can we take delivery of the goods?

Tao；You just present the document of transfer voucher to the shipping company, and the consignment will be yours.

Lee ；I see. I hope you'll be able to grant us a more favorable method of payment if we get a repeat order in the near future.

Tao；Yes, we will.

Lee；Thank you.

Sample Dialogue 2. Payment in Installments

Mr. Howard is Deputy Managing Director of an Australian company, which has just obtained the purchasing right to coal for several thermal power plants. He is now discussing with Li Xin, President of Jinfeng Coal Export Corporation, on the purchase and payment.

Li Xin；Hello, Mr. Howard, welcome to our corporation.

Howard；Hello, Mr. Li. It's a great pleasure for me to meet you.

Li Xin；Me, too.

Howard；I know you're very busy. So I'd like to get down to business.

Li Xin；OK.

Howard；Our company's just obtained the coal purchasing right for several Australian thermal power plants. We'll need one million two hundred thousand tons a year and we'd like to know the availability.

Li Xin；There's no problem. Do you need the supply in one shipment or in several installments?

Howard；We hope it'll be in equally six lots, one shipment every other months. So they can have two months' stock reserves.

Li Xin；That's all right. You mean every shipment's two hundred thousand tons.

Howard；That's it.

Li Xin；How would you like the price? I mean CIF or FOB?

Howard:We'd like FOB. We'll send ships to the port here to collect the goods.

Li Xin:And payment? Certainly by irrevocable letter of credit payable by draft at sight, if the credit is issued by a small bank, it'll have to be confirmed by an internationally well – known bank. But payment once for all or in installment?

Howard:We think it's better to be in installment. The L/C is to be established before each shipment.

Li Xin:That's OK. I'm sorry, but I'll have to leave you to our Vice President as I have a provincial conference to attend. You can go into details with him. I'll give a dinner in the evening in your honor. See you then.

Howard:Thank you. See you.

Sample Dialogue 3 . Payment by Revolving L/C

Miss Lanks is a clerk of the Accounting Department of an Australian import company, which just signed a contract with a Chinese export company for the purchase of 1.2 million tons of coal. She goes to the McGreeBank to open an L/ C and Miss Mains receives her.

Mains:Good morning, Miss Lanks. What can I do for you?

Lanks:Good morning, Miss Mains. I'm here to open a letter of credit.

Mains:Congratulations. Your company has made a purchase of great quantities of coal.

Lanks:Thank you. It's about 1.2 million tons of coal to be shipped in six equal installments.

Mains: Uhuh, it's a big contract involving a huge amount of money.

Lanks:You can say that again. Our department manager is worrying about how to raise such a sum of money for such a short time.

Mains:Why not pay by revolving letter of credit, then? Only one-sixth of the total amount is to be paid each time.

Lanks:Revolving L/C? What's a revolving letter of credit?

Mains:A revolving letter of credit is a letter of credit where under the terms and conditions the amount is renewed without specific amendment. It is particularly useful in situations where there are regular shipments of the same type of goods. It just suits your case.

Lanks:Oh dear! That's just the thing we want. We open a revolving letter of credit to pay for the first installment and when the second shipment is made, the same revolving L/C works again and goes on like this until the last shipment.

Mains: Right on! Under a revolving credit, the amount of the credit is automatically reinstated after a drawing or after a specified period of time. What is more, a revolving letter of credit avoids the need for repetitious arrangements for opening, checking and amending of the credit.

Lanks: You see, I've got a lot to learn in money matters.

Mains: Don't worry. You'll soon pick it up.

Lanks: Thank you, Miss Mains. I must go back and talk about this matter with our department head. Maybe we'll have to get in touch with the Chinese company for their confirmation. I'll come again for the actual formalities. Bye for now.

Mains: Bye.

Sample Dialogue 4. We Insist on This Customary Practice

J: Well, we have settled the question of price, quantity and quality and shipment. Shall we discuss the mode of payment?

Z: Yes. As a rule, we only accept confirmed irrevocable Letter of Credit payable by draft at sight.

J: I see. Could you agree to accept D/A?

Z: I'm afraid not. As you know, Letter of Credit is the normal terms of payment universally adopted in international business. We insist on this customary practice.

J: To tell you frankly, it's expensive to open an L/C. When I open a Letter of Credit with a bank, I have to put a deposit in it. That'll tie up my money and increase the cost of my import.

Z: But you know it very well, an confirmed irrevocable Letter of Credit gives the exporter the additional protection of the banker's guarantee.

J: To meet you half way, what about 50% by L/C and the balance by D/A?

Z: I'm sorry, but I'm afraid I can't accept it. As I've already said, we require payment by L/C. That's the rule of our company, though we know for certain that an enterprise of your standing will never default.

J: Well, I agree to your payment of L/C. Another thing, how long should our L/C be valid, that's, when should we set the expiry date?

Z: The L/C is valid for fifteen days after the shipment date.

J: Very good. Well, thanks to your cooperation, our discussion has been very pleasant and fruitful. I sincerely hope we'll find alternate terms for our future business.

Z: To be frank, D/A is impossible at the present. But perhaps after more business between us in the future, we could agree to D/P terms.

J:Good. I hope you do business more flexibly and leave us some leeway in future terms of payment.

Sample Dialogue 5. We Agree to Use Payment by D/P at Sight

C:Now what about the terms of payment?

W: Mr. George, we only accept payment by irrevocable L/C payable against shipping documents. It's adopted universally in the international trade.

C:Mr. Wang, it's expensive to open an L/C. Furthermore, we need to put a deposit in the bank and thus tying up the capital of a small company like ours. Could we adopt D/P or D/A?

W :I'm sorry, we can't make an exception. As I've said, we can't accept any other terms of payment. Furthermore, China's silks enjoy a good reputation in oversea markets. The products you are interested in are in great demand and sell especially well. I assure you the quick turnover will offset your L/C expenses and give you a considerable profit.

C:As far as I know, you do sometimes accommodate your customers by accepting D/A or D/P.

W :Yes, but only under very unusual circumstances.

C:Don't you think ours is a special case?

W: In order to finalize business, we agree to use payment by D/P at sight.

C:Could you do me a favor and accept D/P after sight?

W:I'm afraid not. But we will try to make delivery one month earlier.

C:Good. If you promise to effect shipment one month earlier, we will agree to use D/P at sight. Since we have agreed to adopt D/P at sight, the documents will be checked and paid immediately after we receive them. However, we will beg your pardon for refusal of payment in case the papers are not in conformity with the contract.

W:We advocate fair play. Of course, payment might be refused if anything goes wrong with the documents. But in that case you must give all the reasons for refusal to the bank once and for all. Mind you, only one refusal of payment is acceptable to the bank. Two or more refusals are not acceptable. Furthermore, please note that you ought to pay us the bank interest once payment is wrongly refused.

C:I don't think anything like that will happen. We believe you would never ship us shoddy products.

W : Of course not. We always value reputation and we don't think you will refuse to pay.

Sample Dialogue 6. Terms of Payment

The letter of credit (L/C) is the most commonly used method of payment for imports and exports in the world and China is no exception. Today international traders often request a longer period for settlement of an account. Clearly, if one can delay payment, the funds can be put to other uses in the interim Mr. Sanchez is a South American importer in the chemicals trade. He wants to obtain more favorable terms.

Sanchez: Mr. Yin, we'll make arrangements with our bank to open a confirmed, irrevocable L/C to cover our shipments from Shanghai to Callao.

Yin: That's fine. Payment should be made by sight draft.

Sanchez: How long should our L/C be valid, that is, when should we set the expiry date?

Yin: The L/C is valid for twenty-one days after the shipment date.

Sanchez: Could you tell me what specific documents you will provide?

Yin: Together with the draft, we'll also send you a complete set of bills of lading, an invoice, an export license, an insurance policy, a certificate of origin, and a certificate of inspection. I assume that's all.

Sanchez: You didn't mention the consular invoice. We need that as well.

Yin: All right. I'll make a note of it.

Sanchez: Mr. Yin, is it possible to find alternate terms for our future business? What about documents against acceptance?

Yin: I'm sorry, but we can't accept D/A terms. Payment by L/C is our method of financing trade in such commodities.

Sanchez: You see, our government is reluctant to approve of credit. If D/A is possible, it will help ease the licensing problem. If not, would documents against payment be better?

Yin: To be frank, D/A is impossible. But perhaps after more business together, we could agree to D/P terms.

Sanchez: Good. I hope you will leave us some leeway in future terms of payment.

Sample Dialogue 7. A Heated Negotiation

Ms. Hayes is a sales technician with ACME Machine Tools Ltd. It's the company's first transaction with China, so she has been haggling over the payment terms with her Chinese buyers, Mr. Fu and Ms. Ma. Now Ms. Hayes thinks she is on the verge of success. Mind you, one shouldn't rejoice too soon.

Hayes: Thank you for these 50 sets of Offset Printing Machines XCI. We've struck a deal at last. But what will the payment be? What arrangements will you make?

Fu: We shall open a letter of credit in your favor, to be settled in US dollars.

Hayes: That's good. When will you open the letter of credit?

Fu: 30 days before shipment.

Hayes: Fine, but this L/C must be a confirmed and irrevocable one. That's the rule of our company, though we know for certain that a national enterprise of your standing will never default.

Fu: We can do that, but Ms. Hayes, since this is a rather substantial order, and since we have never bought such machines from you before, our customers demand that 90 percent of the credit amount be paid at sight, that is, against the presentation of documents. The rest...

Hayes: Yes?

Fu: The rest is to be paid after the machines have arrived here, and after they are proved satisfactory on trial.

Hayes: No, Mr. Fu, that can't be done. We have never done business on such terms.

Fu: Such terms are quite common in the machinery trade.

Hayes: Look, Mr. Fu, we ask for full payment at sight, because we guarantee 90 percent mechanical efficiency for all our products. Do you have the same guarantee from other suppliers?

Fu: 90 per cent mechanical efficiency. That's under your terms of sales. It's the seller's responsibility to supply goods up to their standard.

Ma: In fact, because the climates vary everywhere, mechanical efficiency could hardly go beyond 85 percent. The usual percentage is between 82 to 83.

Hayes: I know our products extremely well. That's why I promise such high efficiency. If you like, we could send fitters to China to help fix the machines to ensure good operation. We guarantee you'll be satisfied with our equipment. But the total amount must be paid in full upon receipt of the documents.

Ma: But other suppliers are offering better terms. Some even allow payment 60 days after sight.

Hayes: If that's so, I'm afraid I'll have to walk out of this meeting room disappointed.

Fu: Did you say you could send fitters here to ensure good operation?

Hayes: Yes. We often send technicians abroad to offer after-sales service to our customers.

Fu: If your fitters would come along with the machines to help with the fixing, to ensure that all machines run properly, and if after-sales service is provided, we agree to make payment in full.

Hayes: I'm more than pleased to accept your terms. Thank you, Mr. Fu, but you nearly upset the apple cart. Just now I thought the last two weeks of negotiations would be a wasted effort.

Ma: Now, Ms. Hayes, you don't feel disappointed anymore, do you?

Hayes: Oh, certainly not. I'm in high spirits now.

Sample Dialogue 8. Payment Terms

Mr. Kelly is an old European customer of a Chinese company. Mr. Liang, the sales manager of the company is talking with Mr. Kelly on the methods of payment.

Kelly:Mr. Liang, I'd like to say a few words with you about the method of payment.

Liang:Everything goes well with payment. What are we going to talk about?

Kelly:You know, we had only small orders to place with you when we started doing businesses with you. You insisted on payment by cash in advance, first payment on order and a year later payment on invoice.

Liang:True, but we did so because at that time you were unknown to us and we were not familiar with your credit standing. What is more, small orders placed are unnecessary to pay by letter of credit. We were well aware that this method placed the burden for financing the transaction entirely on you, and therefore we gave you preferential prices to make up for that.

Kelly:We fully appreciated it then and even now we are grateful to you for that. Thanks to your cooperation, it helped expand our business and in two years' time our volume of business was growing bigger and bigger. And in turn our orders were also becoming bigger and bigger in quantities.

Liang:Then we changed the terms of payment to that by letter of credit.

Kelly:Right. Soon after, my company was steadily developing with might redoubled and now has become a well-established big company. You've been dealing with us for eight years, have you ever had any trouble getting payment from us?

Liang:Never. You've always paid on the nail.

Kelly: Frankly speaking, payment by a letter of credit is the most ideal method, which is fair and beneficial to both the seller and the buyer. As you well know, the European markets are shrinking and business is not as easy as before. Under such circumstances, we'd like you to consider an easier method of payment for us.

Liang: What's your problem?

Kelly: When I open a letter of credit with a bank, I have to put certain percentage of money into my current account. That will not only tie up my money without any interest and I'll have to pay a commission of 0.5 % of the value of the credit. All these increase the cost of my imports. We're not in any financial difficulty, no at all, but cannot recover the debt owed to us and money is tight at the moment. Sometimes the turnover is not quick enough.

Liang: I'm fully aware of the world economic situation and quite agree with you there.

Kelly: You know, you're one of our biggest suppliers and we are one of your biggest customers in Europe. We're in the same boat and I sincerely hope you'll lend us a hand at a time like this.

Liang: Just say what we can do to tide you over.

Kelly: Thank you. What in particular in my mind is to suggest different dealings by different methods of payment.

Liang: Such as?

Kelly: For orders in value above one hundred thousand euros, payment is still to be made by L/C, but we hope you will consider charging a little bit lower price. For orders in value below one hundred thousand euros, we'd like to suggest paying you by Bill of Exchange. That means you draw on our client at sight and send the draft and other shipping documents to Nordic Bank for collection. And upon receipt of them, the bank will hand over the documents to our client as soon as he pays for the goods.

Liang: It is documents against payment, or D/P at sight. But how can we get complete assurance of payment of drafts on collection basis if the buyer defaults?

Kelly: If in doubt let us act as your delcredere agent. You can charge a slightly higher price and just allow us a slightly higher commission. There is no problem, I'm telling you, as we know our customers well.

Liang: We'll consider it.

Kelly: As for commodities like carpets, they're not fast sellers and if I order a container of them, it takes quite some time to sell them off. It causes the problem for quick turnover of stock. So I suggest payment for this kind of commodities by open account. That is, you dispatch one or two containers of the goods, debit our account and send us the invoice. At some agreed period of time, say once a month or every three months, we send a remittance to you to settle the outstanding balance on the account. In doing so, I'm sure the business will soon go up.

Liang:Good for you, wise and resourceful! It'll be strange if your company doesn't prosper. As for your suggestions, I myself cannot decide and have to talk to our president about it. It is him who OK's.

Kelly:I fully understand. Thank you for listening. I'll be expecting the OK.

Sample Dialogue 9. Presentation of Shipping Documents

Lucia, a junior clerk of the accounts department in charge of presentation of dock, goes to present the shipping documents to Emily, the bank clerk who is in charge of credit matters.

Emily:Hello, Lucia, what can I do for you?

Lucia:Hello, Emily, I'm here to present the letter of credit documents for payment.

Emily: Have you got all the required documents exactly in accordance with the terms of the credit and double-checked them?

Lucia:Of course I did. They suit the L/C to a T.

Emily:I think we'd better check them again. The research department of our bank found that 25 % of the documents were rejected on the first presentation. There're various kinds of errors, which lead to rejection.

Lucia: There's no problem, I guarantee.

Emily: We'd better be on the safe side in money matters, better safe than sorry.

Lucia:You're right, Emily. Would you please help me check them again?

Emily: I'd love to. Now let's check them up one by one. First, what's the L/C's expiry date?

Lucia:The 15th of September.

Emily:OK. There're ten days to go. Then how many copies of the bill of exchange have you worked out?

Lucia: They have been drawn in a set of three: First of Exchange, Second of Exchange...

Emily: Does the amount of money in words and that in figures agree? Does it agree with that in both the L/C and your invoice?

Lucia: Yes, it does.

Emily: Now the other documents called for by the credit. How many copies of the invoice have you had typed?

Lucia: Five copies, all told.

Emily: Is the description or spelling of goods on the invoice different from that in the letter of credit?

Lucia: No.

Emily: Now, the last but not least, is it a clean, on-board bill of lading marked with Freight Prepaid?

Lucia: Yes.

Emily: Was it signed and dated?

Lucia: Yes, again.

Emily: But on what date?

Lucia: The first of September.

Emily: Then the error comes, Lucia.

Lucia: Oh, what's the trouble with it?

Emily: The trouble is very terrible, Lucia. The L/C stipulates that shipment be effected by the end of August. The. error can lead to rejection on the first presentation.

Lucia: Oh dear! What shall I do?

Emily: What happened that made you load the goods on board the ship only one day late?

Lucia: I was told the consignment was carried to the dock on the 29th and was arranged to be loaded on the 31st, but there happened to be a terrible storm that day and the loading could not be conducted. When the goods were loaded into the ship the first mate signed the bill of lading on the first of September.

Emily: There's a way now. It was the shipping company to blame. They should have signed the bill of lading on 29th, but your people ignored it. Go back to your shipping people and ask them to bring the lading back to the shipping company, asking them to backdate it.

Lucia: What a big fool I am! I'd be fired for sure this time without your help.

Emily: Oh, come, Lucia. We are not all saints. Don't blame yourself too much. Remember, in dealing with credit documentation, you can never be more careful.

Lucia: Yes, I will. Emily, I can never thank you enough. All right, I must be going now.

Key Sentences 经典必备句

● 付款方式：

To push the sales of the new product, we'll consider accepting payment by D/P.

为了推销新产品，我们将考虑接受付款交单方式。

In general practice, we require the payment by L/C.

日常操作中，我们要求以信用证付款。

Could you please consider an exception and accept D/A?

您能否考虑一次例外，接受 D/A 的付款方式？

We require100% value, irrevocable L/C in our favor with partial shipment.

我们要求用不可撤销的、金额为全部货款的信用证，允许分批装运。

We prefer to use letter of credit at sight.

我愿意用即期信用证付款。

I suppose we can try D/P or D/A for this time.

我建议这次试用付款交单或承兑交单方式来付款。

We accept flexible terms of payment.

我们采用灵活的付款方式。

L/C at sight is the normal way in our exports to European countries.

我们向欧洲国家出口一般都使用即期信用证。

I am so happy that we finally settled the terms of payment.

我很高兴我们最终谈妥了付款条件。

The terms of payment is confirmed as irrevocable letter of credit.

付款条件确定为不可撤销信用证。

You are requested to protect our draft on presentation.

你们被要求见票即付。

It is the normal terms of payment in international trade.

这是国际贸易中惯用的付款方式。

We won't accept D/P payment for future dealings.

以后的交易我们不接受付款交单方式支付。

You can do the business on 60 days D/P basis.

你们可以按60天付款交单的方式进行交易。

The seller can't accept payment on deferred terms.

卖方不能接受延期付款。

The buyer insists on a letter of credit.

买方坚持用信用证方式付款。

We never accept Cash against Documents on arrival of goods at destination.

我们从不接受"货抵目的地付款交单"方式付款。

They agree to change the terms of payment from L/C at sight to D/P at sight.

他们同意将即期信用证付款方式改为即期付款交单。

The buyer would like to draw D/P against our purchase.

买方想按付款交单方式收这批货款。

They draw on us by their documentary draft at sight on collection basis.

他们将按托收方式向我方开出即期跟单汇票。

What is the mode of payment you prefer to employ?

您希望用什么方式付款?

How about we pay 60% by L/C and the balance by D/P?

我们以信用证付 60% ,其余的用付款交单,您看怎么样?

An irrevocable L/C gives the exporter the additional protection of banker's guarantee.

不可撤销信用证为出口商提供了银行担保。

● 付款操作:

Collection is already paid.

托收款已经照付。

You need to open a letter of credit in USD with a bank in Holland.

你需要在荷兰的一家银行开立美元信用证。

Is the credit at sight or after sight?

信用证是即期的还是远期的?

The wording of"confirmed"is necessary for the letter of credit?

信用证上必须写明"保兑"字样。

It's not convenient for us to make payment in pound sterling.

用英镑付款对我们来说不方便。

Many banks in Europe can open L/C and effect payment in Renminbi.

欧洲的许多银行能够开立信用证,并能用人民币支付。

Your letter of credit should be opened in March.

你们的信用证应该在 3 月初开出。

Payment is to be effected before the end of this week.

这个月末以前应该付款。

Please notify the L/C number by FAX.

请传真通知信用证号码。

We are looking forward to your opening letter of credit in good time.

我们希望你方及时开出信用证。

The bank in London is in a position to open letters of credit against the sales confirmation or contract.

伦敦的银行可以凭销售确认书或合同开立信用证。

The credit is short opened to the amount of US $160.

信用证的金额少开了 160 美元。

The draft will be handed to the bank on clean collection.

汇票将交给银行按光票托收。

The draft has been collected.

汇票之款已经被收进。

The draft was already discount in in Paris.

汇票已经在巴黎贴现。

A cheque for USD 490 is enclosed.

附上 490 美元的支票一张。

We have met these drafts.

我们已经兑付了这些汇票。

We can draw a sight bill in favour of the Bank of China.

我们能开立一张以中国银行为收款人的即期汇票。

We sent our draft through Bank of China for documentary collection on Tuesday.

我们已经于星期二将汇票交中国银行按跟单托收。

The amount has already been remitted by cheque.

款项已经以支票方式汇出。

The supplier has drawn a clean draft on us for the value of this shipment.

供货商已经开出光票向我们索取这批货的价款了。

We will draw on you for payment of the invoice amounting to USD35 000 this afternoon.

今天下午我们会按照发票金额 35 000 美元向你方开出汇票。

Could you tell me when do I have to open the letter of credit?

您能告诉我必须什么时候开立信用证吗?

Our draft will be honored on presentation.

我们的汇票见票即付。

Your L/C NO.35 is short of HK $130.

你方第 35 号信用证少开了 130 元港币。

•拒付：

The decline in prices might lead to refusal of payment.

市场价格下跌会导致拒付。

We refuse to pay until shipping documents for the goods reach us.

没有拿到货物装船单据，我们拒绝付款。

Payment might be refused when anything goes wrong with the documents.

如果单据有问题，可以被拒付。

One refusal of payment is acceptable to the bank.

银行会接受一次拒付。

Your draft NO. 26 is dishonored.

你们的第 26 号汇票被拒付。

Could you give an explanation for your refusal of payment?

你们是否能解释一下你们的拒付吗？

For this wrong refusal of payment, you ought to pay us the bank interest.

因为拒付出错，你们应该偿付我方的银行利息。

Frequently Used Words and Phrases 常用词汇和短语

anticipatory L/C 预支信用证

back to back L/C 对背信用证

reciprocal L/C 对开信用证

Cash With Order（C. W. O）随订单付现

Cash On Delivery(C. O. D)交货付现

Cash Against Documents（C. A. D）凭单付现

Cash Against Payment 凭单付款

clean payment 单纯支付

clean L/C 光票信用证

confirmed L/C 保兑信用证

C&F Cost and Freight "成本加运费"或"离岸加运费"价格

C. I. F. Cost, Insurance and Freight "成本加保险费、运费"或"到岸价格"

C. I. F_Ex Ship's Hold C. I. F. 舱底交货

deferred payment L/C 延期付款信用证

deferred payment 延期付款

dishonor 拒付

documentary L/C 跟单信用证

Documents against Payment（D/P）付款交单

Documents against Payment at Sight（D/P sight）即期付款交单

Documents against Payment after Sight（D/P sight)远期付款交单

Documents against Acceptance（D/A）承兑交单

Ex Dock Duty Paid 目的港码头完税交货价

Ex Warehouse 仓库交货价
Ex Dock Duty Unpaid 目的港码头未完税交货价
Ex Factory 工厂交货价
Ex Ship 目的港船上交货价
Ex Plantation 农场交货价
flexible 灵活的,多变的
F. O. B. Free On Board "船上交货价"或称"离岸价格"
F. O. B. Liner Terms F. O. B. 班轮条件
F. O. B. plane 飞机离岸价(用于紧急情况)
F. O. B. Stowed 船上交货并理舱
F. O. B. Trimmed 船上交货并平舱
F. O. B. Under Tackle F. O. B. 吊钩下交货
FAS—Free Alongside Ship 船边交货价
Irrevocable L/C 不可撤销信用证
payment 支付,付款
payment on terms 定期付款
payment agreement 支付协定
pay order 支付凭证
payment order 付款通知

payment by banker 银行支付
payment by remittance 汇拨支付
payment in part 部分付款
payment in full 全部付讫
progressive payment 分期付款
payment by installment 分期付款
payment respite 延期付款
payment at maturity 到期付款
payment in advance 预付(货款)
pay on delivery(POD) 货到付款
payment in kind 实物支付
payment for(in) cash 现金支付,付现
payment terms 支付条件,付款方式
refusal 拒绝
revocable L/C 可撤销信用证
sales—purchasing 促销,推销
something goes wrong 某事上出问题,出现差错
simple payment 单纯支付
to pay 付款,支付,偿还
the refusal of payment 拒付
the bank interest 银行利息
the mode of payment 付款方式
unconfirmed L/C 不保兑信用证

Useful expressions for negotiation

Responding to a Proposal 回应建议

We've looked at what you have proposed, and we are ready to respond.

After serious consideration, we are prepared to respond to your proposal.

Regarding your proposal, our position is...

Our basic position is...

As far as your proposal is concerned, we think that ...

We would be willing to ..., provided, of course, that ...

We'd be prepared to... However, there would be one condition.

May we offer an alternative? We propose that ...

We'd like to make an alternative proposal. We propose that...

From where we stand, a better solution might be...

What you don't seem to understand is that...

I see what you mean, but if...

I'd like to say something about...

Let me say something about...

I'd like to make a comment about o...

I'd like to make a point about ...

There are other issues/considerations; for example the price...

If we look at this from another perspective...

There are other points to bear in mind. Firstly, we have...

Just to remind you, we are...

To put you in the picture, we are...

To bring you up to date, we are ...

As you probably know, we are ...

You may have heard that we are ...

If you haven't already heard, we are ...

实训综合习题

I. put the following sentences into Chinese.

1. We shall be obliged if you will give US a little more time to settle your account due 1 June.

2. The cash discount given on this bill is an inventive to pay the bill on date due.

3. We have granted you the extra time. and therefore we expect you to live up to your promise.

4. Our standard terms of payment are included in our general terms of sale.

5. I'd appreciate it if you would pay for the first 1 o machines in advance.

6. Sorry, I've not been authorized to discuss credit terms.

7. I have to insist on an advance payment guarantee issued by a reputable bank, though.

8. We are not prepared to bear the exchange risk.

9. Payment unless otherwise specifically agreed is to be made by letter of credit established immediately upon receipt of confirmation of order.

10. In accordance with this plan, we shall look for the first payment on September 1.

11. Please send US your cheque to settle the matter.

12. We enclose a cheque for $50 00 in payment of your invoice of the 1 0 December.

13. We are duly in receipt of your letter of May 5. enclosing a draft, value $50 000 in check. which has been credited your account as requested.

14. We inform you that we have opened an irrevocable credit with the London Bank in your favor.

15. Documents will be checked and paid immediately after receipt if there is no discrepancy.

16. What kind of installment payment do you have in mind?

17. Accepting D/P or D/A makes no great difference to you, but it certainly does to me.

18. I can't be of any help in this respect. L/C is the only term of payment we can accept.

19. If you agree to accept D/P. we can compromise on other terms.

II. Substitution Exercises.

Drill 1　I wonder if you could ...

　　　　　Complete the above sentence by using the following:

　　　　　— accept Document against Payment

　　　　　—tell us the quantity of the goods you want

　　　　　—work out the FOB price for this particular item

　　　　　—tell us what particular items you're interested in

Drill 2　In order to... can you bend the rules a little?

　　　　　Complete the above sentence by using the following:

—close our deal

—sign the contract tomorrow

—decide the date of delivery

—come to an agreement on price

Drill 3　To be on the safe side, we insist on ...

Complete the above sentence by using the following:

—making a trial purchase

—seeing the samples first

—exploring other possibilities

—receiving payment by Letter of Credit

Drill 4　It looks like we've settled everything in connection with this transaction except ...

Complete the above sentence by using the following:

—the term of payment

—the claim procedure

—the date of delivery

—the insurance premium

Drill 5　For the payment of this order...

Complete the above sentence by using the following:

—we require German marks

—please make it by way of L/C

—we'd appreciate it if you could send us a sight L/C

—an irrevocable, transferable L/C would be most appropriate

Drill 6　To avoid having our funds tied up...

Complete the above sentence by using the following:

—would a usance L/C be all right

—we've got to speed up cash flow

—a sales promotion has to be initiated

—we should open a revolving L/C（循环信用证）

Drill 7　Since you're our old customer, I agree. However, you'll have to ...

Complete the above sentence by using the following:

—send us the L/C within 40 days

—buy products from one of our joint ventures

—open a confirmed L/C at the National Westminster Bank

—open a bank account at a bank that we have business relations with

Drill 8　I have another question to ask you. Do you think you could...

Complete the above sentence by using the following:

—reduce the deposit a little

—advance the date of delivery

—accept new orders for the time being

—change one item in our sales contract

Drill 9　We'd like to make the payment by ...

Complete the above sentence by using the following:

—sight L/C

—installment

—documents against payment

—documentary collection（跟单托收）

Drill 10　I need to check with my company as to whether ... is okay.

Complete the above sentence by using the following:

—a time draft

—a clean bill

—a banker's bill

—a commercial draft

Drill 11　To my knowledge, you can make the payment by ...

Complete the above sentence by using the following:

—collection（托收）

—remittance（汇付）

—loan on credit

—deferred payment

Drill 12　We're not in a position to ...

Complete the above sentence by using the following:

—promise you a deferred payment

—provide you with a loan on credit

—guarantee you a low interest rate

—allow you to make the payment after its expiration date

Drill 13　Since a/an ... would be more appropriate.

Supply the missing words in the above blanks by using the following:

—a prompt payment is difficult, installment

　　　　　　—D/A causes a lot inconvenience to us, D/P at sight

　　　　　　—the opening of a L/C is expensive, a loan on credit

　　　　　　—the interest rate on installments is high, prompt payment

Drill 14　To … is okay, but there're still a lot of details which need
　　　　　to be worked out. Complete the above sentence by using the following：

　　　　　　—make the payment by L/C

　　　　　　—meet you half way on price

　　　　　　—sign the contract tomorrow

　　　　　　—make the delivery within a month

Drill 15　In the meantime, I'd appreciate it if, you could …

　　　　　Complete the blank in the above sentence by using the following：

　　　　　　—send us some samples

　　　　　　—open L/C before Christmas

　　　　　　—ship the goods within two months

　　　　　　—make the payment 50% by L/C and 50% by D/P

Drill 16　From the exporter's point of view, the term of payment which can offer
　　　　　the best protection is …

　　　　　Complete the blank in the sentence by using the following：

　　　　　　—irrevocable, transferable L/C

　　　　　　—irrevocable, confirmed, sight L/C

　　　　　　—L/C with T/T reimbursement clause（带有电报索汇条款的信用证）

　　　　　　—irrevocable L/C payable against shipping documents

III. put the following sentences into English.

1. 如果可能的话,我是愿意通融一下的。但在付款这方面,我们只接受信用证。

2. 若是你们同意接受付款交单的话,别的方面我们可以让步。

3. 请问你们打算委托哪家银行开证?

4. 如果在六个星期后还收不到你们的信用证,我们的发货工作就要受到影响了。

5. 这一点请尽管放心。你方不收跟单托收,我们按信用证的方式做好了。

6. 根据惯例,信用证应在装船前 15 到 20 天由买方开出。

7. 为了保险起见,我们的一贯做法是只接受不可撤销信用证。

8. 从现在国际金融市场的角度来看,我们更愿意你们用日元来作为支付手段。

9. 你知道作为卖方来讲,我们也有资金被占用的问题。所以请你们开即期信
用证。

10. 我们是不能接受远期汇票这种支付方式的。

11. 我现在无权对您的要求作出答复,我得和我们公司总部联系一下。

12. 具体的费用请你们与你方的开证银行联系。

13. 如果是老客户,我们可以按照承兑交单来做;但对新客户,我们都按信用证的方式来做。

14. 在分期付款和延期付款上,我们对客户加收的利率是一样的。

15. 最主要的是,我们需要你方议付行开出的保兑信用证。

16. 其他都好说,但这笔生意需要一笔很大的定金。

17. 我们所关心的是信用证的开户银行什么时候能够支付这笔款项。

18. 这笔买卖不知你是否可以通融一下,按50%付款交单,50%承兑交单来做?

19. 这样可以避免占用我们的资金,又帮助我们解决了资金周转问题。

20. 考虑到您是我们的老客户,我们可以让您用远期信用证的方式来支付,利息按国际市场上的价格来计算,您看可以吗?

IV. Role. Play.

Work in pairs.

Make up a dialogue on one of the following situations.

Task 1

You represent Suzhou Arts & Crafts Imp. & Exp. Corp. , selling paper mnbrellas. An American businessman has ordered a total of USD20, 000 worth of your products. But since this is the first time you are doing business together, you want to be careful about every detail. So you point out that the L/C should be "irrevocable", because L/C without the word "irrevocable" provides no protection for the exporter.

Task 2

Mr. Clive, a businessman from England, is in negotiation with you about purchasing Yingchun Brand woollen sweaters. Everything has been going quite well except the problem of payment. As his order is big enough, you finally agree to 50% by L/C and the rest by D/P sight. You make clear to him the process and procedures of such terms of payment.

V. Oral Practice.

Work with your partner. One importer pushes you to accept D/P payment. You explain why you can accept it.

VI. Topics for Group Discussion.

1. In what way will an irrevocable L/C protect the seller's interests?

2. On what grounds would you accept different kinds of payment such as D/A and D/P?

第 8 章　运输

Shipment（Ⅰ）

Lewis：Let's have a word about delivery under FOB terms, shall we? But before we start, I must confess I'm quite a layman in import and export business. Sometimes terms like shipping advice or shipping instructions keep puzzling me and very often I can't tell which is which. I do feel a bit nervous at times.

Xiong：Everybody has a beginning; so don't feel nervous at all. As to these two terms, let me tell you once and for all. Shipping advice is issued by the seller, to advise the buyer that the goods have been shipped on board, while shipping instruction is issued by the buyer, to instruct the seller of the name of ship and its sailing date.

Lewis：Excuse me, please. Shipping advise advising the buyer ...shipping instruction instructing the seller ... They get confused very easily. But I'll learn it by and by. One lives to learn.

Xiong：In this transaction, you are the buyer. As buyer, you are to charter a ship or book the shipping space.

Lewis：That's understood

Xiong：Then you should advise us, or rather, instruct us by fax, name of ship and its sailing date. In another word, you are to send us a shipping instruction so that we can make necessary arrangements for shipment beforehand.

Lewis：That's also understood. Will you make clear to me your responsibility?

Xiong：We'll see the goods pass over the ship rail and our responsibility ends there.

Lewis：It's you who should bear all the charges of transportation of the goods, am I right?

Xiong：We bear all the charges up to the time the goods are on the hooks.

Lewis：What do you mean by all the charges?

Xiong：They are Customs duties as well as any service charges on exporting goods.

Lewis：As I understand it, you are also to inform us of the contract number, name of commodity, quantity, loading port and the estimated date when the goods will reach the port of loading. Is that so?

Xiong: Exactly. We'll fax you 30 days before the month of shipment.

Lewis: Excellent. So far we have a mutual understanding on everything concerning our respective responsibilities. I hope we'll both discharge them as well.

Words and Expressions

layman 外行	respective 各自的
shipping advice 装船通知	discharge 卸,履行(职责)
shipping instruction 装船须知	have a word about 谈谈关于……
board 甲板	at times 有时候
charter 租船	once and for all 一劳永逸地
rail? 扶手,栏杆	ship on board 装上甲板
hook 钩,钓钩	one lives to learn 活到老学到老
customs 海关	or rather 或者说
duty 关税	up to the time 知道……时间
load 装载	

Shipment (II)

Jebb: Now that we've satisfactorily dealt with the question of payment terms, I'm eager to know if it's possible to effect shipment during March?

Tian: I'm sorry we can't effect shipment in March.

Jebb: When is the earliest we can expect shipment?

Tian: By the middle of April, I think.

Jebb: That would be too late. These goods are urgently required by our customers for the shopping season in May. Also, our customs formalities will take quite a long time. You must deliver the goods before April, or else we won't be able to catch the shopping season.

Tian: It's all very well for you to say that. But the problem is that our factory has a lot of back orders on hand. And all of these orders have to be dealt with in strict rotation. As a result, it's very difficult for us to improve any further on the time.

Jebb: Can't you find some way for an earlier delivery? It means a lot to us. If we place our goods on the market at a time when all other importers have sold theirs at profitable prices, we shall lose out.

Tian: Let me see. How is this then? Considering our long-standing business relations, we'll make an effort to negotiate with our manufactures again and request them to advance shipment to the beginning of April. That is to say, advancing shipment by 10 days. But then the workers will have to work three shifts for that. I think this is the best we can do at present.

Jebb：That's terrific. Then I'll take you at your word. May I suggest you put it down in the contract My letter of credit will be issued early in March. Other terms and conditions remain the same as in previous dealings.

Tian：OK. On our part, we'll do everything we can to ensure punctual shipment.

Jebb：I don't know how to thank you enough. I hope the volume of trade between us will be even greater in future.

Words and Expressions

satisfactorily 令人满意地

formality 手续

rotation 旋转, 轮流

profitable 有利可得

deal with 与……打交道

shopping season 销售季节

back orders on hand 在手的过期未交货的订单

It's all well for you to say that 你那么说倒轻松

in strict rotation 按严格顺序

at a time when 当……的时候

lose out 失去, 亏本

I'll take you at your word 我就认定你这句话了

put it down in the contract 在合同中写进去

Key Sentences 经典必备句

●交货日期：

A timely delivery means a lot to the buyer.

及时交货对买方来说关系重大。

After shipment, it needs at least 4 weeks before the goods can reach our retailers.

从交货到零售商收到货物至少需要 4 个星期。

Your prompt reply will speed up the shipment.

你们的及时答复将会加速装船。

Can Our order of 1 000 accordions be shipped as soon as possible?

我们订的 1 000 台手风琴能尽快装运吗？

We can effect shipment of the order in June.

我们能在 6 月份装运这批货。

Could you do something to make a prompt shipment?

你们能不能设法即期交货？

We will highly appreciate if you can manage to hasten the delivery?

如果你们能加快装运我们将十分感激。

We are so sorry to inform that we can't advance the time of delivery.

我们非常抱歉地通知您,我们不能把交货期提前。

I'm sorry that we are unable to give you a definite date of shipment till now.

很抱歉,现在我们还无法告诉您确切的装船日期。

We are terribly worried about late shipment.

我们非常担心货物会迟交。

Please hold shipment till you get our instruction.

请在我们通知之前暂停装货。

We are so happy to hear that the order is all ready for shipment.

我们很高兴听到货物已经准备好待装运了。

Since the order NO. C209 is urgently in demand, we have to ask you to speed up shipment.

由于第 C209 号订单所订货物我们急需,请你们加快装船速度。

Is there any possibility to ensure a prompt delivery of the goods?

还有任何可能可以确保即期交货吗?

We can assure you that shipment will be made no later than the end of August.

我们可以向你保证交货期不会迟于 8 月底。

We hope you can effect shipment in November at the latest.

我们希望你们最晚 11 月份交货。

We try to ship as you desired.

我们尽力按你们的要求装船。

Can we short-ship 60 boxes?

我们可以少装 60 箱吗?

They suggest to ship from Dalian instead of Tanggu?

他们建议把交货港由塘沽改为大连。

Shipment can be effected from Hong Kong, if you hope to receive the goods much earlier.

如果你们希望可以更早些收到货物,可以安排在香港交货。

There is no difference to us, wherever you ship—Shantou or Zhuhai.

无论你们从哪里装货——汕头或是珠海,对我们来说没有什么不同。

It may cause problems in our shipment.

这可能给我们的发货带来问题。

Our experience tells us, it's better to designate Tanggu as the loading port.

我们的经验表明,在塘沽装货比较合适。

The facilities for shipping goods in Southeast Asian countries have changed a lot.

东南亚的货物的装运条件已大大改善了。

It is to inform that the shipment has arrived in good condition.

特此告知,运到之货情况良好。

There are more sailings at Shanghai, so we have chosen it as the loading port.

上海的船次多,我们把这里定为装货港。

They found an over-shipment of 320 lbs.

他们发现货物多装了 320 磅。

Clients are willing to choose big ports as the loading ports.

客户希望选择较大的港口作为装运港。

We have had a brief talk about the loading port.

我们已经就装运港问题简短地谈过了。

We designate Tanggu as the loading port because it is near the producing area.

我们把塘沽定为装运港是由于它离货物产地比较近。

We insist that Dalian is the proper loading port.

我们坚持大连是适合的装运港。

We regret to inform you that a part of your goods were damaged in transit.

我们很遗憾地通知您,您的一部分货物在运输途中受损。

Sea transportations are preferred because of the higher cost of railway transportations, although it is quicker to move the goods by railway.

因为铁路运输费用相对要高些,大家更愿意走海运,尽管铁路运输较快。

The buyer prefers to have the goods dispatched by sea for such a big order.

鉴于订货很多,买方更愿意走海运。

From what I've heard you're ready well up in shipping work.

据我所知,您对运输工作很在行。

How do you usually export your agricultural machines?

你们出口农用机器通常采用什么运输方式?

If the goods are to be transshipped from one means of transportation to another during the course of the entire voyage, it's called "combined transport". We don't count on this kind of combined transportation.

如果货物在运输途中交换交通工具,这便是"联运"。我们并不相信这种联运方式。

When you are ready to reserve the cargo space, please send us the necessary application forms.

当你们准备好需要预订货舱时,请将订舱表寄给我们。

A lot of problems may occur in the multimodal combined transport.

联运中可能出现很多问题。

It's easy to cause a delay in shipment or even lose the goods in a combined transport.

联运中货物容易误期，甚至出现丢失。

Please have the goods dispatched by air.

请空运此批货。

Since there is no direct vessel. I am afraid you have no choice but a multimodal combined transport by rail and sea although it is troublesome.

由于没有直达船只，恐怕你们只能接受海陆联运了，尽管麻烦。

Sometimes, combined transportation has the complicated formalities.

联运常会手续烦琐。

The goods are now in transit.

此批货物正在运输途中。

At last, the two sides made an agreement on the mode of transportation. Both of them agree to employ "combined transportation" to ship the goods.

最终双方就运输方式达成了协议。双方都同意"联运"货物。

Let's discuss the transportation mode of the timber we ordered.

我们现在讨论一下所订木材的运输方式吧。

We specialize in arranging shipments to any part of the world.

我们承揽去世界各地的货物运输。

We don't think it is proper to transport the goods by railway,

我们认为此货不适合用铁路运输。

The buyer would prefer to have goods carried by road and not by railway.

买方宁愿用公路运输而不用铁路运输。

What is your specific transport requirement?

你们要求什么样的运输条件?

● 运费：

Please quote your current tariffs.

请报你公司的最新运费表。

Who will bear the extra freight charges?

多出的运费由谁负担?

The bill of lading should be marked as "freight prepaid".

提单上应该注明"运费预付"字样。

Insurance covers both sea and overland transportation.

保险应包括水陆两路的运输。

Have you done any chartering?

你们已经租船了吗?

We will pay the freight for shipment from Dalian to Hongkong.

从大连到香港的运费由我方负担。

It should be the transportation company who pay the damage occurred during the transit.

运输过程中出现的货物损坏应由运输公司赔偿。

Frequently Used Words and Phrases 常用词汇和短语

unloading/discharging 卸货

cargo freight 运费

cargo mark 货物装运标志

cargo space 货舱

carriage 运费

Combined Transport Documents(CTD)
联合运输单据

combined transportation 联运

direct vessel 直达船只

entire voyage 整个运输过程中

facilities 条件,设施

forward shipment 远期装运

initial shipment 第一批货

late shipment 迟交

load off 卸货

load time 装货时间

loaded on deck(货物)装于甲板上

loading certificate 装货证明书

loading charge 装船费

loading days 装货天数,装载时间

loading list 装船单

loading 装货

Male's Receipt 大副收据

means of transportation 运输方式

mode of transportation 运输方式

move 运输

multimodal combined 联运,多式联运

shipment as soon as possible 尽快装运

shipment 装运

shipping advice 装船通知

shipping documents 装船单据

shipping instruction 装船单据

shipping instructions form 装船指示单

shipping mark 装运标志

shipping order 装货单

shipping 装运的

short-shipment 少装

through B/L 联运提单

tough transport 联运

time of delivery 交货期

time of shipment 装运期,装运时间

to arrange transport 安排运输

in transit 正在运输

to do charter 租船

to effect shipment 交货,装运

to effect shipment 装运

to make delivery of the goods 交货

to make shipment 交货,装运

to ship 装船,装运

to speed up 加速

to take delivery of the goods 提货

to transport by railway 陆运

to transport by sea 海运

Train. Air. Truck（TAT;TA）"陆. 空.
陆"联运;或"陆空联运"

near shipment 近期装运

over-shipment 多装

preferential duty rates 优惠利率

prompt delivery 即期交货

prompt shipment 即期装运

transport charge 运输费

transport 运输

transportation business 运输业

transportation by sea, land, air, and
mail 海、陆、空、邮运输

transportation company（corporation）
运输公司

transportation cost 运输成本

way of transportation 运输方式

Sample Dialogues 1. Hurry Up

Both sides have reached an agreement on price terms. Now they go on a discussion about shipment...

A:If we place an order at this moment,when can you ship the goods?

B. 1 am afraid it should be in October. We are fully committed at the moment. It is impossible for us to commit ourselves beyond what the production schedule can fulfill.

A:Is there any possibility for you to arrange a prompt shipment before October? I am afraid our stock doesn't allow us to wait too long.

B:Well,as this is our first transaction,I wish we can make a deal. We will try our best to advance the shipment before October. Perhaps some other orders will be canceled. We'll keep you informed.

A:Let me put it in this way. We concluded the deal on a FOB basis. Even if you deliver the goods at the beginning of October,we need to spend about two weeks to go through the Customs. If you can do us a favor to manage a delivery two or three weeks earlier,everything will be fine and we will be able to make it.

B:The best we can do is to effect shipment at the end of September. Anyway,we will do anything to advance the shipment.

A. I think I have got your promise on the shipment at the end of September. That's very kind of you. I'm looking forward to receiving your advice of shipment as early as possible.

B:OK. You take my words. But your L/C should be opened early before September.

A: I promise

Sample Dialogue 2. Have to Wait at the Port

Finally, the seller fails to catch the liner designated by the buyer...(Now they are on the phone)

Seller: Mr. Philip?

Buyer: Yes?

Seller: This is Li Kun. I am sorry to inform you that we didn't catch the liner.

Buyer: What is up?

Seller: Since you enlarged the order, we spent two more days to prepare the goods. And then we had no enough time for the commodity inspection and watched the vessel leaving the port helplessly.

Buyer: Well, what shall we do? You know it is hard to get a ship right now.

Seller: But our goods are at the port. If there is no ship, they will be moved back to the stock place. For that, we need to pay additional fees including stock returning, warehouse rental, and even interest to your end according to the fine clause.

Buyer: I understand. We will try our best to arrange another ship as earliest as we can. We will let you know the name of the ship and date.

Seller: Thank you. By the way, since the delay was caused by your change in the quantity of goods stipulated in the contract, the fine clause for the overdue shipment should be invalid. And we will share the additional fees occurred by storing goods at the port.

Buyer: Of course, it is not an overdue shipment. Our problem is to find a ship quickly. Otherwise, we'11 have a real problem. Let me do that right now, OK? I will call you back later.

Sample Dialogue 3. Date of Shipment

When a buyer places his order, he often demands that the delivery meet his sales requirement. To avoid possible disputes, the date of shipment should be stipulated as clearly as possible in the contract. Mr. Wei from the Shanghai Foodstuffs Import & Export Corporation has had much experience in this area.

Myer: Now, Mr. Wei, a word about delivery. Can you make prompt shipment?

Wei: "Prompt shipment", well, such terms are ambiguous. People can interpret this phrase differently.

Myer: We must have the seafood for the winter sale. That's all I want.

Wei: For the winter sale? Why, that would mean the goods must arrive at London in early November. We're now in late September. Even if we had the goods ready I don't think we could ship them right away.

Myer: I know there's a great demand on shipping lately.

Wei: That is so. I was informed by our shipping department yesterday that liner space for Europe up to the end of next month has been fully booked. I'm afraid we can do very little about it.

Myer: We understand tramps are still available.

Wei: Yes, but tramps are scarce. Generally, no refrigeration facilities are provided on them, and I'm not sure whether there would be enough tonnage to make a full cargo, even if a tramp could be obtained.

Myer: Is there any chance if transshipment is allowed?

Wei: But transshipment adds to the expenses, risks of damage and sometimes may delay arrival, because there's also a shortage of transshipment space for Europe. Anyhow, we'll try. We have good connections with the China Resources Shipping & Storage Co., Ltd. in Hong Kong. This company has a great reputation for its competence in the shipping world. And since it has long-term agency agreements with many world famous shipping companies, it can easily meet the clients' varied demands.

Myer: We prefer direct shipment, of course, but if you can't get hold of a direct vessel, we may agree to have the goods transshipped at Hong Kong. You know, good quality, competitive prices, all would mean nothing if goods could not be put on the market on time.

Wei: Yes, fully understand. We'll find out the situation about the connecting steamer right away.

Myer: As far as I know, Jardine Shipping Agent (HK) Ltd. Has a liner sailing from Hong Kong for Europe around mid-October. If you could manage to catch that vessel, everything would be all right.

Wei: It's very hard for us to accept a designated on-carder as there are many factors that might make the goods miss the intended sailing. Besides, are you sure the vessel will call at London? And is she already carrying a full load?

Myer: I guess if we start immediately, there's still hope. And if worst comes to worst, please ship the goods to London or Liverpool. How about Liverpool as an optional port of destination?

Wei: Good. Then what would you say if we put it like this: "Shipment: first available steamer in October. Port of destination: London or Liverpool. Transshipment at Hong Kong allowed. " I think this is the earliest possibility.

Myer: Fine. It seems I've no alternative. Thank you, Mr. Wei. I'm sorry if these arrangements cause you a lot of inconvenience.

Wei: Oh no, we're only too glad to help you in any way we can.

Sample Dialogue 4. Negotiating Delivery Periods

In this dialogue, the buyer is negotiating delivery periods for machines he has ordered with the supplier.

Supplier: Well, let's get started. You know, with this delivery problem I'm sure there's room for negotiation.

Buyer: Well, let's see how we get on.

Supplier: Right, well this is how we see it. We can deliver the first machine in ten weeks, and install it four weeks after that.

Buyer: How do you justify such a long delivery period?

Supplier: Well, these are in fact the usual periods. It's pretty normal in this kind of operation. Did you expect we could deliver any quicker?

Buyer: This is how we see it. We would expect a delivery period of six weeks as a maximum, and would expect installation to take about four weeks.

Supplier: I see what you mean, but that would be very difficult. You see we have a lot of orders to handle at present, and moving just one of these machines is a major operation. Look, if I can promise you delivery in eight weeks, does that help?

Buyer: I'm sorry, I can't accept that. You'll have to do better than that, I'm afraid. It's too late.

Supplier: Ah-ha! Well, look. er... You want the machine in six weeks. Now that is really a very short deadline in this business. You said that you couldn't take it any later, but couldn't your engineers find a way to re-schedule just a little, say another week?

Buyer: I have my instructions. I'm afraid I can't agree to another week.

Supplier: Well, you really are asking us for something that is very difficult. I've already offered you seven weeks. I'll have to consult with my colleagues and come back to you, but I can't see what we can do.

Buyer: May I make a suggestion? If you can promise to deliver to us in six weeks, then we may be able to discuss the possibility of a further order.

Supplier: Well, on that basis I suppose we might be able to look at some kind of arrangement. In fact, if you can promise another order I think we could accept your terms.

141

Buyer: Good. Let's just summarize the terms: 6 weeks for delivery; 4 weeks for installation; and we'll come to a decision about a further order by the 26th of this month.

Supplier: Exactly. If you could confirm this in writing, everything would be settled.

Sample Dialogue 5. Discussion on Delivery Time

Mr. Frank Murphy, Export Manager of an American company is discussing with Mr. Eric Blare, Import Manager of Scanska Co. , about the terms of the contract on Diesel Engine.

Murphy: Well, Mr. Blare, let's go on to the next point, shall we?

Blare: Okay. It's the question of the delivery date, Mr. Murphy.

Murphy: As for the delivery date, What's your time limit?

Blare: I'm afraid we'll have to insist on not later than September 20th. You see, we have a very strict timetable and we also have other orders to be filled.

Murphy: Yes, quite.

Blare: And many things will depend on the installation of the engine...

Murphy: Yes, of course.

Blare: You see, Mr. Murphy, it's essential for us to have it before the 30th. Otherwise...

Murphy : Yes, but let me explain the position.

Blare: Certainly. Go ahead, please.

Murphy: As you know, we had a disastrous hurricane here not long ago and part of our workshop was damaged and our production had a standstill for quite some time.

Blare: Yes, you told me.

Murphy: So, er, there's a backlog of orders to fill.

Blare: Mm?

Murphy: We're working at full capacity at present, but the best we can do is the last week in September as the shipment date.

Blare: I'm not altogether satisfied, I'm afraid.

Murphy : Why not?

Blare: I do hope you'll appreciate our problem, Mr. Murphy, because you have to arrange the delivery date not later than September 20.

Murphy: Mm—I think we can compromise on this.

Blare: And then when?

Murphy:What about making September 25 the official shipment date?

Blare:Why the 25th?

Murphy:That's the last liner scheduled to sail for your port in September.

Blare:Let me see...it'll take about a week to ship the engine to the destination and we'll have to install the engine on the 5th of October.

Murphy:But we'll do our best to meet an earlier date.

Blare:Okay,let's make it 25th. But we must insist absolutely on September 25 as the last possible date.

Murphy:Fair enough.

Blare:All right, then. Let's make it the 25th of September. But the earlier the better.

Murphy:Splendid. Now Let's come to the next point.

Sample Dialogue 6. Expecting a Delivery

Zhao Bin, who is the manager of the Delivery Section of Goodluck Forwarding Co., is now getting in touch on the phone with Andrew Mellon, the manager of the Logistics Department of a foreign-owned KMW Co., making arrangements to deliver the components and parts KMW's imported.

Mellon:Good afternoon. Logistics of KMW Co.

Zhao:Good afternoon. This is Zhao here from Good luck Forwarding. I'd like to speak to Mr. Mellon, head of the department.

Mellon:Mellon speaking. Mr. Zhao. How are you?

Zhao:I'm fine, thank you. And you?

Mellon:Not too bad, thanks. What can I do for you?

Zhao:I think you should have said what I can do for you.

Mellon:What gives?

Zhao:I was phoning to inform you that the steamer carrying your imports docked at Tianjin Port this morning and has started unloading in the afternoon.

Mellon :Ah, yes, that's good news. I was just about to call you about it. Er... would you tell me when we can expect the consignment to arrive in our warehouse?

Zhao:Yes, as far as I know, there're eight containers in all.

Mellon:Say no more!

Zhao: We'll need four lorries to carry them, two on one lorry. The lorries should arrive late Thursday or early Friday, it depends on traffic and weather. Er... what time will you accept deliveries?

Mellon: The latest time we can start unloading is 4 p. m. , but we can start at as early as 8.30 a. m. Er... could you tell me Whose lorries are delivering the goods?

Zhao: Yes, certainly. Two of them will be ours, and the others are on hire from the Safe trip Transport. But their drivers are absolutely reliable.

Mellon: Fine. Mr. Zhao, could you let me know if they will arrive on the same day?

Zhao: Yes. I'm not entirely sure about that, but... er... two will be setting off at least half a day earlier, they should arrive on Thursday. And the other two will arrive towards midday on Friday.

Mellon: Could you let me know how long it proximately takes to unload a lorry?

Zhao: Yes, er ... it'll take about an hour.

Mellon: I think you should know that we can't unload more than two trucks at a time.

Zhao: Well, I see. Thank you very much for the information. I wonder if you can tell me what'll happen if one of the trucks arrives later and can't be unloaded on Friday. Do you know if it can be unloaded on Saturday?

Mellon: I'm afraid not. You might have to wait till next Monday. Er... I'll talk about this matter with our warehouse manager and come back to you tomorrow. What do you say?

Zhao: Good. Thank you very much. It's nice to talk to you. I'll be expecting your call tomorrow. Till then, goodbye.

Mellon: Goodbye.

Sample Dialogue 7. Requesting for Late Delivery

Mr. Jackson is the marketing manager of ABD Co. There is some-thing wrong with their production. As they cannot fill on schedule the orders they have accepted, he goes to call on some of their customers and tries to persuade them into agreeing to delay their supplies.

Jackson: I'm not going to waste time making excuses and talking about our problems. The fact is we're not going to be able to fulfill your March order on time. But I'm hoping we can reschedule deliveries so that we can fit in with your production priorities.

Dobson: I do appreciate your difficult situation, but I have my own difficulties too. At the time of ordering, we had quite attractive offers frown some of your competitors.

My directors didn't want to order from your company. If I have to go to them now and say, ABD Company can't meet their next delivery dates- that will be unpleasant for me. And also for your company.

Jackson: Yes, I understand. But your current order is a large one. Are you sure you need all these components urgently?

Dobson: I didn't follow you.

Jackson: Well, according to our records, you've ordered ten thousand transistors per month right through to the summer. Surely there's some seasonal variation in your production schedules?

Dobson: It's true that we reduce production a little bit in the summer.

Jackson: So some of the components would be held in stock until autumn.

Dobson: Perhaps you may be right. When my assistant joins me later, I shall get him to check the situation.

Jackson: Would you please try to reschedule the quantity of your orders for the next two months if possible? It would be in both your interest and ours. I'll get in touch with you tomorrow for the results. See you tomorrow.

Dobson: See you tomorrow.

When Mr. Jackson leaves DDH Co., he goes to visit Mr. Walter, another customer who has also been ordering transistors from them.

Jackson: You see, Mr. Walter, the purpose of my visit is to see whether you have any change in your orders for transistors.

Walter: Oh, yes, that is what I just wanted to get in touch with you for. We've developed a new design, much smaller and also cheaper.

Jackson: I see. I expect you'll be using integrated circuits for the new model.

Walter: That's right. The advantage of integrated circuits is very obvious to our competitors as well as to us. So we want to put it on the market as soon as possible.

Jackson: I'm sure we can supply you with what you'll need for the new model.

Walter: Now-the problem is about the components that had been ordered for the old model...

Jackson: Er yes...the transistors...

Walter: We don't really need them any more.

Jackson: Well', we'll be very pleased to cancel the order. What about the stocks you're holding?

Walter: We hold quite large stocks. More than we need, in fact.

145

Jackson: I can take some off your hands, if that helps you.

Walter: That's marvelous. How many would you take. ?

Jackson: As many as you like!

Walter: Hang on a moment. I'll check...Oh about twenty thousand.

Jackson: OK, I take them all. Thank you for helping me solve a big problem.

Sample Dialogue 8. Urging Delivery

Mr. Lin, the manager of a Chinese-owned company newly established in London, is talking on the phone with Miss Catherine, the sales manager's secretary of the furniture company, urging delivery of the desks and chairs they have ordered for their new office.

Mr Lin: Hello?

Catherine: Hello, the sales manager's office.

Mr Lin: Can I speak to the sales manager, please.

Catherine: I'm afraid Sales Manager is engaged at the moment. Can I help you?

Mr Lin: Yes, my name is Lin from Huaying Co. , London. I was promised delivery of four desks and chairs a week ago, and they still haven't arrived.

Catherine: I'm sorry to hear that, Mr. Lin.

Mr Lin: You sent an invoice, though, and I'm certainly not going to pay it until I get the goods.

Catherine: Of course not, it goes without saying, Mr. Lin. Could you give me the invoice number?

Mr Lin: AD1811.

Catherine: Thank you. I'll ask the sales manager to look into the matter as soon as I can get hold of him.

Mr Lin: And please tell him we need those desks and chairs urgently.

Catherine: Of course. I'm very sorry there's been a delay.

Mr Lin: You'll ring me back later this afternoon, then?

Catherine: Yes, of course, as soon as we can.

Mr Lin: Right. I look forward to hearing from you. Goodbye.

Catherine: Goodbye, Mr Lin.

Sample Dialogue 9. Dealing Properly with Wrong Delivery

Mr. Sun's company makes a serious mistake in delivery, but the buyer Mr. Palette helps deal with the problem to the satisfaction of the both parties, thus enhancing the friendship between the two companies.

Palotti：Good afternoon... Oh, sorry, I should have said: good morning. This is Palotti from Marpolo Co. , Italy. Could I speak to Mr. Sun, Sales Manager?

Sun：Speaking. Hello, Mr. Palotti, good afternoon. Can I help you?

Palotti：Hello, Mr. Sun, yes. Well, I think there may have been some misunderstanding about our last order.

Sun：Oh dear, what seems to be the problem?

Palotti：The consignment arrived at the port here yesterday in time, but when the tracks brought the containers to our warehouse we've just found, while unloading, that the quality of the goods doesn't appear to be Class A1 as we ordered.

Sun：Goodness gracious! I'm terribly sorry. Let me just check this on the computer Er... oh dear, yes, I'm afraid there has been a slip-up in our shipping department. I'm very sorry, but it's certainly our fault. what would you like us to do about it?

Palotti：Oh, no. Well, we can keep the goods and try to find another buyer for it, if you will charge us 25% less for the shipment and ship us a load of Class A 1 right off.

Sun：That sounds fair enough. Thank you for your cooperation. But just let me check our stock position... Yes, we can ship by the first available steamer... actually there's one scheduled to sail the day after tomorrow. We'll try our best to make an immediate arrangement for the shipment.

Palotti: Oh, yes, that'll be fine. I hope the steamer will arrive on schedule and we can have the goods by the middle of next month.

Sun：We'll stress this point to the shipping company and keep you in touch.

Pallotti：Oh yes, that's fine.

Sun：Mr. Palotti, thank you very much for your kind cooperation.

Palotti：Well, friend in need is friend indeed, We hope you will lend us a hand when we're in difficulties in the future.

Sun：Yes, of course. Whenever you need our help, do be free to let us know and we'll try our utmost to help. That's a promise for sure.

Sample Dialogue 10. To Advance the Shipment to Early April

Jebb：Now that we've satisfactorily dealt with the question of payment terms, I'm desirous to know if it's possible to effect shipment during March?

Tim：I'm sorry we can't effect shipment in March.

Jebb：When is the earliest we can expect shipment?

Tim：By the middle of April, I think.

Jebb：That would be too late. These goods are urgently required by our customers for the selling season in May. Besides, our Customs formalities will take quite a long time. You must deliver the goods before April, or else we won't be able to catch the shopping season.

Tim: It's all very well for you to say that. But the problem is that our factories have a lot of back orders on hand. I'm afraid it's very difficult to improve any further on the time.

Jebb: Can't you find some way for an earlier delivery? It means a lot to us. If we place our goods on the market at a time when all other importers have sold theirs at profitable prices, we shall lose out.

Tim: How's this then? We'll make an effort to advance the shipment to early April.

Jebb: All right I take you at your word. May I suggest you put it down in the contract? My letter of credit will be issued early March. Other terms and conditions remain the same as in previous dealings.

Tim: OK. We'll do everything to advance the shipment.

Jebb: Thanks ever so much for your help. I hope the volume of trade between us will be even greater in future.

Sample Dialogue 11. Another Possibility to Ensure a Prompt Delivery

Forest: It has just occurred to me that there is still another possibility to ensure a prompt delivery of the goods.

Xiang: And that is?

Forest: How about making Hong Kong the port of shipment instead of Shantou?

Xiang: I'm afraid we can't agree to that. We concluded the business with you here in Guangzhou, and the goods you ordered are manufactured in Shantou. We wish to point out that all orders accepted by us are shipped from Shantou or Huangpu. Hong Kong is out of the question.

Forest: It's like this. There are only one or two sailings a month from Shantou to Osaka, while sailings from Hong Kong are quite frequent. If shipment were effected from Hong Kong, we could receive the goods much earlier.

Xiang: I see. You want to have your goods shipped from Shantou to Osaka via Hong Kong, where they can be transshipped. Is that the idea?

Forest: Yes, exactly, because I want these goods on our market at the earliest possible date.

Xiang: Your idea may be a good one, but the trouble is that there are risks of pil-

148

ferage or damage to the goods during transshipment at Hong Kong. How about shipping them from Huangpu instead of Shantou? You may choose either one as port of shipment. It makes no difference to us. There are more sailings from Huangpu than from Shantou.

Forest: It sounds all right to me, but I'll have to think about it. I'll give you a definite answer tomorrow. If I choose Huangpu, will it be possible for you to ship the goods by the end of March?

Xiang: We'll try our best. Anyway, we assure you that shipment will be made not later than the first part of April.

Sample Dialogue 12. Jacob needs advice from the seller about transportation…

A: Since it is our first time to import from China. Could you give me some ideas about the transportation?

B: Don't worry. Our CIF prices will release you from the mass of arranging transportation. Normally, we choose multi-model combined transport by rail and sea. That is, we will send the goods to Tianjin by rail and then from Tianjin to Amsterdam by sea.

A: One of my friends told me that we can make transshipment in Honking. How is that?

B: Do you mean that we manage to catch a certain vessel heading to Europe from Hong Kong? Then we need take the risk of missing the intended sailing. Another possibility is, the designated vessel is already carrying a full load when Our goods are ready in Hong Kong. Besides, the transshipment also increases the probability of damages.

A: But the combined transport also may cause a delay in shipment or even a loss, doesn't it?

B: Risks exist in all ways of transportation. As far as I know, delay and loss never happened in our transshipment of European-bound cargoes at Tianjin port.

A: Good. Then, how about the formalities? Are they complicated?

B: But we will handle them at our end. What you need to do is to pay on the arrival of the shipping documents for the transshipment from Tianjin.

A: OK.

Sample Dialogue 13. Out of Our Reach

A Chinese company located in Wuhan decides to import fertilizers. They are talking about the shipment since Wuhan is an inland port which the buyer can't reach directly through sea shipping…

Tang: May we have the price of CIF Wuhan?

Timothy: If I am right, Wuhan should be an inland port.

Tang: Yes. Wuhan is the capital of Hubei province. It is a landlocked city located on the bank of ChangJiang River.

Timothy: I am afraid that we can only ship your goods to a sea port nearest to Wuhan. That is all we can do. I think it should be Shanghai.

Tang: Then, how about the distance from Shanghai to Wuhan?

Timothy: Generally, the buyer prefers to ship the goods by means of some kind of river boat since Changjiang River leads all the way up to Wuhan.

Tang: Understand. So you will quote CIF Shanghai.

Timothy: That is right.

Useful expressions for negotiation

Explanation and Correcting Misunderstanding 解释和消除误解

That isn't quite what I said; you see all the items we sent are...

I'm afraid there seems to be a slight misunderstanding...

Perhaps I haven't made myself clear ...

Let me(just briefly) put it in another way...

To be mo re specific, I think the data...

Allow me to rephrase that...

What I mean is...

What I am suggesting is...

What I am trying to say is...

What I am getting at is...

What I am driving at is...

Let me try that again.

The point I'm making is(that)...

Let me put it this way.

What steps would you suggest to correct that?

I'm sure you don't realize it, but...

Perhaps you didn't understand the consequences that could result from...

Maybe I failed to make myself clear ...

Let me tell you why...

There's a(good)reason for this:

The reason is...

I'm sorry. I can't tell you that(right now).

Can I get back to you on that?

I'll explain(a little)later.

We'll come to that later.

We'll get to that in a few minutes.

Can we save that until later?

In other words.

Let me put it another way.

Let me try to make that clearer.

Put simply…

The bottom line is…

实训综合习题

I. put the following sentences into Chinese.

1. We assure you that shipment will be made before September 1st.

2. What would you say if we ship the goods in installments?

3. To meet your demands, we allow transshipment, but the expenses and risks involved should be borne by you.

4. If the goods are not shipped in February. we'll be compelled to purchase elsewhere and may have to cancel our order.

5. If partial shipment is permitted. we can ship whatever is ready to fill the urgent needs of your end-users.

6. You'd better ship the goods entirely/in one lot/completely.

7. Since there is no direct steamer to your port from Shantou. The goods have to be shipped to Hong Kong for transhipment.

8. It's likely to cause a delay in shipment or even complete loss of the goods if you arrange such a combined transport.

9. As your prompt attention to shipment is most desirable, we hope you will let us have your shipping advice by cable without delay.

10. We greatly regret the delay, which has been due to circumstances beyond our control.

11. The ordered goods must be shipped in Full Container Load.

12. Shipment should be made before October, otherwise we are not able to catch the season.

13. The order is so urgently required that we must ask you to expedite shipment.

14. Shipment by the middle of October will be too late for US.

15. If nothing can be done about it, the goods can only be shipped in September.

16. 1'm sorry we can't effect shipment in March.

17. When is the earliest we can expect shipment?

18. As a rule, the earlier the shipment, the better the business.

19. Your price sounds reasonable, but shipment is too extended.

20. We shall effect shipment as soon as your L/C arrives.

II. Substitution Exercises.

Drill 1   You know, what we've ordered is...

        Complete the above sentence by using the following:

        — needed urgently

        — exceptionally large

        — essentially a seasonal product

        — classified as strategically important

Drill 2   Yes, I understand. We'll definitely ...

        Complete the above sentence by using the following:

        — speed up delivery

        — give it top priority

        — make sure you receive them on time

        — make sure there's some room on this vessel

Drill 3   But by all means please make sure that ...

        Complete the above sentence by using the following:

        — there' re two sailings next month

        — the opening bank of the L/C is reliable

        — we could receive your L/C within six weeks

        — your manufacturer can deliver the goods next month

Drill 4   You can take my word for it that ...

        Complete the above sentence by using the following:

        — our project is going on well

        — we'll send you the confirmed L/C you want

        — the required down payment is not a large sum

        — our installments will be paid off 18 months later

Drill 1   We'd like to have this order sent ...

Complete the above sentence by using the following:

— via air cargo

— in 4 to 5 batches

— in 7 or 8 containers

— by way of sea transportation

Drill 2　In order to effect shipment without delay, I suggest ...

Complete the above sentence by using the following:

— that your order be divided into batches

— valuables and ordinary items be separated

— we adopt both the air and the sea transport

— the actual size of these containers be calculated

Drill 3　We wish to ship a consignment of goods from ... to...

Complete the blanks in the above sentence by using the following:

—Albany, USA; Dalian, China

—Weihaiwei, China; Buffalo, USA

—Alexandria, USA; HongKong, China

— Huangpu, China; Delaware Breakwater, USA

Drill 4　We have ... at Port Xingang ready for dispatch to ...

Complete the above sentence by using the following:

— 100 tons of coal; Osaka（大阪）, Japan

— ten cases of arts goods; Hamilton, Canada

— 150 tons of grain;Kawasaki(川崎),Japan

— three containers of garments;New Orleans,USA

Drill 1　Since this is our seasonal product, we've got to market it before ...

Complete the above sentence by using the following:

— January the first

— February the third

— January the sixth

— February the fourth

Drill 2　Can you do something about it to ...

Complete the above sentence by using the following:

— effect shipment

— speed up the delivery

— send us the L/C earlier

— guarantee the chartering of a ship

Drill 3　That'll be a really hard nut to crack. You see, the problem is...

Complete the above sentence by using the following:

— mode of payment

— date of delivery

— availability of the ship

— the cost of opening an L/C

Drill 4　According to our manufacturer, the earliest possible date of delivery would be ...

Complete the above sentence by using the following:

— the end of march

— the first of April

— the middle, of April

— the end of April

Drill 1　I'll get in touch with ... and make sure ...

Complete the above blanks in the above sentence by using the following:

— our sales agent, the price is correct

— our sales representatives, he has enough stock

— our sales manager, we have the right stuff you want

— our manufacturer, they'll be able to deliver the goods on time

Drill 2　Oh, I almost forgot. Maybe it's a good idea for you to ...

Complete the above sentence by using the following:

— charter a ship right now

— secure a spot on the airplane

— talk to another sales representative

— ask the native produce and animal by products company

Drill 3　Look, about delivery, our manufacturer suggests transportation by ...

Complete the above sentence by using the following:

— air

— sea

— short distance truck

— long distance truck

Drill 4　We'll effect shipment every other month as of this...to...for a total span of six months.

Complete the blanks in the above sentence by using the following:

— January, July

— February, August

— March, September

— April, October

III. put the following sentences into English.

1. 签订合同后,我们就马上向船公司登记,安排发货计划。

2. 这方面也请你理解,如果没有轮船公司的支持,我们也没有办法和你们配合。

3. 关于责任问题,在到岸价的条件下,不能按期装运是发运方的责任。

4. 在离岸价的条件下,由于买方不能按时派船而造成的延误,则是买方的责任。

5. 在特殊情况下,买方可借口对方派船误期而拒绝交货。

6. 请在合同中注明发货方及收货方。

7. 我看还是用集装箱来空运这批贵重物品比较保险一点。

8. 其他的一般货物和大件货物就用海运吧。

9. 我们订的这一批货,季节性很强,错过了季节就没办法赚钱了。

10. 我们的工厂正在加班加点,尽量往前赶。

11. 我们来交易会的目的就是为了赶上我们国内一年一次的季节性销售。

12. 所以,请千万保证船期,使我们不至错过销售旺季。

13. 这个问题可真不好办了。你们的订货量不大,用空运的方式怎么样?

14. 让我这么说吧,要是这次我们的订货能赶得上销售季节,明年我们继续合作。

15. 我这里有两方面的问题。我不仅要和船公司联系,也要和装运港联系。

16. 我们提供的集装箱,可以两头同时打开进行装运。

17. 这种集装箱的防水性能也不错,装货后的封闭也简单。

18. 我们联系了几家船运公司和代理,但他们在下月 25 号之前都没有船。

19. 预期装船将在 7 月 15 日前完成,船到纽约是在 8 月 30 号。

20. 这批货物的装运挺复杂,要均成 6 份,分送给两个目的港。

IV. Role Play.

Suppose you are having a talk with a Japanese merchant about the time of shipment. He asks you to make shipment in April. The reason is that he wants to catch the seasonal demand for swimming suit on the market in time. Since it takes time to find the fight manufacturers locally, you could not promise the shipment. The best you can do is in the middle of May. Of course, if conditions permit, you'll do your best to advance the shipment as he wishes.

V. Oral Practice.

Work with your partner. You have drawn an agreement on the order. But the importer insists on designating a shipping company which will bring you lots of trouble. Try to persuade them to accept your transit.

VI. Topics for Group Discussion.

1. The importance of making punctual shipment in international trade.

2. The difference between Shipping Advice and Shipping Instructions.

3. Are there any other modes of transportation with which you are familiar? Try to compare their advantages and disadvantages with marine transportation.

第9章 包装

Packing(I)

A German company placed an order of tea from one of Chinese companies. They found there is a ready market in Europe. Their representative, Sherman, is talking with John, the sales manager, about the packing before they make another order.

J: Glad to see you again, Sherman.

S: Hi, glad to see you too.

J: Please, sit down. Would you like to try our new tea?

S: Great! The main purpose of my visit today is to place another order of your tea. Actually, we will place regular orders from now.

J: Oh, it is really great news for us. I have told you that our tea won't let you down.

S: That is true. But before that, I'd like to talk something about the packing of the tea.

J: Did you find any problems with the packing?

S: No. What I mean is an improvement of the packing of your tea. There is no doubt that the quality of your tea is good. But we believe the packing is as important as the products themselves, because it is the packing that will give the first impression on customers rather than products themselves.

J: Well, I agree with you. But could you be more specific?

S: Sure. Firstly, we believe the appearance of the package should catch customers' eyes. A beautiful packing is surely a great help in pushing sales. Honestly speaking, your packing is not attractive enough to buyers.

J: Do you mean the color of the design should be more bright and eye-catching?

S: Eye-catching with traditional Chinese style. You see, customers even can smell your culture before they open the box and drink the tea. As you know, one function of packing is to stimulate the buyers' desire to buy.

J: I'll pass your idea onto our designers and ask them to improve on it.

S: Thank you, John. I hope you can understand that the competition from the similar producers is quite tough. Secondly, if it is possible, we would like to advice you to improve your method of packing.

J: Our packing is typical tin for teas. Any questions about this way?

S: Again, how to let the packing speak for the good quality of your tea? Can we find some other packing ways to show off the appealing green and shape of your tea?

J: We can leave an open window on the packing.

S: You got the point. Of course, your designers will be professional to do this. Finally, only a reminder to your designers, flimsy packing can make the feeling of expensiveness lose. People won't believe products of high quality are wrapped inside with a poor packing.

J: Thanks for your suggestions.

Packing(II)

Now, the out packing comes into question in a discussion between the buyer and the seller...

B: How will you pack our order?

S: We have the standard packing for export. Firstly, each item will be individually packed in poly-bag. Then, we put each 10 items into one wooden case.

B: The wooden case will be put into the container directly, doesn't it?

S: You are right.

B: How about dampness protection? Dampness may cause damage during the transportation. It happened in our last order.

S: Well, each wooden case will be lined with plastic sheets from inside. Anyway, no claim of damage caused by dampness was put forward in our export before.

B: I am glad to hear that. But carefulness never hurt. Do you have the sign of "Keep Dry" on the wooden cases?

S: Sure. Along with "Upward".

B: One more question, how is your shockproof packing?

S: We have shockproof cardboards in wooden cases. The safety of packing is something we always pay a lot of attention to. I am sure you don't have to worry about it.

B: That is fine.

Notes

place regular orders 定期下订单（定期购货）

eye-catching 引人注目的，耀眼的

to stimulate 刺激

pass onto 传递

flimsy packing 易坏的包装

standard packing 标准包装

shockproof packing 防震包装

dampness protection 防潮

carefulness never hurt 小心无过错

to be lined with...用……做衬里

Key Sentences 经典必备句

● 包装费用：

In general practice, it is buyers who will bear the charges of packing.

一般来说,包装费用由买方负担。

No charge will be allowed for packages.

包装容器不收费。

Normally, packing charge is already included in the contract price.

一般来说,合同价格中已经包括了包装费用。

Our packing charge is about 2.5% of the total cost of the goods.

我们的包装费用占货物总值的 2.5% 。

● 产品外包装：

An eye-catching packing will help push the sales.

醒目的包装有助于推销产品。

Our packing is beautiful and quite well-done.

我们产品的包装美观讲究。

We improved the packing in order to give ur clients satisfaction.

为了使我们的客户满意,我们改进了包装。

It is necessary to improve the packaging.

改进包装方法十分必要。

Different packing is used for different articles.

不同商品需要不同的包装。

Packing affects sales directly.

包装直接影响到产品的销售。

Our packing also attributes to the reputation of our products.

我们的包装也对赢得产品的声誉作出了贡献。

The necklace is elegantly placed in a satin—covered small box, lined with beautiful silk ribbon.

项链被精致地装在一个锦缎小盒里,再用一条漂亮的绸带系在外面。

The unique design of the packing will help you promote the sale.

独特的包装将有助于你们推销。

● 运输包装：

Both suppliers and buyers should pay great attention to packing.

供货方和买方都应该注意包装的情况。

We use cardboard boxes for export.

我们出口用硬纸板箱包装。

Each carton is lined with foam plastics to protect the goods against press.

每个箱子里垫有泡沫塑料以免货物受压。

Each pill is sealed into a small box with wax.

每个丸药被用蜡密封入小盒。

Each100 should be packed in a case marked TM and numbered from No. 1 upward.

每 100 个装一箱,刷上唛头 TM,从第一号开始往上循序编号。

We don't think the cardboard boxes are strong enough for ocean transportation.

我们认为纸箱对于远洋运输来说不够结实。

It would cost more to pack the goods in wooden cases than in cartons.

使用木箱包装成本高于硬纸箱。

The outer packing is marked with "Fragile" and "Handle with Care".

外包装上标明了"易碎品"和"小心轻放"字样。

Our packing will be on a par with that of any competitors in Europe and America.

我们的包装可以与欧洲和美国的竞争者相媲美。

Please fax US the packing and marks.

请传真给我们包装及唛头式样。

Please make an offer with an indication of the packing.

请报价并说明包装情况。

For fruit jars, it is important to make them airtight.

对于果酱罐来说,密封很重要。

Please mark the bags as per the drawing enclosed.

请按所附图样在袋上刷唛头。

Wool sweaters should be packed in plastic-lined water-proof cartons.

羊毛衫应放在内衬塑料防水的箱子里。

After the canned goods are to be packed in cartons, the cartons should be strapped.

罐装货物被装入纸箱里后,外面应该再加箍。

The key point of packing is to protect the goods from moisture.

包装的关键是防潮。

The eggs must be packed in cartons with beehives lined with shake-proof paper board.

鸡蛋一定要用带蜂房孔、内衬防震纸板的纸箱包装。

For ocean transportation, the goods are to be packed in strong cases and securely strapped.

对于远洋运输来说,货物应该用坚固的木箱包装,并且牢牢加箍。

Packing must protect machines against dampness, moisture, rust and shock.

机器的包装必须保护机器,具有防湿、防潮、防锈、防震的作用。

We are glad to see the packages are intact and the packing is beautiful when the consignment arrived.

我们很高兴在货物到达时,包装完好无损,很美观。

The packing must be strong enough to withstand any rough handling in transit.

包装必须十分坚固,以承受运输中可能的粗鲁操作。

We prefer smaller containers to pack the goods.

我们主张用小容器包装这批货。

The buyer insists on using wooden cases for outer packing.

购买方坚持要用木箱做外包装。

We reach an agreement on the stipulations about the packing and shipping mark.

我们关于包装和运输唛头的条款达成了协议。

According to the contract, we use a polythene wrapper for each shirt.

根据合同规定,我们每件衬衣都用聚乙烯袋包装。

We use metal angles at each comer in order to strengthen the carton.

我们每个箱角都使用金属角,以便加固箱子。

We pack two dozen into one carton. whose gross weight is around 30 kilos.

我们一纸箱装两打,每箱毛重 30 千克。

We've informed the manufacturer to adjust their packing as per your instruction.

我们已经通知厂商按你们的要求改进包装。

We will reinforce the packing with metal straps.

我们会用铁箍加固包装。

Your opinions on packing have been passed on to the manufacturers.

你们对包装的意见已经被转达给了厂商。

Frequently Used Words and Phrases 常用词汇和短语

bales 包件

barrel 琵琶桶

be in bad order 破损,(包装)不合格

be in good order 完好

box 盒子

breakage-proof 防破损

bundle 捆,束

can/tin 罐装,听装

canvas 帆布

cargo in bulk 散装货

carton 纸板箱,纸箱

case 箱

cask 桶

casket 小箱 chest 箱

coil 捆,盘装

collective packing 组合包装

consumer packing 消费包装

container 集装箱

corrosive 腐蚀性物品

crate 板条箱

customary packing 习惯包装

dangerous When Wet 遇水燃烧品

drum 圆桶

explosive 爆炸品

fireworks 礼花

flexible container 集装包

foam plastic bag 泡沫塑料袋

fragile 易碎品

glass jar 玻璃瓶装

gunny bag 麻袋

handle with care 小心轻放

indicative mark 指示性标志

inflammable gas 易燃气体

inflammable liquid 易燃液体

inflammable solid 易燃固体

inflammable 易燃的

inner packing 内包装,小包装

intact 完整的,未损伤的

iron drum 铁桶

keep away from boilers 远离锅炉

keep away from cold 请勿受冷

keep away from heat 请勿受热

keep dry 防湿

keep in a cool place 在冷处保管

keep in a dry place 在干燥处保管

keep upright 勿倒置

keg 小桶

kraft paper 牛皮纸

leakage—proof 防漏

mark 唛头

marten overcoats 貂皮大衣

metal hoop 铁箍

neutral packing 中性包装

not to be tripped 勿倾倒

nude cargo 裸装货

ocean transportation 远洋运输

organic peroxide 有机氧化物

outer packing 大包装,外包装

oxidizing agent 氧化剂

pack test 包装试验

pack 包装,装罐

package design 包装设计

package engineering 打包工程

package in damaged condition 破损包装

package materials(packing supplies)包装材料

package 包装(指包、捆、束、箱等);打包

packaging 包装方法

packaging industry 包装工业

packed cargo 包装货

packet 包裹,封套,袋

packing and presentation 包装装潢及外观

packing charge 包装费用

packing clause 包装条款

packing cost 包装成本 packing credit

打包放款,包装信用证

packing expenses 包装费用

packing extra 包装费用另计

packing letter of credit 包装信用证,红条标信用证

packing list/note/slip 装箱单

packing specification 包装标准化

packing 包装

pallet 托盘

parcel post 包裹邮寄

parcel 小包,一批货

plastic bag 塑料袋

poison gas 毒气

poison 毒剂

polythene 聚乙烯

radioactive 放射性物品

rough handling 粗率的处理(搬运,装运货物)

satin-covered 缎包装的

seaworthy packing 适合海运包装

seller's usual packing 卖方习惯包装

shake proof 防震

shipment packing 运输包装

silk ribbon 绸带

single packing 单件包装

smaller container 小容器

sound-proof 隔音

spontaneously combustible 自燃物品

substantial 坚固的

tastefully 精美的

the canned goods 罐装货

this side up 此端向上

to be on a par with 与……相媲美

to be packed in bag 用袋装

to be packed in paper bag 用纸袋装

to reinforce the packing 加固包装

upward 向上,由下往上

use no hooks 请勿倒挂

warning mark 警告性标志

water-proof 防水

well—done 美观,讲究

wooden case 木箱

wooden cask 木桶

Sample Dialogue 1. To Submit to the Regulations of Our Government

W: In my opinion, overly strict regulations are just another way of restricting imports.

F: Ah, there's something in what you're saying. According to the present FDA regulations, the Ma Ling labels as they are cannot be used if the lichee is to be offered for import into the United States.

W: Why not? Our canned lichee and other canned provisions have already been widely sold in various markets abroad, and Ma Ling label has now been accepted by most overseas customers and importers. Is it impossible for you to use the Ma Ling labels as they are?

F: I'd be quite willing to if I could, but we must comply with the label requirements according to our law, or we can't clear the consignment of lichee through the

Customs.

W: In that case, what can we do to help you?

F: Would you consider quoting us for the order with neutral (unlabelled) cans on a CIF basis for delivery in Hong Kong? Our associated company there will have the labels printed to comply with the FDA regulations.

W: Do you think that's the only way out? You know we usually do the labeling ourselves, as we are responsible for the brand labels of our products.

F: Well, the present label won't do. Is it possible for you to get round the Ma Ling Factory to print different labels for us?

W: Yes, I think they might consider it as long as your requirements are reasonable.

F: This is great. I could wish for nothing better.

W: Well, let's hear what idea you have in mind.

F: The FDA insists that only two languages be used on the labels. Since there are two principal display panels on the label, one can be in English and the other in Chinese. The important point is to have information on one of the panels in English only.

W: The German or Dutch description on the current labels is to be deleted then, isn't it?

F: Yes, that's what we want.

W: Any other changes?

F: Yes, just one more thing. The net weight must be indicated in a type of required size, that is, one-eighth of an inch minimum, and placed in the lower 30% of the panel.

W: I see. We shall give it our immediate attention.

F: Thanks for your help.

Sample Dialogue 2. Keep Making Improvements in Packing

S: Shall we discuss the packing now, Mr. Liu?

L: All right. Bathrobes are packed in cartons of 20 dozen each.

S: Do you think cartons are strong enough for a long sea voyage?

L: It doesn't matter much. We strengthen the cartons with four nylon straps outside.

S: But you should know that dampness may get into cartons during long distance shipping. This would make bathrobes spotted. And it may bring us a great deal of loss.

L: You can be assured. The cantons are lined with waterproof plastic sheets. Besides, we use a transparent polyethylene bag for each bathrobe.

S:That's good. The transparent packaging gives the consumer a clear view of the beautiful colors of the bathrobe and facilitates its marketing in super-markets, department stores and other retail outlets.

L:That's true. We keep making improvements in our packing method in order to meet the demands of competition in the international market. By the way, do you have any other questions or requirements regarding packing?

S:The inner packing needs to be improved. It does not look attractive enough to customers. Although your bathrobes are reliable in quality, you lose out to others just because you fail to pack the goods properly.

L:That's a good suggestion, but can you be more specific?

S:You should have color designs on each transparent polyethylene bag. In this way, the bathrobes can be more eye-catching. They will be more popular in our market.

L:Good ideas. We'll see to it that the packing appeal to the eye as well as to the purse. I will pass your ideas on to our designers. Any other suggestions?

S:No, nothing else. I suppose everything concerning packing is clear now. I'm very much satisfied with your packing this time. If everything goes smoothly, we're likely to place larger orders with you before long.

L:Thank you. I'm looking forward to your good news!

Sample Dialogue 3. Packing and Packaging

Proper packaging is almost as important as the quality of the product itself. Poor packaging can damage the chance of success just as much as a bad product can. Mr. Jeffery is a regular buyer of China's exports. He often comments on the packaging of the products. Ms. Yuan Ming from the Shanghai Home Textiles Corporation is one who is receptive to new ideas and suggestions.

J:(Examining some of the cartons in the corner) Mm.

Cartons of this sort are not quite sea-worthy. Ms. Yuan, you may remember we once had a serious problem with a shipment of your towels. Most of the cartons were broken and damaged. We had to repack the goods. Just think of the trouble that caused us.

Y:As soon as I got your fax I went to the factory and asked them to use stronger cartons and double straps. Later shipments were all right, weren't they?

J:They were perfect. You're very cooperative, Ms. Yuan.

Y:It is a minimum requirement to ensure that the goods are safe from breakage.

J:Many foreigners have great respect for the quality of China's products. You can compete successfully on the world market in a good many commodities, but you lose out to others just because you fail to pack the goods nicely. Look at this. It's a good one. But if a customer can see the goods or a picture of the goods on your box or package, it helps him see what he's buying.

Y: That's only the outer packing. Inside there's a transparent poly bag. (Take the Cotton Velvet Bedcover out) This should catch the customer's eye! Sales appeal is certainly quite important. The buyer sees the package and its contents as a whole.

J: That's right. A well-designed package helps sell the goods. The buyer will probably be very influenced by the package.

Y: He should also learn that appearances are deceptive sometimes. (Both laugh.)

J: That's true. And naturally, when marketing products, the quality of the goods is still most important.

Y: We've made some improvements in our packaging lately. For instance, with bath towels, we've introduced two packaging lines, each handling goods for specific sales requirements. We can either offer you normal packing, that is solid design but assorted colors, or assorted designs and colors.

J: Ms. Yuan, you mentioned assorted designs. How many can you put in a poly bag?

Y: Two or three. For four or more designs, we charge extra.

J: And your normal packing is still ten dozen per carton?

Y: That's right.

J: But Ms. Yuan, that isn't enough. You know, nowadays many firms have opened up new selling channels over the Net, which means commodities are sold through mail order houses. Therefore, packing should be improved accordingly.

Y: I understand that many consumer products are being sold through mail order houses.

J: Oh yes, the mail order business is booming. So you'll need to change your packing to suit this new development.

Y: What type of packing do you want? I mean for bath towels.

J: We prefer special cartons of 30cm ×60cm with two or three dozen to each carton because it's convenient and easy to handle. Can you make this adaptation, Ms. Yuan?

Y: Yes, we can, but I'm afraid the cost will go up by 5 ~ 8 percent and there's also the freight rate.

J: I think it's worth it. Maybe I can order a small quantity for a trial sale next time. One more point, a second development in packaging is that some customers are asking for "consumer packs", that is, a pack which allows the products to be put directly onto the store shelves.

Y: Yes, I know. With the boom of hypermarkets or supermarkets and convenience stores, there has been a trend toward prevailing smaller packages to suit costumers' needs and requirements.

J: Packaging is a real skill. One lives and learns. All right, Ms. Yuan, thank you for giving me so much of your time. I must leave now.

Y: It's a pleasure talking with you, Mr. Jeffery.

Sample Dialogue 4. To Make Sure That the Packing Is Seaworthy

F: What about the outer packing?

L: We'll pack them 10 dozen to one carton, gross weight around 25 kilos a carton.

F: Cartons?

L: Yes, corrugated cardboard boxes.

F: Could you use wooden cases instead?

L: Why use wooden cases?

F: I'm afraid the cardboard boxes are not strong enough for sea transportation.

L: The cartons are comparatively light, and therefore easy to handle. They won't be stowed with other heavy cargoes. The stevedores will see to that. Besides, we'll reinforce the cartons with plastic straps. Shirts are not fragile goods. They can stand a lot of jolting.

F: Maybe you are right, but the goods are to be transshipped at Hong Kong. If the boxes are moved about on an open wharf, dampness or rain may get into them. This would make the goods spotted or ruined.

L: No need to worry about that. The cartons are lined with waterproof plastic sheets, and as the boxes are made of cardboard, they will be handled with care.

F: Well, I don't want to take any chances. Besides, cartons are easy to cut open, and this increases the risk of pilferage.

L: Tampering with cartons is easily detected. I should say that this rather discourages pilferage.

F: Maybe so, but I'm afraid that in case of damage or pilferage, the insurance company will refuse compensation on the ground of improper packing, or packing unsuitable for sea voyage.

L :But cartons are quite seaworthy. They are extensively used in our shipments to continental ports. There are never any complaints from our clients, and such packing has also been approved by our insurance company for W. P. A. and T. P. N. D. coverage.

F:If you could guarantee compensation in case the insurance company refuses to honor a claim for faulty packing, we would be quite willing to accept cartons.

L:I'm sorry, but we can't take on any responsibility that is beyond our functions and powers. We'll make sure that the packing is seaworthy, but we can't commit ourselves to being responsible for every kind of mishap.

F:I can understand your position. Perhaps I'm asking too much.

L:We'll use wooden cases if you insist, but the charge for that kind of packing will be considerably higher, and it also slows down delivery.

F:Well, I'll cable home immediately for instructions on the matter.

L:Please do. I'll be waiting for your reply.

Useful expressions for negotiation

Expressing Disagreement 表示异议

I really don't think so, because...

Your point is well-token, but...

I have my own thought about that.

I'm afraid I can't accept that.

I don't think you are right about that.

That's not how I see it.

I see your point, but...

I can't go along with your view.

I don't see why.

Surely not.

I'm afraid I have a different opinion.

I see things rather differently myself.

I am not sure if I agree...

Maybe, but don't you think that...

I can't say I share your view on this...

I feel I must disagree...

I wouldn't say that...

I respect your opinion, of course, but on the other hand...

That might be OK, but...

While I don't agree with your conclusion, you certainly have the right to your opinion.

Would it be possible for you to recheck...

Unfortunately, we must decline your offer for the following reason(s).

I'm sorry, but we must respectfully decline your offer.

I'm sorry, but I am opposed to the proposal.

I'm sorry, but I can't support the proposal.

I'm sorry, but I don't think that's such a good idea.

I'm afraid I think that would be a mistake.

I'm afraid that doesn't sound very good to me.

That sounds like a bad idea to me.

Quite honestly, I think that would be a big mistake.

We seem to be talking at cross purposes(与目的相反的结果).

实训综合习题

I. put the following sentences into Chinese.

1. How would you pack the goods we have ordered ?

2. We hope the packing could be more attractive, the design and the color will suit European taste.

3. Your recommendation on improving packing would be appreciated.

4. We hope that you can make more improvements in the packing. Attractive wrapping would help us sell the goods.

5. Packing should be suitable for transport by sea. Could you use wooden cases instead?

6. Please make sure to use shockproof packing.

7. The goods are to be packed in wooden cases containing 20 dozen each.

8. Each package should be marked "Fragile".

9. Each case should be lined with foam plastics in order to protect the goods from pinch.

10. Don't forget to stencil "Handle With Care" and other relative marks on the cartons.

11. I must make it clear that for different materials. expenses will be different.

12. In my opinion, customers should get an idea of what is packed inside through outer packing.

13. We could use wooden cases for packing if you insist. This kind of packing costs more.

14. When you pack, please put 2 or 3 different designs and colors in each box. This will make distribution to the retailers.

15. We usually do the label ourselves, as we are responsible for the brand labels of our own products.

16. The packaging must be seaworthy and strong enough to Stand rough handling.

17. The new packing of the porcelain is of typical Chinese style.

18. I have to complain about the really careless packing of the last consignment.

19. You should have used stronger cardboard boxes for such a heavy item.

20. Your packers apparently left out the padding and that's why the casing on the printer is cracked.

II. Substitution Exercises.

Drill 1　As for the packing of the products, we'd like to use ...

Complete the above sentence by using the following:

— tins

— crates (板条箱)

— iron drums (铁桶)

— corrugated cardboard boxes (瓦棱纸箱)

Drill 2　This is no big problem. As long as we can ... Complete the above sentence by using the following:

— we have goods in stock, make the delivery

— you agree on the price, sign the contract

— you've made up your mind, lower the price a little

— the offer is good for one more day, give you a definite

Drill 3　For this kind of product we export, each item is individually packed in ...

Complete the above sentence by using the following:

— paper cartons

— plastic sheets

— polyethylene wrappers

— corrugated cardboard boxes

Drill 4　... are packed in a paper carton before shipping.

　　　　Complete the above sentence by using the following:

　　　　— every 6 dozen

　　　　— every 10 boxes

　　　　— every 24 pieces

　　　　— every 12 bottles

Drill 5　Please make sure you use the kind of packing which is ...

　　　　Complete the above sentence by using the following:

　　　　— leakproof

　　　　— seaworthy

　　　　— dampproof

　　　　— shockproof

Drill 6　We'll pack them... in a...

　　　　Complete the blanks in the above sentence by using the following:

　　　　— 5 dozen, crate

　　　　— 6 dozen, wooden case

　　　　— 7 dozen, cardboard box

　　　　— 12 dozen, corrugated cardboard box

Drill 7　I'm concerned about the ...

　　　　Complete the above sentence by using the following:

　　　　— quality of our first order

　　　　— possible delay of the delivery

　　　　— difficulty in pushing the sales

　　　　— sudden change in the market situation

Drill 8　We've got an excellent record on ...

　　　　Complete the above sentence by using the following:

　　　　— aftersales service

　　　　— making our service first rate

　　　　— making our customers satisfied

　　　　— offering the best value you can buy

Drill 9　... is something we always pay a great deal of attention to.

　　　　Complete the above sentence by using the following:

　　　　— the variety of our service

　　　　— the quality Of our service

— our customers' satisfaction

— the competitiveness of our product

Drill 10　We sure can if you want us to, but ...

Complete the above sentence by using the following:

— discount will be low

— we need a separate check for that

— that amount of money will have to be shown somewhere

— the percentage of the commission will have to be written down

Drill 11　Do you mind if I ...

Complete the above sentence by using the following:

— give you a little help here

— ask you for an indication of price

— discuss the issue of packing and delivery

— come back with a definite answer within 3 days

Drill 12　Your products are good, there's no question about that.

Substitute the first sentence "your products are good" by

using the following:

— the demand for oil keeps rising

— business between our two companies is growing

— your products have a ready market in our country now

— our co-operation in the past has been very satisfactory

Drill 13　That's really a good idea. I'll pass it on to our ...

Complete the above sentence by using the following:

— retail stores

— agents abroad

— local manufacturers

— franchise dealers（特许经营商）

Drill 14　Our packing is strong enough to stand ...

Complete the above sentence by using the following:

— jolting

— rough handling

— a long sea voyage

— long distance truck transportation

III. Put the Following Sentences into English.

1. 我想把关于包装的问题再落实一下。

2. 希望你们能在海运箱上注明我们公司的商标,并注明内装何物。

3. 关键的问题是要确信这些箱子适合于海运。

4. 对这一类物品来说,用瓦楞纸来包装是足够好的了。

5. 用纸箱可以减轻重量,节省运费;包装费也不用另外计算。

6. 这种货物的包装有盒装,袋装和一般包装三种;价格都是一样的。

7. 我们的商品都是聚乙烯袋包装的,商品不会脏。

8. 这个散装货码头的装卸能量怎么样?

9. 首先我想了解一下,这批货能不能用中性包装?

10. 我建议你们使用开窗包装,可以直接看到盒内的商品。

11. 我建议你们的五星啤酒采用现在国际上流行的小瓶包装。

12. 另外,瓶盖是否也可该成一拧就开的那种。

13. 在包装这些小瓶啤酒时,6 瓶为一盒,4 盒装一箱。

14. 我们这批货在装运时一定得加倍小心,这都是国家的一级保护文物。

15. 这些盒子都需要里面内衬防震板,外加加固条。

16. 为了使这批录像机对我们的顾客更有吸引力,请你们使用双包装。

17. 除了普通的硬纸箱包装之外,请最好再加上印有我们公司商标的塑料袋。

18. 这样包装后的商品更能显示出它的华贵气派。

19. 但是您说的这种算是特殊包装,我们得向您收取额外费用。

20. 在硬纸箱内我们已经加了硬泡沫塑料衬垫,用于加固和防震。

IV. Role Play.

Work in pairs. Make up a dialogue on one of the following situations.

Task 1

You represent Nanfang Native produce and Animal By-products Imp. & Exp. Corp. A businessman from Korea has ordered a total of USD10 000 worth of your bamboo ware. He is not sure what kind of packing would be most appropriate for his orders. You suggest paper cartons according to different sizes of the products. Now you discuss this issue with him.

Task 2

You sell oolong tea on behalf of Fujian Native Produce & Animal By-product Imp. &Exp. Corp. Now a Japanese businessman has ordered a total of USD18 000 worth of your oolong tea. He wants to make sure the packing is absolutely moisture-proof and seaworthy. You tell him the way you pack the tea and the material you use.

V. Oral Practice.

Work with your partner. One of your foreign importers is not satisfied with the packing of your silk garments. They worry the packing may not stand the rough handling. In the end you make an agreement to improve it.

VI. Topics for Group Discussion.

1. Describe the inner and outer packing of pyjamas.

2. What are the proper ways of packing garments?

第 10 章　代理与佣金

Commission（Ⅰ）

Jones：Mr. Xiong, we are desirous to know your usual practice in giving commission.

Xiong：Actually, we don't give any commission in general.

Jones：I'm afraid it goes against the usual commercial practice not to allow commission.

Xiong：Mr. Jones, you must be aware that the articles under offer are our best sellers.

Besides, the prices we quote are very keen and the profit margin very narrow. It's really impossible for us to make any further concession by allowing you any commission.

Jones：But you see, Mr. Xiong, as commission agents we do business on commission basis. In fact, we usually get a 3 to 5 percent commission from European suppliers.

Xiong：Well, if you'll increase your order we might perhaps consider your request.

Jones：Do you think so? What do you say if we increase the order by 15 000 yards? 15 000 yards is not a small figure, isn't it?

Xiong：In that case we may consider giving you a 3 percent commission. It is only in view of your strenuous efforts in pushing the sale of our products in the past few years that we extend you this most favorable accommodation.

Jones：My heartfelt thanks, Mr. Xiong. But there's one thing I wish to have your special attention.

Xiong：What is it?

Jones：Do not deduct our commission from the value of the consignment.

Xiong：I beg your pardon? I didn't catch your meaning.

Jones：I'm afraid I haven't made myself clear. I mean you write the full value in the invoice just the same. And it's only after you've collected the full payment of the L/C, will you then remit us our commission.

Xiong：I see your point now. We'll do as you wish.

Words and Expressions

strenuous 费力的,艰辛的　　　　　　　concession 让步

175

extend 伸展

accommodation 适应,妥协

heartfelt 由衷的

deduct 扣除

consignment 寄售,货物

invoice 发票

remit 汇寄

collect 收集

in general 总的来说

go against 不符

in view of 鉴于

push sale of 推销

I beg your pardon 请再说一遍

Notes

under offer = being offered under 意为"处于某种状态下"

I've come to make a contract with you for the business under discussion.

我就是来和你就讨论中的这笔买卖订合约的。

Commission (II)

Ali: Now, Mr. Liu, we have gone too far off the point. Let's return to the topic of commission, shall we?

Liu: That's just what I was going to propose.

Ali: Honestly, Mr. Liu, the rate of commission you are going to grant us is far too small. Could you raise it to 5%?

Liu: But 2% is exactly the same as we pay to other grants. Any increase would have to be put onto the price and make it less competitive. Moreover, when other customers get to know it, they are likely to raise questions. It would then be very embarrassing.

Ali: That I know. But then, different problems, different approaches, as your Chinese saying often goes. They have established their markets while we have to start from the very beginning. Besides, it's a new product. In order to promote the sales we shall have to spend a lot of money on advertising. In a nutshell, our operating cost is much higher than others', don't you think so?

Liu: There may be some truth in what you say. They say it is much easier to lose a customer than to win one. It is our first transaction; for the sake of future business we might consider your proposal. But your five percent is far from being acceptable.

Ali: Could we make a compromise? Allow us a higher rate for a certain period of time, say, six months. What would you say to it?

Liu: That sounds more practical. But I can't decide it at the moment. I have to get confirmation from my head office.

Ali: When could you give me a definite answer?

Liu: Will you come around tomorrow afternoon? I think I'll be able to let you know the results by then.

Ali: OK.

Words and Expressions

nutshell 坚果壳	put onto 加到……上
compromise 妥协	in a nutshell 总的来说
far off the point 远离话题	make a compromise 妥协
rate of commission 佣金率	come around 过来

Sample Dialogue 1. We Are Still at the Get-acquainted Stage

Phyllis: I'm very interested in the newly designed hand tools on display in your show-room.

Zhang: Thank you very much for your high comments on our products. Do you think they'll be popular in Australia?

Phyllis: Products with good quality ensure good sales. To market your products effectively in our market you need the services of a well-established firm.

Zhang: You mean you want to act as our agent?

Phyllis: That's right.

Zhang: Well, I must say this is a little surprise to us. We've had only one year of business between us. Though we are quite satisfied with your efforts to push the sales of our hand tools, we are still at the get-acquainted stage. So we don't think it advisable to consider the matter of agency at present.

Phyllis: As a leading importer of hand tools in the local market we have excellent business connections and our reputation is second to none.

Zhang: We appreciate very much your intention to push the sales of our products. But these hand tools are newly-designed models. Usually it takes time to put new models to market successfully. We suggest that you should try our Box Socket Sets first and do a little research of the market at the same time.

Phyllis: How long will the trial time be?

Zhang: 12 months. If you have achieved marked success, we'll take your proposal for agency into consideration.

Sample Dialogue 2. To Continue Your Efforts in Building a Large Turnover

Liu: May I know the conditions as a Sole Agency?

Alien: Mr. Liu, your offering help to push the sales of our products will be appreciated by us. But as we are now only at the get acquainted stage, we consider it rather premature to take into consideration the matter of sole agency.

Liu: What about your suggestion?

Allen: In my opinion, it would be better for both of us to try out a period of cooperation to see how things prove. Also it would be necessary for you to test the market ability of our products at your end and to continue your efforts in building a large turnover to justify the sole agency arrangement.

Liu: How long do you mean the trial period should be?

Allen: One year, we suggest. If everything turns out satisfactory, we shall revert to this subject without delay.

Liu: Mr. Allen, you needn't to spend long testing our market ability of your products. Please be convinced that we will try our best to fulfill the sufficient turnover so as to warrant the sole agency appointment.

Allen: But you should at least let us know your market connection, the effectiveness of your sales organization and your technical ability to handle the goods to be marketed.

Liu: We have more than twenty sales representatives, who are on the road all the year round, covering the whole of the China's market.

Allen: Do you have any middlemen or sell direct to the retailers?

Liu: Through years of efforts, we have set up effective channels of distribution and we canvass the retailers direct without any middlemen.

Allen: Well, if you could pursue your efforts in building a large turnover, we shall be glad to take into consideration your proposal of an agency appointment.

Liu: You can rest assured that we'll do our utmost to do so.

Sample Dialogue 3. To Promote Your Products More Vigorously

Jackson: Mr. Wan, we've spoken before this matter, and I hope we can come to some agreement this time. As you know, Jackson & Co. Ltd. would very much like to act as your agent in the US and America.

Wan: Yes, indeed. I have spoken to our relevant organization, and we are willing to appoint Jacksons as our sole agent for the US.

Jackson: Excellent news. Once the agreement is signed, we'll be able to promote your products more vigorously. Giving sole agency to us will also reduce the number of rivals, which is beneficial for business development. And, as you are aware, we have a broad customer base and deal with many retailers not only in the US but all over America. Thus, we consider that the agency agreement should include the USA and the whole America.

Wan:I see. But we also have a well-established customer base in America, and don't really feel the need for an agent to cover America on our behalf. Besides, we have many old customers in Canada and Brazil. If we signed up with you, we would undoubtedly lose these old and valued customers.

Jackson:Okay. I would suggest that the duration of the agreement should be 3 years and then after that, if it proves satisfactory to both sides, we can extend the agreement.

Wan: Sounds fine. You've clearly given this a lot of thought. What quantity do you propose to sell?

Jackson: I would suggest 30 000 square meters in Year One, 40 000 square meters in Year Two and 50 000 square meters in Year Three.

Wan: Good. We must also clarify what kind of carpets you will sell on our behalf. We can't just say Chinese carpets. That's too general. What we mean is Super Woolens.

Jackson: I'm disappointed that you are restricting the types of carpets we can sell as well as the geographical area we can cover. This will certainly affect our sales.

Wan: Oh, I'm sorry. I obviously haven't made myself clear. You can certainly sell as many different types of carpets as you like. We'd be delighted, of course. You can order them from us in the usual way. You will, however, be required to sell on our behalf the types that you undertake to sell under the agency agreement.

Jackson:I see. That would be fair enough.

wan: Perhaps I could ask you to draw up the agreement.

Jackson: Yes, of course. We'll get it signed tomorrow.

Sample Dialogue 4. Enquiries and Commission

Mr. Fisher, an American importer, is discussing with Mr. Ma, the sales manager of a Chinese company, on his client's enquiries and the commission rate he can get.

M:Good morning. Mr. Fisher. Did you have a good night sleep after the long flight from Los Angeles?

F:Yes, I slept like a log all the night.

M:OK, Mr. Fisher, I'm a busy man and I know you're also a busy man, So I'll get right to the point.

F:Good. What about our enquiry? As I said yesterday, it comes from an important client of ours. I hope you've brought me a firm offer.

M:As a matter of fact, I came just for this matter. We value your enquiry very much, so I think it's better we go into some details before we make the firm offer.

F:Let's.

M:You've got our catalogue and price-lists?

F:Yes, you gave them to me yesterday and I studied carefully in the evening.

M:The price we are going to offer is CIF Los Angeles.

F:That's OK.

M:The special commission we're prepared to grant is 6 percent of the order over a hundred thousand US dollars in value. All right?

F:CIFC6%? It's too little. You see, it can hardly cover our expenses. How about 10%?

M:I'm afraid we can't agree to 10%. You see, the raw materials, distribution charges and costs are going up. In fact, we've been left a small margin of profit.

F:You see, we're your old connection and bring you a good many orders every year. We hope you'll give a special consideration.

M:OK. In that case, let's meet half way. We suggest an 8 % special, commission for an order of US $100 000 and over in value. And it will be paid in two months after the date of invoice.

F:Oh, hold on for a moment. I'll take it down, 8% special discount for orders of US $100 000 and over in value and the usual payment will be made in two months after the date of the invoice. I agree. What about delivery then?

M:Your client will have to open the relevant letter of credit within one month after the signature of a contract and delivery can be assured of, within two months upon receipt of the letter of credit.

F:Yes, an L/C must be opened within one month after the contract is signed and shipment will be made within two months upon receipt of the L/C.

M:OK?

F:It's all right, as I can see it, but I'll get in touch with home office as soon as possible and ask them to fax or e-mail their reply.

M: That's settled. I'll leave to work out the offer.

Sample Dialogue 5. To Be Our Agent?

A Chinese company wants to be the sole agent of an American company. As the representative, Mr. Kong goes to their head office for a further talk...

A:Miss Janis,I am Kong Lin, ,the sales manager of Shengda Company.

B:Hello,Mr. Kong,so nice to meet you face to face finally after so many calls and mails.

A：Nice to meet you too. I am here for your opinion on the possibility of being your agency in China.

B：Yes，we have talked some about it through mails. We appreciate your efforts in pushing sales of our products. But，to be flank，Mr. Kong，we feel that it's not a mature time for you to act as a sole agent for our products.

A：Why not? May I have your opinion?

B：You have placed three orders with us till now with a total of 2 800 cases. I would say you have done well considering you just start to trade with this kind of products. But this figure is far from the annual order and turnover we expect a sole agency should a-chieve.

A：I see. But through our order quantity which keeps the steady increase. you will see our potential ability. And we are planning to invest more on developing market in the next year.

B. That is why we think highly of you and would like to give any support we can. We would rather to suggest you consider starting from the market of Guangdong province.

A. But you know it is far from our expectation. We have a faith in your products.

B：I understand your meaning，Mr. Kong. We very much appreciate your good intentions.

But I hope you also can understand that business lives on actual income instead of prospect. Anyway，you are one of our best customers，so we will give our full support to you.

Sample Dialogue 6. Renew the Agency Agreement

When sole agency agreement will expire in 6 months. a representative is sent to the supplier to renew the agreement…

Agency：I come to renew our sole agency agreement with you for another 3 years.

Supplier：Before we talk it over with you，I would like to thank you for your wonderful work in fulfilling the agreement.

Agency：We are happy that you are satisfied with our efforts. Actually we are ambitious to take bigger part of the local market in the coming years，of course，with your support.

Supplier：That is exhilarating. Let's see what is to be changed in the new agreement. First，the annual quantity…

Agency:We can accept 150 000 bottles for the first year,and an annual increase of 50 000 bottles for next two years.

Supplier:We agree. In the general practice,we need your marketing plan for each year.

Agency:I have brought the plan for the coming year here for your kind reference. Just like what we stipulated in the first agreement,we will keep on sending you the marketing report and feedback periodically .

Supplier:Thanks. You are so efficient. I don't doubt your future success at all.

Sample Dialogue 7. More or Less

The buyer is very curious about what commission the seller can offer...

Buyer:May I know your commission system that you mentioned before?

Seller:Well,we have a baseline for providing commission—the order must exceed 5 000 sets. From 5 000 to 15 000 sets,the commission is 2% of the net invoice amount. From 15 000 to 30 000 sets,the buyer will get 3% . For the order larger than 30 000 sets,it is open to be discussed.

Buyer:Clear. But usually we can get 5% commission from European suppliers.

Seller:As you know, our price is relatively favorable compared with that of our competitors in Europe. It leaves hardly margin of profit to us. And the commission system is fixed as rules of our company which can't be changed easily for a certain order.

Buyer:So,if we place an order of 22 000 sets,we will get 3% of the net invoice amount.

Seller:That is right. We can't go any further.

Sample Dialogue 8. Proposal of Agency

Mr. Harris, manager of an import and export agent wants to be China's Handicraft agent in Marseilles. He is now at the East China Trade Fair and talking to Mr. Jiang Jianming, a representative from the Handicrafts Corporation.

Harris:When I was visiting an exhibition in Paris, I found your handicrafts were very popular with our people. I'm sure there are opportunities for this trade to develop. If you have an agent such as my company to give you help at this end and to establish your marketing channels, your business is sure to develop very quickly.

Jiang: How long have you been in the handicraft trade, Mr. Harris?

Harris:Oh, we represent more than ten firms, but the lines we represent don't compete with yours. Chinese handicraft is a new branch we are thinking of entering.

Jiang: So you are just trying to build up business in this field. Then it will take some time before you know the market well enough to sell successfully.

Harris: But we do have very wide connections. Our reputation in this trade is second to none. We would concentrate more of our efforts on your products.

Jiang: It's very kind of you to say so, Mr. Harris, and I hope we can do mutually beneficial business together, but before we know your sales volume, your plan for promoting our products, the possible annual turnover, and the import license conditions, it's rather difficult for us to consider your proposal.

Harris: Mr. Jiang, you certainly want to see your business expand, to see your products enjoy a lion's share in our market, but what you are doing now, making offers through so many channels, is counter-productive. In fact you are competing against yourselves.

Jiang: Right. Some dealers are rather enthusiastic. Sometimes problems of uncontrolled marketing do crop up, but there are always two sides to every question.

Harris: You may get big orders now, but in the long run your market will never grow. Not until you have an agent in Marseilles.

Jiang: Thank you for your advice. Mr. Harris. I see your point. May we suggest that you try one or two of our articles for a time. Meanwhile do a little research in the field. If one item could be successfully established, it would help the introduction of other products. Step by step we will come to know each other better.

Harris: So you really think my proposal of having your exclusive agent in Marseilles is unworkable at the moment. Well, we'll consider your suggestion. Could you send us catalogues and price lists from time to time? That would help us a lot in introducing your goods to the market. If you think we might be of help in any respect, don't hesitate to let us know. We would be only too pleased to work with you.

Sample Dialogue 9. Asking to Be Entrusted as Sole Agent

Sam Grant is Managing Director of an Australian company. He pays a surprise visit to China and is discussing the matter of agency with Liu Quanmu , who is Marketing Manager of a Chinese company manufacturing white goods.

Liu: Hello, Mr. Grant. Fancy your standing here in my office! It's a long time since we last met.

Grant: Yes, long time no see. I came here last time about eight months ago. But we often communicate by faxes and emails.

Liu: Take a seat and have a cup of tea.

Grant: Thanks.

Liu: When did you arrive? Why not let us know before you came?

Grant: I arrived last night and went straight to the hotel.

Liu: What can I do for you, Mr. Grant?

Grant: I wouldn't come to you if I didn't have something to ask of you.

Liu: How are you getting on?

Grant: Not well as can be expected, under greater pressure day by day. We have to work harder and harder all the year round.

Liu: Now, Mr Grant, I'm quite sure you didn't travel a thousand miles here just so as to complain about your life to me. Now could I know what the trouble is?

Grant: Oh, not about life but over business. To tell you the truth, the greatest trouble we have nowadays is the way of doing business with you.

Liu: Oh dear, the way of doing business with us? Just tell me what we can help.

Grant: Three years ago we started doing business with you. Though your products were completely unknown in our country, we were pretty well aware at that moment there would be great potential prospects for your things in our market. I left no stone unturned to promote sales at our own costs, doing advertising in every way. We invested big and even publicized your products twice on the television. As a result, your products have become popular and, with our business being on the up and up, we have been placing with you more and more orders. You can see that from your records.

Liu: But recently we have found the number and quantity of your orders are shrinking. We are wondering why.

Grant: Why? That is because once your products become popular through our efforts, the other merchants find it possible to stand to gain from this business and start buying direct from you. They are now even undercutting us to carve their way into our traditional markets.

Liu: Oh, I get the picture.

Grant: If it goes on like this, our efforts will go down to the drain. In the end, we will get nowhere and your products will be in a mess in the market.

Liu: That'll be really unfair to you and it'll become a problem. Keep your cool! We shall do whatever we can to prevent such things happening. What do you have in mind?

Grant: As you well know, by our promotion ability and the big increase in our business turnover, we're entitled to be entrusted as your agent, sole or exclusive agent, in our country.

Liu:But a sole agent means more sales, more publicity and more responsibilities.

Grant:Say what you want. The sky's the limit. We'd rather work our finger to the bone at increasing our turnover than cut each other's throat with our competitors.

Liu:We'll never allow such things to happen. Your proposal is worth consideration, but I must talk about it with our President and if he says yes, I'll discuss with you the details of the Sole Agency Agreement tomorrow. Is that OK?

Grant:Yes, very good. Thank you, Mr. Liu. I'll be expecting your good news. See you tomorrow.

Liu:See you.

Sample Dialogue 10. Agency Agreement

Liu Quanmu, Marketing Manager of a Chinese white goods manufacturer, is discussing the details of an agency agreement with Sam Grant, an Australian importer.

Liu:Good afternoon, Mr. Grant. I've got the green-light from our President to entrust you as our agent in Australia.

Grant:That's great! What shall we do then?

Liu:I think we'd better go over the key points before we draw up this agreement.

Grant: Whatever you say. What's the first point, then?

Liu:What kind of an agency would you like to act as?

Grant: Certainly a sole and exclusive agency.

Liu 'OK. Excuse me, but let me take a note of it. A sole and exclusive agency. Then, the next point? What products of ours would you like to represent us for?

Grant:We'll be handling your complete range of white goods.

Liu:But one thing I must make clear is that you'll be not allowed to sell competing lines along with our products.

Grant:Agreed.

Liu:As I understand it, you'll be our sole and exclusive agent for the whole range of our white goods.

Grant:That's it.

Liu:The duration of the agreement will be three years. Is it OK?

Grant:That's quite all right.

Liu:The minimum total amount of sales shall not be less than 4 million US dollars for the first year, not less than 4. 6 million US dollars for the second year and 5. 29 million for the third year.

Grant:Hmm. That's on 15% increase year by year. OK. Our total business volume this year has already reached 3.75 million US dollars.

Liu: The progress of execution shall be examined half-yearly. If your party fails to place orders for minimum business volume within 6 – 8 months without giving sufficient reasons acceptable to us, we shall have the right to offer the agency to other clients or to take alternative measures without being bound by this agreement.

Grant: It's reasonable. But what if something unexpected happens, such as depression or things like that?

Liu: I think that reason is acceptable to us. Now the next point is territory of the representation.

Grant: Of course it includes the whole area of Australia.

Liu: What about the west part of your country, the area around Perth? We received a few. orders from that part of Australia some time ago. You see, it's so far away from the east part.

Grant: It's not so far as it is beyond our reach, Mr. Liu. As a matter of fact, we've set up an office there already with three sales reps working in that part of Australia. Would you be kind enough to consider the representation area including New Zealand? We've also set up an office there. Sales operation goes like clockwork and I'm sure we'll soon reach the market.

Liu: I think it's better to leave the matter of New Zealand until our products reach the market there.

Grant: I go along with you there, but I'm confident we'll reach that target. What next? Commission?

Liu: We fix it at 15% on total sales. This is our usual practice to all our sole agents.

Grant: In that case, we follow suit. How often shall we give you a market report?

Liu: We'd also like you to forward us a half-yearly detailed report on current market conditions and of consumers' comments on our products. For reference purpose, we'd like you to send us from time to time catalogues of similar commodities offered by other suppliers, together with their prices, sales position and advertising materials.

Grant: You can count on us for that.

Liu: The other terms and conditions are fairly simple. The fees on advertising and sales promotion will be shared between our two parties. Last but not least, after-sales service. That's your responsibility.

Grant : I promise you, Mr Liu, that we'll provide fast, reliable and satisfactory

186

service wherever your products are sold by us.

Liu : Shall we have a coffee break? Then we'll discuss again when the draft agreement is typed out.

Grant: Yes, let's.

Sample Dialogue 11. Termination of an Agency Agreement

Mr. Chen, Marketing Manager of a Chinese white goods manufacturer, makes a special visit to Pakistan to notify their agent Mr. Harris of their decision to terminate their sole agency agreement with him.

Harris: Hello, Mr Chen. Welcome to Pakistan.

Chen: Hello, Mr Harris. I know this is an awkward visit for me but I'm sorry, I have to break this news to you. I'm afraid our company has decided to terminate our agency agreement with you.

Harris: Say What? To terminate the agency agreement? There's still a year and a half to run on it.

Chen: I know. But we've no alternative but to do so.

Harris: May I ask why you want to break the agreement?

Chen : For the first year, your total sales were very disappointing, 20% short of the minimum sales amount laid down in the agreement. We believed what you said in your market report. As you were at the sharp end of the business here, we decided to give you a chance. We stressed again that for this type of products after-sales service is of vital importance.

Harris: We really have to fight for every dollar we make.

Chen: That's no excuse. In doing business, everybody has to fight for every cent they make. For the past six months, you failed to reach your sales target, only 60% of it. We were at a loss as to what'd happened here. From the reactions of the users, we've found that their complaints are all about bad after-sales service. We therefore sent a research team to this country to make a study and they reported back to the company that they visited several stores in which our products were on sale and met almost the same scene: customers clustered before our white goods, speaking highly of the design, quality, function, color, etc. but when a person or two who had bought our products came to complain about the after-sales service, they reluctantly turned to other makes. We are sure that the root of the problem is the poor servicing. Under the circumstances, we think we cannot afford to put all our eggs in one basket any more and make this decision. We hope you'll fully appreciate this.

Harris: Is that all my fault, Mr. Chen? You haven't backed me up.

Chen: Don't blame everybody but yourself at this stage, Mr. Harris. It doesn't help the situation. I admit we have our own fault, but this decision will be of benefit to both of us.

Harris: All I'm saying is, can't you give me another chance?

Chen: You still have a chance. We've decided not to appoint an agent in this market for a couple of years at least. If you improve your servicing to the satisfaction of the customers and your sales pick up a lot with an edge over other competitors, you're still hopeful.

Harris: In that case, I have to go along with you.

Sample Dialogue 12. It is Not a Commission

A: Mr. Zhang, shall we go over to talk about commission?

B: Well, Mr. King, you know, in our general practice, we don't allow any commission.

A: But. our business is on commission basis. And commission will surely help to push the sale of your products. You know, it isn't an easy business since there is a strong opposition from European competitors who are firmly established. A strong sales drive and various advertising is necessary but it means a considerable capital outlay.

B: We are pleased to learn that you will do your utmost to open the market. The point is the price is finely calculated, so it is difficult for us to grant you a commission.

A: But your price isn't competitive at all. Nobody wants to lose money in the business.

B: Well, we may find some other way out. We can grant you another amount to support you in the sale of this new line. How is that?

A: Sounds practical. But how large will be the amount?

B: US $3,000.

A: I am afraid this amount definitely can't meet the position.

B: I think we need your budget for marketing so that we can decide the exact size.

A: OK, let's set it. We will give the budget as soon as possible.

Key Sentences 经典必备句

● 谈谈佣金：

We only give commissions to agents.

我们只给代理付佣金。

A higher commission means a higher price.

188

佣金提高意味着价格也要提高。

Buyers prefer to start business on commission basis.

买方更倾向于在佣金的基础上交易。

I am afraid that your price excludes our commission.

恐怕你们的价格不包括我们的佣金在内吧?

How about the commission?

佣金是多少?

The commission rate varies according to the size of orders.

佣金率取决于订货量。

He came to hold a talk about the commission.

他来洽谈有关佣金的问题。

The present commission isn't enough to cover our cost.

现有的佣金不够应付我们的费用。

●提供佣金:

A 3% commission is the maximum we can give.

我们最多给3%的佣金。

For every additional 100 cases sold, we'll give 0.1% more commission.

每笔多卖出100箱,我们多给0.1%的佣金。

Is it possible to increase the commission to 4%?

能不能把佣金提高到4%呢?

We usually offer a 3%~5% commission to our agents in Asia.

我方通常给在亚洲的代理提供3%~5%的佣金。

The quotation is subject to a 3% commission.

该报价包括3%的佣金在内。

The commission that we give you is comparably favourable.

我们公司给您的佣金相对来说比较优惠。

We are pleased to increase the commission to 5% in your favour.

我们很高兴将贵方佣金增至5%。

This offer includes your commission of 3%.

这一报价包括了3%的佣金在内。

Generally, we give 2% commission to our agents.

一般情况下,我们给代理商2%的佣金。

We can offer 3% commission if 15 000 cases are ordered.

如果订15 000箱,我们可以提供3%的佣金。

We'll give you a 3% commission on every transaction.

每笔交易我们都付给3%的佣金。

We're usually paid with a 3% commission of the amount for each order.

我们通常每笔交易付给3%的佣金。

We need your grant of an extra commission of 3% to cover the additional risk.

我们需要从你方获得另外的3%佣金，以补偿额外风险。

● 不能提供佣金：

Their expectation of a 5% commission is unacceptable.

他们5%佣金的期望是不可接受的。

We don't pay any commission on our primary products.

对我们的基础产品，概不付给佣金。

We can't increase the rate of commission unless you enlarge your order to a certain amount.

我们不会增加佣金率，除非你方将订单扩大到某个数量。

In general practice, we don't allow commissions.

我们的惯例是不提供佣金。

Frequently Used Words and Phrases 常用词汇和短语

all commissions 所有佣金

buying commission 代购佣金

commission(com.) 佣金,手续费

commission agent 代理商；代办人；代理贸易商

commission charges 佣金；手续费

commission for collection 代收账款佣金

commission insurance 佣金保险

commission on a sliding scale 递加佣金

commission system 佣金制

commission transaction 付佣金的交易

commissions earned 佣金收入

commission received in advance 预收佣金

overriding commission 追加佣金

rate of commission or scale of commission 佣金率

selling commission 代销佣金

to pay the commission 支付佣金

two or several items of commission 两笔或几笔佣金

Useful expressions for negotiation

That's a good idea.

That's a good point.

I agree.

I think so too.

That's right.

I think you're right.

That's my opinion, too.

You and I are on the same wavelength.

I am with you there.

I think we are on the same mind.

I agree with you entirely.

I agree entirely with your view.

I don't think anyone would disagree.

I'm of exactly the same opinion.

I couldn't agree more.

That's just what I was thinking.

You know, that's exactly what I think.

I tend to agree (with you)

I agree (with you) in principle, but…

l agree (with you) in part, but…

Well, you could be right.

I'll go along with that.

I'll second that.

I like that idea.

That sounds good.

Well, l agree with you on the whole, but then again it…

Well, to a certain extent l agree with you, but…

You definitely have point there, but…

Key Sentences 经典必备句

●成为代理:

We hope to apply for the sole agency of your product in China market.

我们想申请做你方产品在中国市场上的独家代理。

We'll spare no efforts to promote the sale in order to renew the agency agreement when it expires.

我们会尽力促进销售,争取在协议期满后能够续订。

We hope to renew our sole agency agreement for another 2 years.

我们希望把我们之间的独家代理协议延长两年。

The agreement of agency can ben renewed on its expiry.

代理协议在期满时可以续订。

It is our honor to act as your sole agent.

能做贵公司的独家代理是我们的荣幸。

We wish to conclude a long term agency contract with you.

我们期望能与你方达成长期代理合约。

We are ready to take the obligations that a buying agent should take.

我们能负起作为买方代理应负的责任。

● 关于代理申请的答复：

For a sole agent. this annual turnover is evidently conservative.

对独家代理来讲,这样的年销售量显然太保守了。

We are sorry to say that we can't appoint you as our sole agent for such a small quantity?

我们很抱歉,以你们如此少的订货量,我们无法请您做独家代理。

I think it is not mature for you to discuss the question of agency.

我认为现在讨论代理问题对于你们来说为时过早。

Unless there is an increase in your turnover,we can't appoint you as our sole agent.

除非你们营业额有所增加,否则我们无法指定你们作为我方的独家代理。

We haven't taken the question of sole agent into consideration.

我们还没有考虑有关独家代理的问题。

We regret to refuse your proposal of acting as our agency.

我们遗憾地谢绝你们作为我方代理的建议。

We won't consider signing an agency in your market at present.

我们目前不考虑在你地市场设立代理的问题。

We'll leave aside the problem of agency.

我们要搁置代理问题。

We agree to appoint you as the sole agent for our vases for the next three years.

我们同意指定您为贵国市场上我们的产品花瓶的独家代理,为期三年。

For your extensive experience in the field,We are glad to appoint you as the sole agent in our domestic market.

考虑到你们在这一业务范围的丰富经验,我们很高兴指定你们为在国内市场的独家代理。

We decide to entrust you with the sole agency for our products.

我们决定委托你作为我们产品的独家代理。

We were appointed as IBM's agent two years ago.

我们在两年前被指定为 IBM 的代理。

I believe it is right time to make you our exclusive agent.

我相信是时候委托你为我方的独家代理了。

Your application for sole agency is under our careful consideration.

我们正在仔细考虑你方想要独家代理的请求。

We advice you get in touch with our agent in the local market for the supply of the goods you require.

我们建议您与我们的当地代理联系,以提供你们所需的商品。

● 签订代理合同:

We have drafted a sole agency agreement for our reading lamps for a period of 2 years.

我们已经拟订了一个专销台灯的为期两年的独家代理协议。

To make a decision on the agency agreement, we need your marketing plan.

为了让代理协议有个结论,我们需要你方递交一份市场计划。

Since the agency agreement was signed, our turnover has amounted to US $ 150 000.

自从代理协议签订以后,我们的销售额已达 150 000 美元。

The agency agreement for the period of 3 years has been drawn up.

为期三年的代理协议书已经拟订出来。

They are satisfied with the agency agreement and found no loopholes in it.

他们对代理协议书很满意,没有发现有漏洞。

Let's have a talk about the annual quantity for the new agreement.

让我们商讨一下新的协议中的年销售量吧。

When shall we sign the agency agreement?

我们何时签订代理协议呢?

Frequently Used Words and Phrases 常用词汇和短语

agent 代理人

agents or agency 代理方或代理公司

buying agents 购货代理

exclusive agent 独家代理(人)

express agency 明示代理

forwarding agents 运输代理

implied agency 默认代理

principal 委托方

selling agents 销售代理

sole agent 独家代理(人)

the agent carrying stock 储货代理

the agent of necessity 需要时的代理人

实训综合习题

I. put the following sentences into Chinese.

1. We are pleased to offer you a sole agency for the sale of our products in your country.

2. If terms prove workable, we would like to appoint you as our agent.

3. If you can push the sale of our products successfully for the next six months, we may appoint you as our agent.

4. We have no intention of considering exclusive sales in your market at present.

5. Asour sole agent, you are not expected to sell any other competitive line of goods in this market.

6. We'd like to renew our sole agency agreement for another two years.

7. Your total order last year was very small, which in no way demonstrates your ability to act as our agent.

8. Don't you think this annual turnover for a sole agent is rather conservative?

9. As to your suggestion of an agency agreement, we do not think the opportunity has come to maturity for us to consider the matter.

10. We will increase our turnover if you appoint US as your sole agent.

11. The trial period for agency seems rather long for us.

12. As our sole agent, you are not allowed to reexport our goods to any other area outside your own.

13. We regret to inform you that our agency representation has been taken over by someone else.

14. We appreciate the confidence you show in US by offering us an agent for your products.

15. We will not accept your agency on these terms.

16. We are confident that your entrusting US with agency will add a new page to the records of our cooperation.

17. As your agent, we'11 make greater efforts to push the sale of your products.

18. With the sole agency in your hand, you could easily control the market.

19. We'd like to sign a sole agency agreement with you on your electric fans for a period of three years.

20. We think our proposal to be your agent is to our mutual interest and profit.

II. put the following sentences into English.

1. 你们能保证每年最低销售额是多少?

2. 做我们的独家代理就不能销售其他厂商的同类产品。

3. 我们所有做这类商品的代理都只拿5%的佣金。

4. 如果情况令双方满意,协议有效期可以延长。

5. 我们会免费提供一些产品介绍资料。

6. 你做工艺品的生意有多久了?

7. 我们与当地这一行业的主要批发商及零售商有着广泛的业务联系。

8. 我想了解一下你们以前有没有在这一行业为其他供货商做过代理。

9. 我们考虑将业务扩展到俄罗斯,所以希望在那里找一个代理,能够销售我们的产品。

10. 我们很赞赏你方做我们代理的想法,但我们还是建议你们先对市场做一番仔细的调研。

III. Oral Practice.

Work with your partner. One of your buyers asks for an increase in the Commission after several orders You have the right to decide what to do. Then have a talk with their representative.

IV. Oral Practice.

Work with your partner. You want to be the sole agency for a European embroideries producer in China market. You made a proposal to them two weeks ago. They accept your proposal and have a further discussion with you.

V. Role Play.

Task 1

Work in pairs. One of you acts as Mr. Smith who would like to be appointed as the sole agent for the Beijing Shirt Factory and the other as the general manager of the factory. Now you are having a discussion on the problem of sole agency.

Task 2

A businessman from Nepal is invited to China. Since the establishment of diplomatic relations, friendly business connections have been strengthened. Our cotton piece goods have found a ready market there. Having done business with us for many years, he wishes to be the sole agent in his market for Chinese cotton piece goods. In order to fortify our marketing position in his district and expand the range of business, we are willing to enter into some sort of agreement with him.

VI. Topics for Group Discussion.

1. If you are an exporter, what makes you adopt the mode of agency?

2. What are the advantages of distribution to both parties?

第 11 章 保险

Insurance （ I ）

A:Shall we take up the terms of insurance right now?

B:OK.

A:We have a deal on CIF price. It means that it should be you who will buy the insurance. right?

B:Certainly. The premium should be paid by us. All our export goods sold on CIF terms are insured with the PICC. They provide a broad range of marine insurance,such as FPA,WPA,ALL Risks and so on.

A:What kind of coverage will you take out for our order then?

B:Usually we'll only insure WPA for this kind.

A:We hope you can cover the Packing Breakage Risk for us.

B:We can do that for you. But we won't pay this additional premium.

A:We will pay that. So,please insure the consignment against WPA and Packing Breakage Risk for 150% of invoice value.

B:I am sorry, we only can insure goods for 110% of the invoice value. For 150% , the extra premium will be borne by you.

A:OK. By the way,since it is our first time to import from China,how is PICC's service? How about the claim?

B:Don't worry. The People's Insurance Company of China enjoys a high prestige in the international trade. They will give a prompt settlement on claims.

A:Good.

B:Then we made a deal that we will insure this consignment against WPA. and Packing Breakage Risk for l 50% of invoice value. Is there anything else about the insurance clause?

A: I don't think so

Insurance （ II ）

Insurance of goods in transit plays a vital role in foreign trade. Among the documents presented for payment, an insurance policy is essential for a CIF contract. The buyer wants to be sure he is getting the full value of the shipment he has already arranged to pay for. That's why Mr. James is now carefully studying the sales confirmation given by Mr. Liu Hao, manager of the export section of Shanghai Lansheng Group Ltd.

L:Mr. James, is there anything that's not clear in the sales confirmation?

J:Oh, yes. There are a few points, which need to be clarified. I think it's better to get a clear idea of the terms before signing so that there will be no misunderstanding.

L:That's right. Let's go over them one by one.

J:The first thing concerns insurance. What does " I " cover according to your usual CIF terms?

L:It covers All Risks and War Risk for 110 percent of the invoice value.

J:So such risks as breakage, leakage, TPND, hook and contamination damages are all included.

L:Yes.

J:You'll also cover SRCC risks, won't you?

L:If you desire.

J:Don't you think you could make the price CFR for our future business? And how much will you take off?

L:The rates quoted by the People's Insurance Company of China are moderate. They have very little effect on our CIF prices. Roughly speaking, the difference between CIF and CFR is about 0.3 percent. Of course, the premium varies with the nature of the goods, the degree of" cover" required and the place of destination.

J:0.3 percent. That sounds reasonable.

L:The People's Insurance Company has a fine reputation for its good credit as well as its reasonable rates. It has more than 300 surveyors and agents all over the world.

J:Uh huh, they have very good connections. Mr. Liu, you see the reason I asked you about the rates is that we have an open policy with the ABC Insurance Company in London. All we have to do when a shipment is made is to advise them of the particulars. It saves us a lot of tedious formalities. What's more, we are on very good terms with this company. Usually we receive a handsome premium rebate from our underwriters at regular intervals.

L:I can assure you that we could provide the same service. Our relations with the People's Insurance Company are amicable. Their way of handling business is flexible and formalities are simple. If you'd let us effect the insurance, I'm sure things will turn out to our mutual benefit.

J：OK. Mr. Liu, I'll buy on CIF for this first transaction as a trial. Well, so much for insurance. The next point I would like to discuss is…

Notes

take up 开始从事

WPA = With Particular Average 单独海损赔偿，担保单独海损，水渍险

Premium 保险费

prestige 声望，威望，威信

TPND = Theft, Pilferage and Non-Delivery 盗窃和提货不着险

SRCC 罢工、暴动、民变险

have very little effect on 对……影响很小

open policy 预约保险单

tedious formalities 烦琐手续

at regular intervals 每隔一定时间

underwriters 保险商

Key Sentences 经典必备句

A WPA or WApolicy covers clients against partial loss in all cases.

水渍险在任何情况下都会保部分损失险。

Coinsurance clauses request the insured person to pay usually 20 percent of the total expense covered.

共同保险条款通常要求保险人必须付全部费用的20%。

If you cover an All Risks. it means you have every sort of hazard covered.

如果你买了一份综合险保单，那就是说你保了所有的险。

An FPApolicy only cover total loss in the case of minor perils.

平安险只有在发生较小危险时才给保全部损失险。

Generally speaking, marine insurance is much higher than aviation insurance.

海运保险一般要比空运保险贵。

FPA insurance doesn't cover losses on consumer goods.

平安险不包括消费品的损失。

In the insurance business. "average" is simply defined as "loss" in most cases.

在保险业中"average"一词一般定义为"海损"。

It's necessary to read the "fine print" in any insurance policy to know what kind of coverage you are buying.

阅读保险单上的"细则"是必要的，以便了解你要买的保险包括哪些项目。

Not every breakage is a particular average.

并不是所有的破碎险都属于单独海损。

The premium varies according to the type of goods and the circumstances.

保险费根据货物类别和具体情况会有所不同。

You can find the extent of insurance in the basic policy form and the various risk clauses.

你会在基本保险单和各种险别的条款里看到保险的范围。

The underwriters are responsible for any claim within the scope of cover.

保险公司负责赔偿在保险责任范围内的赔偿。

"All marine risks" means less than "all risks."

"一切海洋运输货物险"比"一切险"范围小。

WPAstands for"With Particular Average".

WPA 代表水渍险。

After the goods get loaded on board, they will go to have them insured.

装船后,他们会去给货物投保。

May I have an insurance rate?

我能拿一份保险率表吗?

We need to find out the premium rate for porcelain.

我们需要查一下瓷器的保险费率。

Don't you wish to add the coverage against Risk of Breakage?

您不想增加破碎险吗?

FPA is good enough. FPA stands for "Free from Particular Average".

只保 FPA 就可以了。FPA 代表平安险。

Generally, people try to avoid using the term "all marine risks" in L/C since it is easily misinterpreted.

一般人们尽量避免在信用证中使用"一切海洋运输货物险"的说明,因为这样容易被误解。

The client worries that the WPA. insurance doesn't cover more risks than the FPA.

客户担心水渍险承保的范围并不比平安险的范围宽。

Insurance brokers can quote rates for all types of cargo and risks.

保险经纪人会开出承保各类货物的各种险别的费用。

What exactly insurance does your usual CIF terms include?

你们常用的 CIF 价格条件所保的包括哪些险别?

We require you to insure the shipment for USD7 000 against All Risks.

我们要求你方将这批货物投保综合险美元 7 000 元。

The coverage is WPA plus Risk of Breakage.

投保的险别为水渍险加破碎险。

The goods are to be insured FPA.

这批货需投保平安险。

The insurance rate for this risk will vary according to the goods.

这类险别的保险费率将根据货物种类而定。

I am sorry but the loss in question is beyond the coverage granted by us.

很抱歉，但是这个损失不在我方承保的范围内。

The premium varies with the range of insurance. The rates quoted by us are very moderate.

保险费用要根据投保范围的大小而有所不同。我们所收取的费率是很有限的。

We paid the total premium of 1 300 US dollars.

我们付了保险费总共是 1 300 美元。

Among these kinds of risks, you can choose the proper one suiting your consignment.

在这些险别中，你可以选择那个适合你要投保的货物的保险。

Clients can go to the information office for any information on cargo insurance.

顾客可以前往问讯处咨询关于货物投保方面的信息。

We advice you to extend the coverage to include TPND, because WPA. coverage is obviously too narrow for this shipment.

我们建议你们追加保偷盗提货不成险，因为水渍险对这单货物显然是不够的。

We can provide a broad range of coverage against all kinds of risks for sea transport.

我们可以承保海洋运输的所有险别。

The safest way is to cover the porcelain ware against All Risks.

最安全的方法是为这批瓷器投保综合险。

They will cover insurance on these goods for 10% above the invoice value against All Risks.

他们将会给这些货物按发票金额加 10% 投保综合险。

What is the insurance premium?

保险费是多少？

What insurances are you able to provide for this consignment?

贵公司想为这批货保哪些险呢？

Could you give an introduction of risks that the People's Insurance Company of China is able to cover?

您是否能介绍一下中国人民保险公司能承保的险种？

What risks would you like to cover?

您想保哪些险?

Unfortunately. you have not covered the Leakage.

不幸的是,你们没有投保渗漏险。

How can I have the goods insured?

我怎么给我们的货物投保?

We must cover Risk of Breakage.

我们必须投保破碎险。

You should study not only the benefits but also the terms and limitations of an insurance agreement.

你应该仔细研究保险所能给予保险人的赔偿费用,以及它的条件与限制。

I'm looking for insurance from your company.

我是到贵公司来投保的。

Mr. Zhang met Mr. William in the office of the People' Insurance Company of China.

张先生在中国人民保险公司的办公室接待了威廉先生。

After loading the goods on board the hip, I go to the insurance company to have them insured.

装船后,我到保险公司去投保。

When should I go and have the tea insured?

我什么时候将这批茶叶投保?

All right. Let's leave insurance now.

好吧,保险问题就谈到这里。

I have come to explain that unfortunate affair about the insurance.

我是来解释这件保险的不幸事件的。

I must say that you've corrected my ideas about the insurance.

我该说你们已经纠正了我对保险的看法。

This information office provides clients with information on cargo insurance.

这个问讯处为顾客提供大量关于货物投保方面的信息。

The underwriters are responsible for the claim as far as it is within the scope of cover.

只要是在保险责任范围内,保险公司就应负责赔偿。

The loss in question was beyond the coverage granted by us.

损失不包括在我方承保的范围内。

The extent of insurance is stipulated in the basic policy form and in the various risk clause.

保险的范围写在基本保险单和各种险别的条款里。

Please fill in the application form.

请填写一下投保单。

What risks is the People's Insurance Company of China able to cover?

中国人民保险公司承保的险别有哪些?

What risks should be covered?

您看应该保哪些险?

What kind of insurance are you able to provide for my consignment?

贵公司能为我的这批货保哪些险呢?

It's better for you to can the leaflet, and then make a decision.

你最好先看看说明书,再决定保什么险。

These kinds of risks suit your consignment.

这些险别适合你要投保的货物。

May I ask what exactly insurance covers according to your usual CIF terms?

请问根据你们常用的 CIF 价格条件,所保的究竟包括哪些险别?

It 's important for you to read the "fine print" in any insurance policy so that you know what kind of coverage you are buying.

阅读保险单上的"细则"对你是十分重要的,这样就能知道你要买的保险包括哪些项目。

What is the insurance premium?

保险费是多少?

The premium is to be calculated in this way.

保险费是这样计算的。

The total premium is 800 US dollars.

保险费总共是 800 美元。

The cover paid for will vary according to the type of goods and the circumstances.

保险费用按照货物类别的具体情况会有所不同。

The rates quoted by us are very moderate. Of course, the premium varies with the range of insurance.

我们所收取的费率是很有限的,当然,保险费用要根据投保范围的大小而有所不同。

According to co-insurance clauses, the insured person must pay usually 20 percent of the total expenses covered.

根据共同保险条款,保险人通常必须付全部费用的 20% 。

The insurance rate for such kink of risk will vary according to the kind.

这类险别的保险费率将根据货物种类而定。

Insurance brokers will quote rates for all types of cargo and risks.

保险经纪人会开出承保各类货物的各种险别的费用。

Can you give me an insurance rate?

您能给我一份保险率表吗?

Could you find out the premium rate for porcelain?

您能查一下瓷器的保险费率吗?

You should study not only the benefits but also the terms and limitations of an insurance agreement that appears best suited to your needs.

你不仅要研究各种保险所标明的给予保险人的赔偿费用,还要研究它的条件与限制,然后选出最适合你需要的一种。

I'll have the goods covered against Free from Particular Average.

我将为货物投保平安险。

I know that FPA insurance doesn't cover losses on consumer goods.

我知道平安险不包括消费品的种种损失。

I don't think that the WPA insurance covers more risks than the FPA.

我认为水渍险承保的范围并不比平安险的范围宽。

Free from Particular Average is good enough.

只保平安险就可以了。

The goods are to be insured FPA.

这批货需投保平安险。

What you've covered is Leakage.

你所投保的是渗漏险。

Why don't you wish to cover Risk of Breakage?

您为什么不想投保破碎险呢?

WPA coverage is too narrow for a shipment of this nature, please extend the coverage to include TPND.

针对这种性质的货物只保水渍险是不够的,请加保偷盗提货不成险。

Don't you wish to arrange for WPA and additional coverage against Risk of Breakage?

您不想保水渍险和附加破碎险吗?

Not every breakage is a particular average.

并不是所有的破碎险都属于单独海损。

The coverage is WPA plus Risk of Breakage.

投保的险别为水渍险加破碎险。

Well, obviously you won't want All Risks cover.

显然,你不想保综合险。

An All Risks policy covers every sort of hazard, doesn't it?

一份综合险保单保所有的险,是吗?

We'd like? to cover the porcelain ware against All Risks.

我们想为这批瓷器投保综合险。

We've cover insurance on these goods for 10% above the invoice value against All Risks.

我们已经将这些货物按发票金额加 10% 投保综合险。

An FPA policy only covers you against total loss in the case of minor perils.

平安险只有在发生较小危险时才给保全部损失险。

The FPA doesn't cover partial loss of the nature of particular average.

平安险不包括单独海损性质的部分损失。

A WPA or WA policy covers you against partial loss in all cases.

水渍险在任何情况下都给保部分损失险。

You'll cover SRCC risks, won't you?

你们要保罢工、暴动、民变险,是吗?

As our usual practice, insurance covers basic risks only, at 110 percent of the invoice value. If coverage against other risks is required, such as breakage, leakage, TPND, hook and contamination damages, the extra premium involved would be for the buyer's account.

按照我们的惯例,只保基本险,按发票金额 110% 投保。如果要加保其他险别,例如破碎险、渗漏险、盗窃遗失险、钩损和污染险等,额外保险费由买方负担。

We can serve you with a broad range of coverage against all kinks of risks for sea transport.

我公司可以承保海洋运输的所有险别。

Generally speaking, aviation insurance is much cheaper than marine insurance.

空运保险一般要比海运保险便宜。

In the insurance business, the term "average" simply means "loss" in most cases.

在保险业中"average"一词一般是"海损"的意思。

Are there any other clauses in marine policies?

海运险还包括其他条款吗？

Breakage is a particular average, isn't it?

破碎险属于一种单独海损,对吗？

the risk of breakage is covered by marine insurance, isn't it?

破碎险是包括在海洋运输货物险之内的,对吗？

The English understood by "marine risks" only risks incident to transport by sea.

英国人对"海洋运输货物险"只理解为海洋中的意外风险。

Frequently Used Words and Phrases 常用词汇和短语

All Risks 一切险

average 海损

fine print 细则

General Average(GA) 共同海损

insurance against air risk, air transportation insurance 航空运输保险

insurance against extraneous risks, insurance against additional risks 附加险

insurance against risk 保险

insurance against total loss only(TLO) 全损险

insurance against war risk 战争险

insurance applicant 投保人

insurance broker 保险经纪人

insurance business 保险企业

insurance clause 保险条款

insurance company 保险公司

insurance conditions 保险条件

insurance coverage;risks covered 保险范围

insurance expense 保险费

insurance free of(from) particular average (FPA) 平安险(单独海损不赔)

insurance instruction 投保通知

insurance proceeds 保险(保险收入)

insurance rate 保险费率表

insurance slip 投保单

insurance underwriter 保险承保人

insurance with particular average, basic risks;insurance against all risk:综合险,应保一切险

insurance 保险;保险费;保险金额

insurant, the insured 被保险人,受保人

insure 保险;投保;保证

insured amount 保险金额

insurer 保险人

leaflet 说明书

Marine Losses 海损

ocean marine cargo insurance clauses 海洋运输货物保险条款

ocean marine cargo insurance, marine insurance 水险(海运货物保险)

on deck risk 舱面险

overland Transportation Insurance War Risk 陆上运输战争险

overland transportation insurance, land transit insurance 陆上运输保险

parcel post insurance 邮包运输保险

partial loss 部分损失

Particular Average(PA) 单独海损

PICC(People's Insurance Company of

China) 中国人民保险公司

premium rate 保险费率

premium 保险费

risk insured, risk covered 承保险项

risk of bad odor (change of flavor) 恶味险, 变味险

risk of breakage 破碎险

risk of clashing 碰损险

risk of contamination (tainting) 污染险

risk of contingent import duty 进口关税险

risk of deterioration 变质险

risk of fresh and/of rain water damage (wetting) 淡水雨淋险

risk of hook damage 钩损险

risk of inherent vice 内在缺陷险

risk of leakage 渗漏险

risk of mould 发霉险

risk of normal loss (natural loss) 途耗或自然损耗险

risk of packing breakage 包装破裂险

risk of rust 生锈险

risk of shortage in weight/quantity 短量险 risk of spontaneous combustion 自然险

risk of sweating and/or heating 受潮受热险

risk of theft, pilferage and no delivery (TRND) 盗窃提货不着险

risk 险别

to provide the insurance 为……提供保险

transportation insurance 运输保险

underwriters 保险商 (指专保水险的保险商), 保险承运人

Sample Dialogue 1. We Refuse to Indemnify You for the Losses

L:I'm from Tianjin Foreign Trade Corporation.

J:What can I do for you?

L:I come here for the unfortunate affairs about the insurance.

J:What's the matter?

L:We exported a lot of gloves a month ago. Now the goods have arrived at the destination. Unfortunately, most of them have gone moldy.

J:Have you asked our agent in that country to take samples and photos ?

L:Yes. A spot investigation has been made.

J:How does the survey report say?

L:It said it was the chemical reaction that caused the mould. When the gloves were stored in the factory, they had been moisturized and the moisture and the chemical elements in the leather gloves resulted in the chemical reaction.

J:If that is the case, we refuse to indemnify you for the losses.

L:Why? Our insurance covered All Risks. To cover All Risks, the Insurance company shall be liable for total loss on land or sea of the insured goods.

J: Even though your insurance covered All Risks, there are conditions under which the insurance company is not liable.

L: I don't understand it. Could you explain it in more details?

J: Certainly. The insurance doesn't cover loss or damage caused by the intentional act or fault of the insured.

L: But our damage is not caused by intentional act.

J: I know. Exclusion also includes loss or damage from normal loss, inherent vice or nature of the insured goods.

L: Do you think our damage is caused by inherent vice or nature?

J: That's it.

L: But when the goods came out of the factory, they were intact and in good condition. It was the long voyage that made them moldy.

J: Do you have any certification that can testify the good quality of the goods?

L: No, we don't have.

J: That's why the insurance company refused to admit the liability.

Sample Dialogue 2. Trust PICC

It is the first deal the buyer made in China. They want to know more about PICC…

Buyer: Well, could you give me more information about PICC?

Seller: You mean what?

Buyer: Some basic information like the major categories of risks which PICC will underwrite.

Seller: Usually our goods are carried by sea. PICC provides three major categories of risks for our marine cargo: Free from Particular Average, With Particular Average and All Risks. The insurance can cover the whole way of transit.

Buyer: And what shall I do if an insurance claim happens?

Seller: When you buy the insurance, your insurance policy will designate a claim settlement agent to you. To make a claim, you apply for an inspection from your agent firstly. Then you can submit your formal claim to PICC with all required documents including insurance policy, bills of lading, invoice, and packing list. Don't forget your list of claim.

Buyer: Thank you. I will have a good grip of PICC as we develop our business in China.

Sample Dialogue 3. What If We Change to "All Risks"?

Smith: We would like to ask you some details about this agreement. Have you taken out insurance yet on this shipment?

Wang: Yes, we talked about it with our underwriter, and think that we should get a policy for With Particular Average, considering our deal is based on CIF clause. Is there anything else you would like to know about?

Smith: No, not really. I was just wondering if the breakage of goods is included in this WPA or not. You know this consignment is easy to be broken.

Wang: In fact, not every breakage is included in this WPA. It is included in the WPA when the breakage results from natural calamities and maritime accidents, such as stranding and sinking of the carrying vessel, or is attributable to fire, explosion or collision. Or else it belongs to the Risk of Breakage. We could add this item if you wish.

Smith: But that's an additional risk item, isn't it?

Wang: Yes. And the buyer is usually required to bear the cost for the additional risk coverage.

Smith: I see. What if we change to "All Risks"? Do we still have to pay extra for the Risk of Breakage?

Wang: No, you don't have to. The insurance of All Risks has that item under coverage already. However, all you need to do is to pay a little higher premium rate.

Smith: That really doesn't matter. The value of the goods is just too high. If we lose them our company will lose a lot of money, and may have to close. So the safety of the goods is all that counts.

Wang: Oh, yes, absolutely. I'll have your insurance changed from WPA to All Risks for 110% of CIF invoice value as per the ocean marine cargo clauses of the PICC.

Smith: Very good. Another thing, what about the scope of the insurance coverage? I mean, where does it start and where does it end?

Wang: We adopt the Warehouse to Warehouse Clause, which is commonly used in international insurance. In other words, the coverage is in effect when the cargo has left the consigner's warehouse and all the way through transit to the consignee's warehouse.

Smith: I see. Thank you for your cooperation.

Wang: It's my pleasure.

Useful expressions for negotiation

Asking for Clarification or Further Information 要求给予解释或更多信息
Sorry I don't follow you completely; would you mind explaining this…
Could you be (a bit) more precise?

Could you expand on that?

(I'm sorry.) Whet do you mean?

I'm afraid I don't follow you.

I'm sorry, but I don't see your point.

I'm afraid I don't understand.

Could you be more specific?

What are you driving at?

What are you getting at?

Would you mind clarifying that for me?

Are you saying…

Could you go into more detail on that?

Would you like to elaborate on that?

Could you repeat it for me?

Could you repeat that? I didn't hear you.

Say that again, please? I didn't hear you.

I'm sorry, I didn't catch that.

Sorry, what did you say?

Sorry, what was that?

What do you mean by…

What are you trying to say?

Could you tell me some more about…

Would you mind telling me more about…

I'd like to know more about…

Something else I was wondering about was…

Sorry, that's not really what I mean. What I'd like to know is…

Sorry to keep after you, but could you tell me…

Sorry I don't quite understand why…

实训综合习题

I. put the following sentences into Chinese.

1. I am looking for insurance from your company, and I want to know what types of cover you usually underwrite.

2. We leave the insurance arrangements to you but we wish to have the goods cov-

ered against All Risks.

3. 10 % above invoice value is the usual practice in international trade.

4. Since the premium varies with the extent of insurance. Extra premium is for buyer's account.

5. If you desire US to insure against a special risk, an extra premium will have to be charged.

6. We want broader coverage to include some extraneous risks.

7. We'll insure the goods with the People's Insurance Company of China.

8. As our order was placed on CIF basis, the insurance is to be effected by you.

9. According to your request, we have insured your shipment to the border.

10. Please send us the insurance policy together with your receipt for the premiums paid as soon as possible.

11. They will undertake to compensate you for the losses according to the risks insured.

12. You will have to claim this amount from the underwriters.

13. Will you please quote your terms for providing the required cover, which should include loading and discharging?

14. The rates vary with the nature of the goods, the degree of cover desired and the place of destination.

15. There are three basic covers, namely, Free from Particular Average. With Particular Average and All Risks.

16. As requested, we will arrange insurance on your behalf.

17. As a rule, the extra premium involved will be for buyer's account.

18. The PICC offers a full range of financial and insurance services worldwide.

19. We are able to cover all kinds of risks for transportation by sea, land and air.

20. Please note that our insurance coverage is for 110% of the invoice value only.

II. Substitution Exercises.

Drill 1   According to the CIF clause, is the risk of ... covered in your offer?

Complete the above sentence by using the following:

— contamination

— fresh water damage

— with particular average (W P A)

— theft, pilferage and nondelivery (TPND)

Drill 2   We generally only issue insurance for ...

Complete the above sentence by using the following：

— risk of grease

— risk of breakage

— the total loss only

— risk of short in weight

Dill 3　We would also like to cover... on the cargo.

Complete the above sentence by using the following：

— total loss only

— comprehensive risks

— with particular average

— free from particular average

Drill 4　But since... is a special coverage, the premium is therefore higher.

Complete the above sentence by using the following：

— risk of oil

— risk of grease

— risk of hooks

— risk of contamination

Drill 5　You may...at your end.

Complete the above sentence by using the following：

— make the payment

— file a complaint

— present your claim

— apply for this kind of coverage

Drill 6　I'll have to adjust the price by adding a percentage of ...

Complete the above sentence by using the following：

— processing fees

— insurance premium

— cost for extraneous risks(一般附加险)

— cost for import duty risk(进口关税险)

Drill 7　Should then how would the insurance company handle this situation?

Complete the above sentence by using the following：

— the validity of the L/C expire

— the seller refuse to admit liability

— stranding(搁浅)and sinking of the carrying vessel take

Drill 8　Do you mind telling me...

Complete the above sentence by using the following:

— why they refuse to admit liability

— who is acting as mediator in this matter

— what the difference between WA and WPA is

— which insurance company has underwritten this deal

Drill 9　No, not really. I was just wondering if...

Complete the above sentence by using the following:

— the L/C is still valid or not

— the insurance will cover losses in full or not

— the coverage of "all risks" is requested or not

— the insurance covers the risk of breakage or not

Drill 10　The buyer is usually required to bear...

Complete the above sentence by using the following:

— the cost of additional coverage

— the cost of insurance on FOB terms

— the cost of special coverage under fire

— the cost of taking out a special insurance

Drill 11　I'll have your insurance coverage changed from...to...

Supply the missing words in the above sentence by using the following:

— war & fire, deterioration

— oil & grease, contamination

— stranding & sinking, hooks & breakage

— theft & pilferage, freshwater & leakage

Drill 12　But first things first could you tell me...PICC under-writes?

Complete the above sentence by using the following:

— what major risk coverage

— what minor risk coverage

— what kind of transportation risk coverage

— what kind of family property risk coverage

Drill 13　My pleasure. For we have three major categories.

Complete the above sentence by using the following:

— insurance claim

— sea transportation

— air transportation

— truck-air- truck transportation

Drill 14　We generally do it on the basis of …

Complete the above sentence by using the following:

— contract stipulation

— your authorized consent

— our mutually agreed terms

— what is stated in the document

Drill 15　This may sound complicated, but actually it's not. You begin by …

Complete the above sentence by using the following:

— filing a formal claim

— presenting your claim in writing

— informing your claim settlement agent

— obtaining your claim settlement agent's inspection

III. put the following sentences into English.

1. 请问这个价格是否包括保险在内?

2. 在我们决定价格之前,我们想先了解一下你们准备投保什么险别?

3. 一般来说,附加险是在买方有必要时才买的。

4. 如果按到岸价成交的话,我们要投保哪些险别?

5. 按照国际贸易惯例,附加险的保险费由买方负责。

6. 请解释一下全损险和基本险的区别。

7. 全损险是指在运输过程中,由于自然灾害或意外事故而造成的全部货物损失的保险。

8. 基本险不但包括全损险中货物发生的全部损失,而且在只发生了部分损失时也负赔偿责任。

9. 保险责任的期限是被保险货物在最后卸货港卸货 60 天为止。

10. 保险索赔必须于货物在最后装卸港卸货后 9 个月内提出。

11. 我们的价格是按成本加运费报的,所以保险请你们自己办理。

12. 如果投保险别和金额超过了规定限度,费用请自理。

13. 在离岸价的条件下,货物的保险由买方投保,或由卖方代保险。

14. 在到岸价的条件下,货物的保险由卖方负责。

15. 保险的目的是为了保障货物的安全和投保人的利益。

16. 按到岸价成交,我们一般保水渍险。

17. 我们想投保水渍险,包括仓对仓条款,有效期 60 天。

18. 我们按发票金额的 110% 投保到目的港。

19. 这没问题。但如果你们需要投保其他险别的话,还要额外付款。

20. 请以到岸价发票金额的 110% 为我们投保水渍险。

IV. Role Play.

Task 1

Mr. Michael, an old customer of ours has done business with us on FOB basis for years. This time he requests a quotation on CIF basis for a repeat order of 500 pieces of Alarm Clock Type 835. But he is not very familiar with insurance clauses of the PICC.

Work in pairs. One student acts as Mr. Michael, the other as the clerk from a trading company. Try to explain briefly the Ocean Marine Cargo Clauses of the PICC in the form of a dialogue and sort out the appropriate coverage for this kind of goods for Mr. Michael.

Task 2

Work in pairs. One student acts as A, a foreign merchant who shows little interest in effecting insurance with the PICC. The other as B, a Chinese businessman. B is requested to try to catch the opportunity to convince A and win the insurance for the PICC.

V. Oral Practice.

Work with your partner. For an order the importer insists on adding the risk of packing breakage which you think it is unnecessary. Moreover, they think you should pay for the risk. Try to settle it through a negotiation.

VI. Topics for Group Discussion.

1. What would the insured do if any damage takes place?

2. On what condition would the insurance company undertake to compensate the insured?

3. Following China's entry into the WTO, what changes can we expect to see in the Chinese insurance market?

第 12 章　商检与仲裁

Commodity Inspction（Ⅰ）

A：There is one more thing to be cleared up. It is commodity inspection.

B：All our goods for export will be inspected by the China Commodity Inspection Bureau before delivery at the port of shipment. The Inspection Bureau only releases the goods which are up to export standards.

A：After that, the Bureau will issue an Inspection Certificate to the qualified goods, won't they?

B：Right. The certificate will be made out in both Chinese and English with the official seal and personal chop of the commissioner.

A：Good. But another thing is, as our transaction involves foods, it is necessary to make sure your sanitary standards meet the requirements of our government. We will make a reinspection upon the arrival.

B：Well, the importers have the right to reinspect the goods after the arrival. We hope you can engage a surveyor as soon as possible since the time limit for the reinspection is within 60 days after the arrival of the goods.

A：No problem. My last question is. we need another certificate to show the goods to be free from radioactive. That is a necessary formality when your foods are launched in our local market.

B：Well, I need consult with the Inspection Bureau. I will let you know their answer very soon. And now, about the commodity inspection, are there any other questions?

A：I have no question at my end. Thanks.

Commodity Inspection（Ⅱ）

To ensure the shipment has arrived safety, the seller calls the buyer after the consignment is supposed to be in their warehouse…

Seller：Hi, Ms. Qiao. How is the shipment?

Buyer：Nice to hear you voice, Mike. The consignment is here. But we found some problems.

Seller：What is wrong? We had executed the stipulations of the contract strictly.

Buyer：Take it easy, Mike. It is not your problem. Upon the arrival, some bottles were found broken. We engaged the Dalian Commodity Inspection Bureau as the survey-or. Their inspection certificate states that the fruit juice inside is inedible.

Seller: How could that happen?

Buyer: The shipping company is determined as guilty for their careless loading and unloading. Since we made the deal on the basis of FOB, we are negotiating with the shipping company and expecting their reply.

Seller: Well, I am sorry to hear this. If there is anything we can do, just let us know.

Words and Expressions

Release 放行,释放   surveyor 检查员

official seal 公章，单位印章   be free from 免于…

personal chop 个人印章   radioactive 放射性的，有辐射能的

sanitary standard 卫生标准   inedible 不适于食用的

reinspection 复查

Key Sentences 经典必备句

The inspection of goods is a vital integral part of the contract.

商品检验是合同里的一个重要组成部分。

The inspection rights should be defined.

商检的权力应该加以明确。

It might cause some disputes Over the results of inspection.

这可能导致对商检的结果会发生争议。

You should engage a surveyor.

你们应该联系公证。

It's complicated to get goods tested and reinspected.

货物测试和复验比较复杂。

All inspection certificates are only valid with the official seal and personal chop of the commissioner.

所有证明书以盖公章和局长签字视为有效。

Exporters have the right to ask for inspectation before delivery to the shipping line as while importers have the right to reinspect the goods after their arrival.

出口商在向船运公司托运前有权检验商品,而进口商在货到后有权复验商品。

The inspection of commodity is not so easy.

商品商检不是那么简单。

The inspection should be completed within a month after the arrival of the goods.

商品检验应在货到后一个月内完成。

China Import and Export Commodity Inspection Bureau is taken as one of the best surveyors.

中国进出口商品检验局被认为是最好的公证行之一。

Upon arrival. the buyer is inspecting this consignment of porcelainware to see if there is any breakage.

货到时,买方正在检查这批瓷器是否有破损的。

We can't accept the goods because the result from the inspection before delivery doesn't coincide with that of reinspectation.

因为发货前的检测结果与复验的结果不一致,我们无法收货。

There is a time limit for the reinspection。

复验有一个时限。

Where do you wish to reinspect the goods?

您希望在哪里复验商品?

We may need another certificate to show the goods is free from radioactive contamination.

我们还要另一份证明书,以证明货物没有受放射线污染。

Frequently Used Words and Phrases 常用词汇和短语

inception of carriage 货车检查

inspect 检验

Inspection Certificate of Health 健康检验证书

Inspection Certificate of Origin 产地检验证书

Inspection Certificate of Quality 质量检验证书

Inspection Certificate of Quantity 数量检验证书

Inspection Certificate of Value 价值检验证书

Inspection Certificate of Weight 重量检验证书

Inspection Certificate 检验证明

Inspection of commodity 商品检验

inspection of loading 监装检验

inspection of material 材料检验

inspection of packing 包装检验

Inspection of risk 被保险物价的检查

inspection of storage 监装

inspection of voucher 凭证检验

inspection 检验

inspector of tax 税务稽查员

inspector 检验员

reinspect 复验

reinspection 复验

Sanitary Inspection Certificate 卫生检验证书

surveyor 检验行,公证行

to inspect A for B 检查 A 中是否有 B

商品检验常用语 （一）

Shall we take up the question of inspection today?

今天咱们讨论商品检验问题吧。

The inspection of commodity is no easy job.

商检工作不是那么简单。

Mr. Black is talking with the Chinese importer about inspecting the goods.

布莱克先生与中方进口商就商品检验问题进行洽谈。

As an integral part of the contract, the inspection of goods has its special importance.

作为合同里的一个组成部分,商品检验具有特殊的重要性。

We should inspect this batch of porcelain ware to see if there is any breakage.

我们要检查一下这批瓷器是否有破损的。

The exporters have the right to inspect the export goods before delivery to the shipping line.

出口商在向船运公司托运前有权检验商品。

The inspection should be completed within a month after the arrival of the goods.

商品检验工作在到货后一个月内完成。

How should we define the inspection rights?

商检的权力怎样加以明确呢?

I'm worried that there might be some disputes over the results of inspection.

我担心对商检的结果会发生争议。

We'll accept the goods only if the results from the two inspections are identical with each other.

如果双方的检测结果一致,我们就收货。

Words and Phrases

inspection 检验	inspector 检验员
inspect 检验	inspector of tax 税务稽查员
to inspect A for B 检查 A 中是否有 B	inspection of commodity 商品检验

商品检验常用语 （二）

Where do you wish to reinspect the goods?

您希望在哪里复验商品?

The importers have the right to reinspect the goods after their arrival.

进口商在货到后有权复验商品。

What's the time limit for the reinspection?

复验的时限是什么时候?

It's very complicated to have the goods reinspected and tested.

这批货测试和复验起来比较复杂。

What if the results from the inspection and the reinspection do not coincide with each other?

如果检验和复验的结果有出入该怎么办呢?

Words and Phrases

reinspect 复验   reinspection 复验

商品检验常用语 （三）

Who issues the inspection certificate in case the quality do not confirm to the contract?

如果货物的质量与合同不符,由谁出具检验证明书呢?

The certificate will be issued by China Import and Export Commodity Inspection Bureau or by any of its branches.

检验证明书将由中国进出口商品检验局或其分支机构出具。

The Inspection Certificate will be signed by the commissioner of your bureau.

检验证明书将由商检局局长签字。

Our certificates are made valid by means of the official seal and personal chop of the commissioner.

我们的证明书以盖公章和局长签字为有效。

As a rule, our certificate is made out in Chinese and English.

通常证明书是用中文和英文开具的。

You may have another certificate showing the goods to be free from radioactive contamination.

你们还要出具另一份证明书,以证明货物没有受放射线污染。

Our goods must be up to export standards before the Inspection Bureau releases them.

我们的货物只有在符合出口标准后,商检局才予以放行。

Our Inspection Bureau will issue a Veterinary Inspection Certificate to show that the shipment is in conformity with export standards.

商检局将出具动物检疫证明书以证明货物符合出口标准。

Is it convenient for you to engage a surveyor?

你们联系公证方便吗？

We have the best surveyor, China Import and Export Commodity Inspection Bureau.

我们有最好的公证行,即中国进出口商品检验局。

Words and Phrases

Inspection Certificate 检验证明

Inspection Certificate of Quality 质量检验证书

Inspection Certificate of Quantity 数量检验证书

surveyor 检验行,公证行

Additional Words and Phrases

Inspection Certificate of Weight 重量检验证书

Inspection Certificate of Origin 产地检验证书

Inspection Certificate of value 价值检验证书

Inspection Certificate of Health 健康检验证书

Sanitary Inspection Certificate 卫生检验证书

Veterinary Inspection Certificate 兽医检验证书

inspection of packing 包装检验

inspection of loading 监装检验

inspection of material 材料检验

inspection of risk 被保险物价的检查

inspection of storage 监装

inspection of voucher 凭证检验

inception of carriage 货车检查

inspection of document 单证检查

inspection of fixed asset 固定资产检查

inspection of incoming merchandise 到货验收

Inspection Certificate on Damaged cargo 验残检验证书

Inspection Certificate on Tank 验船证书

Certificate of Measurement & Weight 货载衡量证书

Authentic Surveyor 公证签订人

inspection on cleanliness 清洁检验

inspection on cleanliness of dry cargo hold 干货舱清洁检验

inspection on cleanliness of tank 油舱清洁检验

inspection and acceptance 验收

inspection before delivery 交货前检验

inspection after construction 施工后检验

inspection during construction 在建工程检验

inspection between process 工序间检验

inspection report 检验报告

inspection tag 检查标签

Inspectorate General of Customs 海关稽查总局

inspection and certificate fee 检验签证费

to issue(a certificate) 发……(证明)

Sworn Measurer 宣誓衡量人　　　　验室
Underwriters Laboratory 保险商实　　Loyd's Surveyor 英国劳氏公证行

Arbitration（Ⅰ）

The buyer and the seller are discussing where to hold arbitration if it is necessary…

Buyer: I don't think you will refuse to add the arbitration clause into the contract.

Seller: I won't. Where do we hold arbitration then?

Buyer: Can we leave the place for arbitration and the arbitral organization open till it is needed? When a dispute arises, we can designate an arbitral body temporarily through a discussion.

Seller: Frankly speaking, it is not a good idea. Suppose there is a dispute, and we can't agree on the place of arbitration, the problem will still be pending. In our usual practice, arbitrations are conducted in China.

Buyer: If it is in China, the arbitration will be conducted according to China rules. But we know nothing about China rules. May I recommend Tokyo?

Seller: Well, to be fair, we can adopt the customary practice that has been used in Sino-Japan trade.

Buyer: Yes?

Seller: The arbitration should be held in the country of the defendant. It means if I submit the case for arbitration, the arbitration will be conducted in your country.

Buyer: Good. I agree. Then how about the fees for arbitration?

Seller: Of course the losing party will pay that.

Arbitration（Ⅱ）

Two parties are ready to sign the contract after a double check…

A: Well, I can find no loophole in this contract. Just to ensure, suppose there is a dispute in our trade and it comes to arbitration, according to this contract, must the arbitration be conducted only in China?

B: It can be conducted either in China or in other countries. But if we declare it so in the contract, it must be in China. What is wrong?

A: I just have no idea about Chinese rules. If in China, the arbitration must apply Chinese rules of procedure, right?

B: Yes. But I can assure you that it is unnecessary to worry about the justice. Actually, CIETAC will arrange and supervise the procedures for each arbitration case undertaken in China. The arbitrators always question and try to get sufficient facts in order to settle a case. And each party in the arbitration will be entitled to present his positions and evidence.

A:In the arbitration, we can only employ a Chinese lawyer, right?

B:No, you can employ a foreign lawyer either. Furthermore, Our new rules allow foreigners to be included in the panel of arbitrators. I think this will release your upset.

A: Yes. thanks. But how is a final decision made?

B:The final decision is made by arbitrators' voting according to the applicable legal principles, after an analysis. And it is final and no appeal is permitted.

A:If one party refuses to accept the decision...

B: Then. the People's Court in China will enforce it at the request of the other party. Anyway, there is never a single dispute which is not settled by friendly negotiation in our history.

A:I don't mean that. We have known your good reputation for a long time. I just want to know more about China to keep the pace with our rapid business development in China. Let's come back to our business. I am ready to sign on behalf of our corporation.

Words and Expressions

arbitration 仲裁	justice 审判
arbitral organization 仲裁机构	arbitrator 仲裁人
dispute 争论	evidence 证据
designate 指定, 指派	panel of arbitrators 仲裁人团
pending 未决的	appeal 上诉
defendant 被告	enforce 强迫, 执行
plaintiff 起诉人, 原告	keep pace with 并驾齐驱
loophole 遗漏	

Key Sentences 经典必备句

As per the dispute, we hope that it can be first settled through friendly negotiation.
至于该争议,我们希望首先能够通过友好协商的方式解决。

To settle the dispute, if negotiation fails, we should turn to conciliation.
为了解决争端,如果协商失败,我们会要求调解。

The correct way is to find out what the problem is and what the liabilities are.
正确的办法是要找出问题所在并找出责任所在。

Since the joint conciliation doesn't work, we have to submit the case to arbitration.

由于联合调解没有起到作用,我们不得不提请仲裁。

The process of arbitration is simpler and faster than the court procedure.

仲裁比法律程序更简单快捷。

In the arbitration hearing, all parties can present the facts and position before the final decision is made.

在仲裁听证过程中,最终决定做出之前,所有各方都能够表述事实和立场。

Usually, it is stipulated in the arbitration clauses that the arbitration decision and award will be the final and can not be appealed. Otherwise it can be enforced through leagal procedures.

通常,在仲裁条款中会规定仲裁决议和仲裁结果是最终结果,不得提起上诉。

Arbitrators are neutral experts chosen by the disputing parties.

仲裁人是由争议双方共同选出的中立的专家。

The facts of the case will be reviewed by arbitrators.

案件所涉及的事实会由仲裁人来审查。

When the claimant submits an application for arbitration, he has to pay a reasonable arbitration fee in advance.

当原告提出仲裁申请时,他要预付一部分合理的仲裁费用。

The arbitration decision and award is made by majority vote.

仲裁决定和结果通过多数投票来做出。

For arbitrations in China, foreign parties are allowed to employ foreign lawyers.

在中国进行的仲裁,外方可以雇佣外国律师。

Arbitration is always supervised by local courts.

仲裁一般由当地法庭监督管理。

If it is necessary. the court has the power to break an arbitration agreement and hear the case itself.

如果有必要,法庭有权力终止仲裁决定并自行进行听证。

Frequently Used Words and Phrases 常用词汇和短语

arbitration 仲裁

arbitrator 仲裁人

arbitration clauses 仲裁条款

arbitration heating 仲裁听证会

arbitration organization 仲裁组织

appeal 上诉

conciliation 调解

customary practice 惯例

enforcement 执行

equitable 公平的

litigation 诉讼

make the award 作出裁决

temporary arbitration court/tribunal 临时仲裁庭

the claimant 原告   the defendant 被告

Sample Dialogues 1. Inspection and Arbitration

Mr. James has scanned the Sales Confirmation for quite sometime. He believes one can never be too careful. Anyhow, the discussion is drawing to an end. There are only two minor points left.

James: Mr. Liu, here, under Article 3: Quality & Weight, you phrase it like this: Based on the inspection certificate issued by the Shanghai Commodity Inspection Bureau. Do you mean that you sell on shipped quality and quantity? If the goods are found disqualified or short on arrival, are we entitled to lodge claims?

Liu: You have the right of reinspection. And you may lodge claims against us if you find that the quality or quantity does not conform to the contract or the bill of lading. There's no risk involved.

James: No, I hope not. How do you stipulate the inspection clause for your imports?

Liu: Inspection must be conducted before shipment by recognized surveyors. Their reports may be taken as the basis for negotiating payment. After the goods arrive, our bureau at the port of destination shall reinspect the goods. The inspection certificate issued by them shall serve as the basis for filing a claim.

James: Very reasonable. The interests of both the buyer and the seller are taken into account. Oh, I nearly forgot. Why is there no mention of arbitration?

Liu: We have the arbitration clause in our general terms and conditions, but not in the sales confirmation. As a matter of fact, most disputes can be settled in a friendly way, with a view to developing a long-term relationship. Arbitration is generally the last resort.

James: I agree. I also believe in developing friendly business relations. Well, I suppose that's all I want to know. Mr. Liu, thank you very much for being so patient with me. I hope you don't think I'm a bore. It's business.

Liu: No, not at all. That's what I'm here for. You must be very tired after a whole morning's talk. If you like, I suggest we go to "Xin Tian Di" this afternoon to relax; it is one of the most famous resorts for entertainment and leisure in Shanghai. Maybe you have already heard of it?

James: Fabulous! Thank you for your thoughtful arrangement for me.

Liu: Please wait in the hotel lobby at 1:30 p. m. We will send our car to pick you up.

James: Thank you. See you this afternoon.

Liu: See you.

Sample Dialogues 2. No Objection to Arbitration Conducted in China

Zhao: Almost everything has been talked over and argued upon, what should we do next?

Smith: Since it's the first time I'm doing business with you. I'm afraid I'm not quite clear on the arbitration clause.

Zhao: Anything particular you want to know?

Smith: Please explain it in general, Mr. Zhao.

Zhao: All right. Generally speaking, we think all disputes can be settled amicably by negotiation.

Smith: If negotiation fails, then what?

Zhao: The case may be submitted for arbitration.

Smith: Do you permit arbitration in a third country?

Zhao: Yes. But our usual practice is that arbitration, if any, will be conducted in China.

Smith: Maybe arbitration in a third country is a fairer and more equitable solution to the problems.

Zhao: If you insist, our contract clauses permit arbitration in a third country.

Smith: I have no objection to arbitration conducted in China. I think amicable discussions are sometimes the best to settle disputes without involving arbitration.

Zhao: I agree. I'm glad we have the same idea. How about this way?

Smith: Please say it directly.

Zhao: We'd better not regulate the location for arbitration and the arbitral organization now. We may discuss to agree upon a temporary arbitral body when needed.

Smith: It sounds reasonable. The clause should be like this: "Any disputes arising from the execution of this contract shall be settled in a friendly way. If no settlement can be reached through consultation and conciliation, the disputes shall be submitted for arbitration by a mutually nominated arbitrator. The arbitrator's decision on the disputes is final and binding upon both parties."

Zhao: Fine. Only one thing is not mentioned. How is the cost of the arbitration to be divided?

Smith: Generally speaking, all the fees for arbitration shall be borne by the losing party.

226

Zhao：It's acceptable. And I hope there are no disputes at all.

Smith：So do I. That will benefit both of us.

Sample Dialogues 3. To Include an Arbitration Clause in the Contract

Y：Oh, Mr. Kinch, the arbitration clause suddenly occurred to me just now. This transaction is rather different from usual. Besides the large quantity, the computers we have ordered are very valuable. In case disputes arise, we should include an arbitration clause in the contract.

K：Arbitration clause? Mr. Yu, I think it doesn't matter whether there is any arbitration or not. If any disputes arise, I'm sure that they can be settled through an amicable negotiation.

Y：Yes, that sounds fine. But the provision of arbitration is really of primary importance and a matter of great concern to both of us.

K：OK, we have no objection then. But I wonder where to hold the arbitration?

Y：Is it agreeable for us to adopt usual practice of international business arbitration?

K：All right. If arbitration is to take place in China, what procedural rules will apply?

Y：The CIETAC procedural rules will apply, of course. CIETAC stands for China International Economic and Trade Arbitration Commission. But if arbitration is to take place in a foreign country, then the rules of the foreign arbitration institution will be used.

K：That's fair. What about the costs of arbitration in China? Is it very expensive?

Y：No, it isn't. When the claimant submits his application for arbitration, all he has to pay is a reasonable arbitration fee in advance according to the Arbitration Fee Schedule.

K：The award should be final and no appeal be permitted. That's right, isn't it?

Y：Right.

K：How about enforcement?

Y：Should the award not be carried out by one party, then the People's Court in China can enforce it at the request of the other party.

K：In my opinion, conciliation should be combined with arbitration.

Y：Yes. This combination is a unique feature of arbitration in China. Chinese arbitrators may conduct conciliation in the arbitration proceedings. This is quite different from the practice in the West, I believe?

K：Yes, it is. Take the U. K. for example. Here conciliation and arbitration are two separate procedures. They are dealt with separately.

Y:Yes, indeed. If conciliation succeeds, the case is solved to the satisfaction of all concerned.

K:If it fails?

Y:The case is referred to arbitration in accordance with the arbitration clause.

K:If necessary, foreign citizens should be invited to join the Chinese panel of arbitrators.

Y:OK. New rules enable foreigners to be included in the panel of arbitrators.

K:Acceptable. Arbitration will be generally the last resort if there is no alternative. But I hope we'll never use it.

Y: So do I.

Sample Dialogues 4. We should try to iron out Our Differences

H:Mr. Chirac, the medical equipment we discussed yesterday are quite valuable.

C:Yes, Mr. Hong, the equipment is of high quality, and very useful. So they're certainly valuable.

H:The design of the equipment is sophisticated, and therefore, the inspection is no easy job. I am worried that there might be some disputes over the results of inspection.

C:You needn't worry about that. There is an arbitration clause in the contract, isn't there?

H:Right. We always attach importance to the arbitration clause of a contract.

C:OK. As the Chinese saying goes "To get prepared against a rainy day", we had better think more of the possible problems which might happen afterwards.

H:You are right. In case of any dispute, we should try to iron out our differences through amicable negotiations. If we fail to reach a settlement, we will then submit the case in dispute for arbitration to an international arbitration organization.

C:Where do you think the arbitration will be held?

H:Would it be agreeable to you to adopt the customary practice that has been used in the Sino-France trade

C:I don't know the customary practice in Sino-France trade regarding the place for arbitration. Will you explain it to me in this regard?

H:It is in the country of the defendant. That is to say, if we submit the case for arbitration, the place for arbitration is in France and if you submit the case for arbitration, the place for arbitration is in China.

C:That's OK. If so, which party will pay the arbitration fee?

228

H：Well, generally speaking, all the fees for arbitration shall be borne by the losing party unless otherwise awarded by the tribunal.

C：And how is the arbitral award made?

H：By the decision of the majority of the arbitrators.

C：And the arbitral award is final and binding on the parties, isn't it?

H：Yes, it is.

C：I have another question. Is an arbitral award made in China enforceable in another country?

H：Yes. China is a signatory to the 1958 New York Convention.

C：Well, personally I should say it's so much better to resolve the dispute through friendly negotiations between the two parties.

H：I agree with you. Arbitration is only the last resort. Now let us go over the stipulations of the arbitration clause of the contract.

C：That's right. I agree.

Useful expressions for negotiation

Asking for Confirmation 要求确认

Am I correct in assuming that the terms of delivery are...

Basically, what you are saying is that...right?

Could you send us confirmation by e-mail, by Wednesday?

Perhaps I misunderstood. Are you saying that...

Let me see if I understood this. Would I be correct in assuming

that you feel...

Oh, and then don't forget...

Make sure you remember to...

Oh, be careful not to...

So in other words, you think...

Basically, what you are saying is...

If I understand you right, you think...

If I understood you correctly, you're saying that ...

Correct me if I'm wrong, but do you mean that ...

When you say do you mean that ...

Are you saying that ...

Would I be correct in saying that you think...

Am I making myself clear?

Did I make everything clear?

Is that clear to you?

I am not really sure what you are getting at.

I'm not quite clear what you mean.

If l understand right...

So what you mean is right?

So what you really saying is...

Let's just confirm the details, then.

Let's make sure we agree on these figures (dates/etc.) .

Can we check these points?

Identifying and Analyzing Obstacles 确定和分析谈判障碍

The main obstacle to progress at the moment seems to be .

The main thing that bothers us is...

One big problem we have is ...

What exactly is the underlying problem here?

Let's take a closer look at this problem.

I would like to analyze this situation and get to the bottom of the problem.

In return for this, would you be willing to ...

We feel there has to be a trade-off here.

It seems to me that the problem is...

My concern is that we may not have enough .

Please explain this to me. There appears to be an error...

What is the main problem?

What is the real issue (here)?

(I think) the major problem is...

Our primary concern is ...

The crux of the matter is ...

(As I see it) , the most important thing is...

The main problem we need to solve is...

We really need to take care of ...

The problem with that is...

That raises the issue of ...

实训综合习题

I. put the following sentences into Chinese.

1. Our products are well known for their fine quality.

2. The material is absolutely of prime quality.

3. We can supply woolen sweater of first class/first grade quality.

4. Our products are superior (good/excellent) in quality.

5. The goods have enjoyed world renown for their excellent quality.

6. The quality of our products is much admired in Asian market.

7. The quality is appreciated by users abroad.

8. Our commodity has always come up to the international standard.

9. The quality conforms in every respect to your requirements.

10. Our television set is one of the best in the world and it surpasses all other models on the market.

11. Our products surpass all other makes in quality while are moderate in price.

12. Our cotton goods are of unsurpassed quality and appearance.

13. Our silk has no equal/rival in quality in the South east Asia market.

14. If the quality is suitable, we may order in quantity.

15. If the quality proves to be satisfactory. there is no question of further order.

16. The quality of the goods you sent US is far below the sample against which we placed our order.

17. The goods are inferior in quality to your samples.

18. We are disappointed to find your goods so unsatisfactory.

19. The goods didn't turn out to our expectation.

20. The goods didn't come up to our standard.

II. put the following sentences into English.

1. 怀特先生与中方进口商就商品检验问题进行洽谈。

2. 如果双方的检测结果一致,我们就收货。

3. 如果货物的质量与合同不符,由谁出具检验证明书呢?

4. 进口方有权在目的港对商品进行复检。

5. 作为合同里的一个组成部分,商品检验具有特殊的重要性。

6. 商检的时间和地点在该合同中有明确而详细的说明。

7. 检验证明书将由中国进出口商品检验局或其分支机构出具。

8. 经检验这批商品并不具有放射性污染,同时其含铅量和含镉量均未超标。

9. 如果对商检的结果有争议该怎么处理?

10. 中国进出口商品检验局是商检的权威部门,也是全国最好的检验部门。

III. Oral Practice.

1. Work with your partner. Upon the arrival, the reinsertion issued by the local Commodity Inspection Bureau states that some products are rusty. The cause should be the inferior quality. Make a negotiation to settle it.

2. Work with your partner. After arrival, you find some cartons broken and goods damaged. You ask for the reason and solution with your supplier.

第 13 章　索赔

Claim（I）

Jones calling for a claim of inferior quality found in their last order.

A：Hello, Mr. Jones. It is a surprise to see you. How are you so far?

B：Hello, Mr. Wang. I am fine. Thanks. I am so sorry to drop in. I hope it does not interrupt you.

A：It's all right with me. How is our last shipment?

B：That is why I am here. My head office informed the arrival of the consignment. Unfortunately, they found leakage in many of tins of bamboo root.

A：You don't say!

B：But that is true. Upon the arrival, the Health Officers made a close inspection. The result shows that the content was considered unfit for human consumption.

A：I'm sorry to hear that. But we have scientific processing controls and packing process. Thousands of tons of this product have been exported by us and this is the only case. Have they discovered what could be the cause?

B：The report showed that the leakage is caused by careless handling instead of inferior package.

A：But it never occurred before.

B：Our cargo handling staff found the leakage was brought about by damaged tins when they arrived. Obviously, it occurred in the loading in Dalian dock.

A：What would you suggest for a settlement then?

B：Since our terms are CIF Amsterdam, it is fair that you pay for the loss caused by careless handling. We'd rather have the loss reduced from the total value. and set against our future purchases of your canned food.

A：To start up a long-term business relationship with you, we hope to settle this issue amicably. Could you offer the certificate issued by the Health Department, and the quantity of damaged tins?

B：I'm so glad to hear of your ready agreement. We will send you a letter to confirm this with the certificate enclosed.

A：As soon as we received your letter, we will give a prompt reply.

Claim（Ⅱ）

Upon the arrvial, the buyer found a short weight, they turned to the seller for a claim…

Buyer：We found a short weight in your last consignment.

Seller：Wait a moment. The consignment should be 6 500 tons coal.

Buyer：But there is a 45 tons short weight on the arrival.

Seller：How can that be?

Buyer：It is true. Here is the copy of the inspection certificate from Melbourne port.

Seller：But we also hold the inspection certificate from our Commodities Inspection Bureau which states the consignment was up to the standard for export.

Buyer：The only possibility is your Inspection Bureau may select a few packages at random. But the whole consignment was not as dry as they expect. The short weight is supposed to be caused by the excessive moisture. So we claim for the compensation for the loss.

Seller：Well,let me have a look at the report of your Inspection Bureau. Er…can we have the retained samples on which you made the analysis? I am afraid we only can give our opinion after we have the samples re-checked here.

Buyer：All right. We will send you the samples as soon as possible.

Words and Expressions

inferior quality 次质量

drop in 顺便走访，不预先通知的拜访

leakage 泄漏，渗漏

at random 随便地

retained samples 留样

Key Sentences 经典必备句

● 索赔：

If we fail to make the delivery on schedule,you can claim on the delayed shipment.

如果我们没有按时装运货物,你们可以对延期发货提出索赔。

According to claim clauses, the seller should compensate the inferior quality of goods or quality changes.

根据索赔条款,卖方应该就货物的低劣质量或是质量改变作出赔偿。

Shortweight is caused by packing damage or shortloading.

短重是由包装破损或装运短重引起的。

Claims occur frequently in international trade.

国际贸易中经常发生索赔现象。

If the damage occurs in the transit. the shipping company or insurance company might be responsible for the claim.

如果损坏是在运输途中发生的,也许船公司或保险公司应负责赔偿。

Here is a claim on shortweight.

这是短重索赔。

We propose you compensate us the loss of all broken tins plus inspection fee.

我们希望你们赔偿我们所有破损罐头的损失,另外加上商检费。

We are looking forward to your reply on the claim.

我们正在等着你们的索赔答复。

The client has lodged a claim against us.

客户已经向我们提出了索赔。

We have filed a claim against the seller for the delayed shipment.

关于延期发货的问题,我们已经向你方提出索赔。

We want to register a claim for US $2 400.

我们要提出索赔 2 400 美元。

We ask for the compensation by 13% of the total amount of the contract.

我们要求赔偿合同全部金额的 13%。

● 索赔答复:

We will give your claim our careful consideration.

我们会就你们提出的索赔进行仔细考虑。

We are undertaking a careful investigation of the claim.

我们正在对这个索赔案件做详细的调查研究。

We regret we can't accommodate your claim.

很抱歉我们不能接受你方索赔。

They expressed that they are not in a position to entertain our claim.

他们表示不能接受我们的索赔要求。

We decide to waive our claim immediately.

我们决定立即放弃索赔。

The American company agreed to compensate us for the inferior quality by 6% of the total value.

美国公司同意就质量不合格问题向我们赔偿总价值的 6%。

We have received your letters with full details of this claim.

我们已经收到了你们内容详尽的索赔信件。

It is to inform the arrival of your remittance in settlement of our claim.

特此通知我们已经收到你方解决我们索赔问题的汇款。

We are considering the possibility of withdrawing the claim.

我们正在考虑撤回索赔要求的可能性。

We regret for the loss you have suffered and agree to compensate the total loss.

我们对你方遭受的损失深表歉意,并同意向你们赔偿全部损失。

Frequently Used Words and Phrases 常用词汇和短语

claim against carrier 向承运人索赔

claim for compensation 要求补偿

claim for damage 由于损坏而索赔

claim for indemnity 要求索赔

claim for inferior quality 由于质量低劣而索赔

claim for loss and damage of cargo 货物损失索赔

claim for short weight 由于短重而索赔

claim for trade dispute 贸易纠纷(引起的)索赔

claim indemnity 索赔

claim letter 索赔书

claim on the goods 对某(批)货索赔

claim on you 向某人(方)提出索赔

claim report 索赔报告

claim 索赔;赔偿;赔偿金

claimant 索赔人

claimee 被索赔人

claiming administration 索赔局

claims assessor 估损人

claims department(commission board)索赔委员会

claims documents 索赔证件

claims expenses 理赔费用

claims rejected 拒赔

claims settlement 理赔

claims settling agent 理赔代理人

claims settling fee 理赔代理费

claims statement 索赔清单

claims surveying agent 理赔检验代理人

claims 索赔;债权

claimsman 损失赔偿结算人

compensate 赔偿,补偿

in settlement of 解决

inability 无能力

insurance claim 保险索赔

Sales Confirmation 销售确认书

to bring up a(one's)claim 提出索赔

to file a(one's)claim 提出索赔

to lodge a(one's)claim 提出索赔

to make a(one's)claim 提出索赔

to make a claim for(on)sth. 就某事提出索赔

to make a claim with(against)sb. 向某方提出索赔

to make an investigation 调查研究

to put in a(one's)claim 提出索赔

to raise a(one's)claim 提出索赔

to register a(one's)claim 提出索赔

to settle a claim 解决索赔(问题)

to waive a claim 放弃索赔(要求)

to withdraw a claim 撤销(某项)索赔

Useful expressions for negotiation

Closing a Negotiation 结束谈判

We're running out of time.

We are running short on time.

We only have three minutes left.

We have to watch our time. It's almost two-thirty.

Can you go a little faster? We don't have much time left.

Can you make it short? We only have three minutes left.

I'm afraid our time is up. We'll have to finish this next time.

It looks like our time is over. We'll have to continue this next time.

To summarize, we decided that ...

Just to remind you, we decided that ...

To re-cap the main points, we decided to ...

Barry is going to check on the ...

Sally is going to find out about ...

It's been great talking with you.

I'm afraid I have to leave now.

Thanks for taking the time to talk with us.

Well, I think we've covered everything.

I think that takes care of everything.

It looks like that's everything for today.

I'll give you a call.

I'll send you an e-mail.

I'll put a packet in the mail for you.

We'll send out that information right away.

I'll have my secretary schedule an appointment.

Could you send me a brochure/some more information?

Could I contact you by e-mail/at your office?

How do I get in touch with you?

How can I reach/contact you?

Let me give you my business card.

Here's my e-mail/office number.

Let's keep in touch by e-mail.

We'll be in touch.

Call me if you have any questions.

That's it then. (informal)

The meeting is adjourned. (very formal)

Sample Dialogues 1. Inadequate Packing

Mr. Su Shenrong, a representative of the Shanghai Textiles Import & Export Corporation in Sydney office, is now looking into the claim they have had on their latest shipment of cotton fabrics to Barbara Trading Co., Ltd. He is talking on the telephone with Ms. Java, purchasing manager of that company.

Su:Mm... I'd like to see things myself, Friday morning, at 10:00. Ok, I'll be there. Thank you. Goodbye.

(Friday morning at 10:00, Su and Java are walking towards a warehouse.)

Java:On the whole, your delivery has been quite satisfactory. We have little to complain about, yet the latest shipment is so disappointing. We feel we must make a complaint.

Su:We are very sorry that this has happened. You said a number of bales were damaged. Is it that serious?

Java:Some were water-stained, some soiled. I suppose you won't be convinced until you have seen it with your own eyes.

(In the warehouse, packages are piled here and there. Several bales lie open, fabrics badly soiled and stained. They go nearer for closer examination.)

Java:These bales appear to have been improperly packed. They have become sodden.

Su:But the goods were in fine condition when shipped.

Java:The result of our investigation said the damage was caused sometime in transit, but it is the inadequate packing that allowed the packages to open in the first place.

Su: Goods for export are specially packed. Our packing is usually suitable for ocean transportation. Are you sure it wasn't caused by improper handling? Even the strongest packing can give way under rough handling, you know.

Java:I often come to watch the handling of cargo on the dock personally. I can assure you rough handling is not common here. We fully follow the standard procedures.

Su: Have you checked how much of the content of the damaged bales can still be used?

Java:Yes. Most of the bales can be used. Here's the surveyor's report.

（Su reads the report.）

Java：Mr. Su, We are very anxious about this. We had counted on receiving the shipment to complete several orders. Now we'll have to keep our clients waiting. I'm sure we can count on your support to help us overcome the present difficulty.

Su：We fully understand your position, Ms. Java. In fact, that's one of the reasons I'm here. Well, what do you suggest for a settlement?

Java：You won't agree, I know, to our returning the goods to you. The handling and shipping charges would cost a lot. Since we have very good relations with you, we are willing to accept the shipment if you will allow 20 percent reduction in price.

Su：That's a little too high. The report says that only 10 percent is unusable.

Java：Yes, but it's quite a job to sort out the unusable fabrics.

Su：Ms. Java, let's make some compromise, say a 10 percent reduction in price on this shipment. And for your next order, we'll give you some favorable terms in addition to what you are getting from us now.

Java：I appreciate your quick decision, Mr. Su. We accept the proposal. I'm glad we found a solution.

Sample Dialogues 2. Inferior Quality

Whenever disputes arise, the supplier feels thrown on to the defensive and will be inclined to resist the charges or may even reject them. Therefore it is the buyer who has to support his claim with justifiable proof. Let's see how Mr. Wu Yuexiang from the Shanghai Metals & Minerals Import & Export Corporation, is lodging a claim against a Steel Plates exporter, represented by Mr. Todd.

Todd：Mr. Wu, I'm here to settle the account concerning 20 000 tons of Hot Rolled Steel Plates under contract No. SA008624. The goods were dispatched in June. But your bank refused to pay. May I know why?

Wu：Our letter of credit is negotiable against presentation of the documents, which include a set of clean bills of lading. You gave us foul ones.

Todd：I can explain that...

Wu：The goods arrived here last month. After reinspection piece by piece, we found 12 pieces out of the whole lot had been seriously corroded with rust. When the rust was cleaned off, one could see pits and even dents in the plates, some with depths up to 2mm. The others were also found to have various defects. You can see from the photos how serious the case is.

（Handing over the photos）

Todd: I'm really very sorry about this, but if the plates arrived in this state, they must have been damaged during the long sea voyage. You see, the bill of lading says "Slightly rust-stained", that is, the plates were by no means found seriously rusted when shipped.

Wu: I don't think I can agree with you there, if the goods had been loaded on the deck, a long ocean voyage might have harmed them, but that's not the case. If signs of leakage had been found inside the holds, we could hold the shipping company liable for the damage; but during the course of discharge, our surveyors went on board and found the holds all in sound condition. Therefore, the serious rust must have existed before shipment.

Todd: But the Bill of Lading only mentions "Slightly rust-stained". The master would have inserted a stronger clause if the plates had been covered by heavy rust. We simply cannot accept your claim. You'd better go to the shipping company for settlement.

Wu: Mr. Todd, you have been in the steel business for sometime. You know the general practice, of course. It is usually stipulated in the bill of landing that the shipping company will not hold themselves responsible for rust damage on metals such as iron and steel. It's the seller duty to ship goods according to contract stipulations. If the plates had been in sound condition, why did the master mark the bill of landing with the phrase "Slightly rust-stained"?

Todd: It only means that the surface of the plates showed some atmospheric rust. That's something inherent in the material. It does not affect the use of the plates in any way.

Wu: The goods are still lying on the wharf. You can go there and see them for yourself.

(On the wharf)

Wu: Atmospheric rust would never lead to such a drastic condition.

Todd: But rust can hardly be avoided while the material lay bare on the wharf for shipment during the whole rainy season.

Wu: Now Mr. Todd, you've said it yourself. The rusty corrosion is the result of storage on the wharf during the whole rainy season. The corrosion existed before shipment when the goods were still in your hands.

Todd: But usually no rust claim is to be accepted for nude cargo.

Wu: Yes, if the claim is against atmospheric rust. But I must remind you, Mr.

Todd, that we are now lodging a claim along more serious lines.

Todd: Erh... Mr. Wu, I'm sorry I don't know very much about these things as I'm in the sales department, but I'll pass the message on to our relevant department immediately.

Wu: This seems to be a clear case now. We hope you'll make a prompt settlement.

Todd: Needless to say, the sooner we clear this case up the better it will be for both of us. And I do hope this undesirable incident will not stand in the way of our future business.

Sample Dialogues 3. Complaint over Damaged Goods

Walter Keynes, Managing Director of London Tableware Co., rings up Zhao Xiang, Sales Manager of China Ceramics Import and Export Co., complaining about the damaged goods.

Zhao: Good morning. Sales Department. Zhao Xiang speaking.

Keynes: Good morning, Mr. Zhao. This is Walter Keynes from London Tableware Co.

Zhao: How are you, Mr. Keynes?

Keynes: I'm fine, thank you. I've got a bone to pick with you, Mr. Zhao! Over your last shipment of the 100 Coffee Sets supplied to our Order No. BT 118. We received them, but I'm sorry to find that, 15 sets of them were badly damaged.

Zhao: That must be due to the rough handling of the shipping company. I advise you to take up the matter with them.

Keynes: We've talked with them about it already. They said that as the cartons containing the coffee sets appeared to be in apparent good condition, they were not responsible for it at all. That was also the reason why we accepted and signed for them without question.

Zhao: Did your people handle them carefully?

Keynes: Yes. Our people are all specially trained for this and unpacked the coffee sets with great care. Therefore, we can only assume the damage must be due to careless handling at some stage prior to packing.

Zhao: I'll look into the matter soonest possible. Could you tell me the cartons' serial numbers please?

Keynes: Yes, they're TC501104, 501107 and 501110.

Zhao: OK. Now what's your opinion about the settlement of this matter?

Keynes: I hope you'll replace all the 15 sets as soon as possible.

Zhao: I go along with you there. We'll send the replacement by air on the first a-vailable airplane.

Keynes: Thank you, Mr. Zhao. By the way, we've put the damaged coffee sets a-side in case you need them to support a claim on your suppliers for compensation.

Zhao: Thank you, Mr. Keynes. It'll be unnecessary for you to keep the damaged coffee sets and they can be disposed as you like.

Keynes: OK, we'll do as you say.

Zhao: Mr. Keynes, thank you for calling me. I assure you that we'll do our best to improve our methods of handling so as to avoid further inconvenience to any customer. I do hope this incident will not affect our future business relations.

Keynes: No, Mr. Zhao, never, but I'm greatly moved by the way you're dealing with the matter. I'm sure our business relations will be further strengthened.

Zhao: I hope so, too. Thank you, Mr. Keynes, for the trouble. Bye.

Keynes: Bye, Mr. Zhao.

Sample Dialogues 4. Claiming Compensation

Mr. Mathew imports a consignment of Color TV sets but when the shipment arrives at Amsterdam Port, it is found that some of the TV sets are badly damaged. He goes to see Mr. Li, the head of a Chinese company's office in Holland from which he imports the goods, to inquire about the matter of compensation.

Li: Hello, Mr. Mathew, please come in and be seated.

Mathew: Hello Mr. Li, Thank you. I'm here for the consignment of Color TV your home office has shipped to us.

Li: Hold on, before you go further, Mr. Mathew, could you let me know the con-tract number, please?

Mathew: Oh, it's CHT012/04.

Li: Thank you. I'll just make a note of it. Now then, what's the problem?

Mathew: The shipment arrived at Amsterdam port yesterday, but we're sorry to find fifteen sets in one of the containers have been badly damaged. I must say, they are a complete write off.

Li: You don't say so? What on earth happened?

Mathew: We're not sure either. When the container was opened, it was found that some cartons were crushed and the TV sets in them were damaged beyond repair.

Li：Mm, it sounds as if the container was accidentally dropped on the ground while being loaded or unloaded. You'd better get the independent surveyor to inspect the cargo right away.

Mathew：We've already done that.

Li：Er, this contract is on the CIF basis. The insurance company is PICC and their agent here in Amsterdam is Dutch Insurance Company. Well, there are two alternatives I'd like to advise you. One way is that you send a copy of the insurance policy together with the surveyor's report to Dutch Insurance Company, putting forward a claim against PICC for the damaged TV sets, and ask them to pay the compensation on behalf of PICC. Another alterative is that you could forward us your insurance policy and the surveyor's report together with a letter of attorney and ask us to lodge a claim against PICC on your behalf. We'll ask our people back at home to take the matter up with our insurance company for compensation in China.

Mathew：I'd prefer the first alternative. I think we'll first have a try here in Amsterdam. It may take less time and we can get compensated earlier.

Li：Oh, it's up to you.

Mathew：But we still need replacement TV sets because we can't keep our customers waiting for too long.

Li：No, of course not. We'll get in touch with our home office and ask them to dispatch another fifteen sets as soon as they can. If possible, the replacements are a small lot, and may be forwarded by air. But the freight may cost a lot more.

Mathew：That's very kind of you. If they are sent by air, we'll pay the extra transport charges.

Li：OK. Now it's all settled. Would you please get in touch with Dutch Insurance Company quickly?

Mathew：Yes. Bye.

Li：Bye.

Sample Dialogues 5. Wrong Delivery

Tianjin Hi-Tech Co. receives the order they placed with a foreign company but finds the order is wrongly delivered. Mr. Li, Purchasing Manager of the company, phones up Mr. Melady, Sales Manager of the foreign company for this matter.

Melady：Good morning. Sales Department.

Mr. Li：Ah, Good morning, this is Li Ming here from Tianjin Hi-Tech Co. Can I speak to Sales . Manager Mr. Melady?

Melady:Melady speaking. Hallo, Mr. Li. How are you getting along?

Mr. Li:Not so well, I'm afraid.

Melady:I'm sorry to hear that. Can I help?

Mr. Li:Yes. I'm phoning up for our Order No. THT0206 placed two months ago. We have just received the consignment of what I expected to be XJ30s but find they are in fact XJ40s. Now that this has been made quite clear, there is no excuse, and if I don't get those XJ30s by the end of the month there'll be trouble, we shall cancel the order under the terms of the contract. Have you got that?

Melady:Yes. Let me check on my computer. Oh dear, you're right. I deeply apologize for that. You see, our computers were attacked by a hacker not long ago, and our whole computerization system was in a mess. Though it was repaired and restored to normal, it was easy to make a slip. It's 20th today and there's 10 days to go. OK. You may rest assured that we'll try our best to deliver XJ30s to you by the end of this month. As for the XJ40s we've sent you, I'd like to have your opinion.

Mr. Li:Don't worry. We'll try to find another buyer for them. The most important thing for us is to get XJ30s as stated as our client needs them badly.

Melady:Thank you, Mr. Li. I assure you that the order will reach you in time.

Sample Dialogues 6. Our End Users Made a Strong Protest

J:Mr. Zhang, I need to talk with you about the canned food we purchased from you last time.

Z:Go ahead.

J: Well, do you remember that last autumn we contracted with you for canned food?

Z:Yes. It's the shipment under Contract No. 11250.

J: You may well remember that I warned on many occasions about your poor packing. And you agreed to make sure that your cartons would meet our requirements. But to our regret many of the cans arrived here dented. As a result the consumers refused to buy such dented canned goods. What's more, the Canadian Consumer Associations also warn the consumers against them, for which we encountered poor sale and sustained great loss.

Z: It's not for me to disagree with you there, but so far as I know the goods under Contract No. 11250 were in perfect condition when they were shipped. As for the dented cans, I'm inclined to think they were due to rough handling during shipment or during loading and unloading. In that case, I think it better that you refer the case to the shipping company.

J: But the result of our investigation shows that the dented cans were caused by faulty packing. Our end users made a strong protest against it. Unless you improve your packing method, you will be losing our market.

Z:Come, come, Mr. Johnson. It seems you were trying to put the blame of rough handling on us. You should have laid the blame on the right person. The truth is, we've always paid great attention to the method of packing. The customers have so far never complained about our packing. Your case was rather a singular one.

J: But the case is true, you know.

Z:Of course. You see, even the strongest packing will give ay under rough handling.

J: In a way, it is so. Anyhow we are sure you don't like to see your goods lose market in this area. So, in order to save the situation and to hold the market, mind your packing, or rather improve it.

Z:You are right. Although it is not our fault, for the sake of good business, we will take care about it. But at the same time, would you contact the shipper to make further investigations to prevent rough handling in future transactions?

Sample Dialogues 7. The Case is Too Serious to Be Overlooked

S:I've something very unpleasant to talk over with you, Mr. Zhang.

Z:Do you mean the quality of the mushrooms you mentioned in your letter of August 1 5?

S:Yes. The case is too serious to be overlooked, so I decided to come and have a face-to-face talk with you. I demand a full refund of the amount paid.

Z:Just be patient, please. Any criticism on our products is sincerely invited. But won't you sit down and tell us the whole thing first?

S:Well, you see, according to the contract we ordered well dried mushrooms of fine quality, but the goods you sent us are not up to the standard and unfit for consumption. We have to lodge a claim against you for inferior quality.

Z:Could you tell us the exact cause of the inferior quality? You see, the damage may be caused by a variety of factors.

S:Here's a survey report by a well-known lab in London. It says that the packing of the goods is sound and intact at the time of survey. So it is clear that the mushrooms were not well dried before packing.

Z:But let me inform you that the goods in question were strictly inspected by the

China Commodity Inspection Bureau at the time of loading, with your representative on the spot. Their report showed that the goods were well dried and up to the standard for export. So the damage must have taken place during transit. We suggest you make a further investigation into the matter.

S:If that's really the case, who do you think we must turn to for our claim?

Z:The goods were bought on FOB basis. And it was you who booked the shipping space and had the goods insured. So you may approach the shipping company or the insurance company for compensation.

S:All right. I think I'll take your advice.

Sample Dialogues 8. The Content Not Up to Your Own Standard

C:Shall we proceed to the next point?

S:An analysis was made of the shipment and the BPL content was only 70.89%, lower than required, so we are lodging a claim of $22 000 for inferior quality.

C:A shipment, as in this case, is designed to come out with the approximate content of 73%.

S:Then how would you explain the BPL content not up to your own standard?

C:The method of sampling is crucial too. If you take samples from the ship, you'll be taking rocks of larger granulation, which are lower in BPL content than the smaller ones. If the correct method was used, we do not feel it is possible to have a difference of 2% as you suggested.

S:The method used was the one you recommended and the percentage is there in the report in black and white.

C:Yes, I know. In this case, I'll have to ask you again for your samples for sending them back for reanalysis.

S:The method of analysis adopted by our Inspection Bureau was in conformity with the methods recommended.

C:We still feel the BPL content would be very largely calculated by the method of sampling. You will note, too, that the analysis from the two laboratories shows quite a difference between the analysis made on the original shipping samples and your samples on arrival.

S:That might be the case, Mr. Carlos, but it's a fact that BPL content is lower than stipulated.

C:It's most unfortunate and my home office has instructed me to do my best to remedy it.

S:We appreciate your efforts.

C:As we wish to settle the claim with you and the BPL difference is entirely due to the method of sampling used, my home office proposes to settle on the basis of a 50/50 between the original analysis on our shipment and the reanalysis of your returned samples.

S:Your proposal is reasonable and, in view of this satisfactory conclusion of the matter, we will also waive our claim for the inspection fee.

C:Thank you. We appreciate your cooperation in settling this unfortunate affair.

实训综合习题

I. put the following sentences into Chinese.

1. I have to complain about the pocket calculators you sent us last week.

2. The last batch we received from you was faulty.

3. The goods arrived damaged.

4. The goods you sent us do not correspond with the sample we gave you.

5. The report you sent US about our new customer is too superficial. We are disappointed.

6. There's a serious problem. The case contained completely different goods from the ones we ordered.

7. The containers are not the size and shape we ordered.

8. Three typewriters are missing from the consignment.

9. I ordered 75 and you sent me 57. Are you shipping clerks dyslexic or something?

10. We are wondering why there is such a long delay. Have the compressors left the factory yet?

11. You seem to have overlooked our order. We should have received the disk drives last week.

12. You did not secure the cartons with metal straps as we had suggested.

13. The Medical Health Officer has issued a "Stop Notice" on them. We are lodging a claim for inferior quality.

14. You should be responsible for the loss.

15. We can not entertain your claim. Your claim should be referred to the insurance company.

16. We hope you will effect a full settlement of our claim.

17. In view of our friendly business relations. we are prepared to meet your claim for the 35 tons short weight.

18. Your claim is not reasonable. We can not accept it.

19. We have to ask for a compensation of $550 to cover the loss incurred.

20. We regret for the loss you have suffered and agree to compensate you by $ 1 000.

II. Translation Exercises.

1.货到上海后我们进行了复验,发现品质与合同规定不符。

2.有20%的包都破了,包内的货物严重污损。

3.这项索赔属保险公司责任范围,我们不能对此负责。

4.八月份的洪水影响了运输以致不能按期交货,我们很抱歉,但确实无能为力。

5.我们保证,今后交货不会再发生类似情况。

6.我们建议这批货在你方市场销售,同时我们降价25%,怎么样?

7.我们对这批货的短量向你们提出索赔。

8.令我们不满意的是,我们发现真丝睡袍有色差。

9.我们一调查完情况就来谈赔偿的事。

10.实际上,这批羊绒衫的质量还是很不错的,只是有些被雨水浸湿了。

III. Role Play.

Task 1

Student A acts as a businessman from China National Machinery Imp. & Exp. Corporation, lodging a claim for the rust of the rollers against a Japanese seller, who is acted by student B. A shows the records and photos identifying the rust problem and photos to B. Then A presents his view of the case. After heated discussion, the case is brought to a happy conclusion. B agrees to give compensation and to ship new rollers to replace the defective ones. He/She also agrees to meet shipping expenses.

Task 2

Work in pairs. One student plays the role of a French merchant, who raises a claim against China National Foodstuffs Imp. & Exp. Corporation for quality deterioration of 800 bottles of Straw- berry Preserves. The other plays the role of a sales manager, taking up the claim on behalf of the corporation. Finally the manager succeeds in rejecting the claim because the claim was raised out-side the claim period stipulated in the contract.

IV. Topics for Group Discussion.

1. Suppose you are the seller. When receiving a claim from buyers, what would you do with it?

2. There are kinds of claims for losses in international trade, such as claims for inferior quality, short weight, wrong delivery, faulty packing, short payment, late delivery and so forth. Choose one of the above mentioned and discuss how you would settle it.

V. Oral Practice.

Work with your partner. Make a claim on the shipment arrived 2 days ago. After examination, you found many of the sewing machines are severely damaged though the cases themselves show no trace of damage. You believe the damage attributable to improper packing.

参考文献

[1]邱革加,杨国俊.现代商务英语谈判[M].北京:中国国际广播出版社,2006.

[2]王乃彦.外贸英语口语[M].北京:中国商务出版社,2002.

[3]刘醒吾,陈坚.经贸英语口语[M].北京:外语教学与研究出版社,1994.

[4]顾乾毅.商务英语口语900句[M].广州:广东世界图书出版公司,2004.

[5]秦川.外贸英语会话[M].北京:中国对外经济贸易出版社,1997.

[6]吴云娣.国际商务谈判英语[M].上海:上海交通大学出版社,2002.